The Harcourt Casebook Series in Literature

Walt Whitman

A Collection of Poems

THE HARCOURT CASEBOOK SERIES IN LITERATURE
Series Editors: Laurie G. Kirszner and Stephen R. Mandell

DRAMA
Athol Fugard
"Master Harold" . . . *and the boys*

William Shakespeare
Hamlet

POETRY
Emily Dickinson
A Collection of Poems

Langston Hughes
A Collection of Poems

Walt Whitman
A Collection of Poems

FICTION
William Faulkner
"A Rose for Emily"

Charlotte Perkins Gilman
"The Yellow Wallpaper"

Flannery O'Connor
"A Good Man Is Hard to Find"

John Updike
"A&P"

Eudora Welty
"A Worn Path"

The Harcourt Casebook Series in Literature
Series Editors: Laurie G. Kirszner and Stephen R. Mandell

Walt Whitman

A Collection of Poems

Contributing Editor

J. Michael Léger
University of Texas at Arlington

Harcourt College Publishers

Fort Worth   Philadelphia   San Diego   New York   Orlando   Austin   San Antonio
Toronto   Montreal   London   Sydney   Tokyo

Publisher	Earl McPeek
Acquisitions Editor	Bill Hoffman
Project Editor	Elaine Richards
Art Director	Van Mua
Production Manager	Linda McMillan

ISBN: 0-15-507472-5
Library of Congress Catalog Card Number: 99-67816

Harcourt College Publishers will provide complimentary supplements or supplement packages to those adopters qualified under our adoption policy. Please contact your sales representative to learn how you qualify. If as an adopter or potential user you receive supplements you do not need, please return them to your sales representative or send them to: Attn: Returns Department, Troy Warehouse, 465 South Lincoln Drive, Troy, MO 63379.

Address for Domestic Orders
Harcourt College Publishers, 6277 Sea Harbor Drive, Orlando, FL 32887-6777
800-782-4479

Address for International Orders
International Customer Service
Harcourt, Inc., 6277 Sea Harbor Drive, Orlando, FL 32887-6777
407-345-3800
(fax) 407-345-4060
(e-mail) hbintl@harcourtbrace.com

Address for Editorial Correspondence
Harcourt College Publishers, 301 Commerce Street, Suite 3700, Fort Worth, TX 76102

Web Site Address
http://www.harcourtcollege.com

Printed in the United States of America

9 0 1 2 3 4 5 6 7 8   066   9 8 7 6 5 4 3 2 1

Harcourt College Publishers

ABOUT THE SERIES

The Harcourt Casebook Series in Literature has its origins in our anthology *Literature: Reading, Reacting, Writing* (Third Edition, 1997), which in turn arose out of our many years of teaching college writing and literature courses. The primary purpose of each Casebook in the series is to offer students a convenient, self-contained reference tool that they can use to complete a research project for an introductory literature course.

In choosing subjects for the Casebooks, we draw on our own experience in the classroom, selecting works of poetry, fiction, and drama that students like to read, discuss, and write about and that teachers like to teach. Unlike other collections of literary criticism aimed at student audiences, the Harcourt Casebook Series in Literature features short stories, groups of poems, or plays (rather than longer works, such as novels) because these are the genres most often taught in college-level Introduction to Literature courses. In selecting particular authors and titles, we focus on those most popular with students and those most accessible to them.

To facilitate student research—and to facilitate instructor supervision of that research—each Casebook contains all the resources students need to produce a documented research paper on a particular work of literature. Every Casebook in the series includes the following elements:

- A comprehensive **introduction** to the work, providing social, historical, and political background. This introduction helps students to understand the work and the author in the context of a particular time and place. In particular, the introduction enables students to appreciate customs, situations, and events that may have contributed to the author's choice of subject matter, emphasis, or style.

- A **headnote,** including birth and death dates of the author; details of the work's first publication and its subsequent publication history, if relevant; details about the author's life; a summary of the author's career; and a list of key published works, with dates of publication.

- The most widely accepted version of the **literary work,** along with the explanatory footnotes students will need to understand unfamiliar terms and concepts or references to people, places, or events.

- **Discussion questions** focusing on themes developed in the work. These questions, designed to stimulate critical thinking and discussion, can also serve as springboards for research projects.

- Several extended **research assignments** related to the literary work. Students may use these assignments exactly as they appear in the Casebook, or students or instructors may modify the assignments to suit their own needs or research interests.

- A diverse collection of traditional and nontraditional **secondary sources,** which may include scholarly articles, reviews, interviews, memoirs, newspaper articles, historical documents, and so on. This resource offers students access to sources they might not turn to on their own—for example, a popular song that inspired a short story, a story that was the original version of a play, a legal document that sheds light on a work's theme, or two different biographies of an author—thus encouraging students to look beyond the obvious or the familiar as they search for ideas. Students may use only these sources, or they may supplement them with sources listed in the Casebook's bibliography (see below).

- An annotated model **student research paper** drawing on several of the Casebook's secondary sources. This paper uses MLA parenthetical documentation and includes a Works Cited list conforming to MLA style.

- A comprehensive **bibliography** of print and electronic sources related to the work. This bibliography offers students an opportunity to move beyond the sources in the Casebook to other sources related to a particular research topic.

- A concise **guide to MLA documentation,** including information on what kinds of information require documentation (and what kinds do not); a full explanation of how to construct parenthetical references and how to place them in a paper; sample parenthetical reference formats for various kinds of sources used in papers about literature; a complete explanation of how to assemble a List of Works Cited, accompanied by sample works cited entries (including formats for documenting electronic sources); and guidelines for using explanatory notes (with examples).

By collecting all this essential information in one convenient place, each volume in the Harcourt Casebook Series in Literature responds to the needs of both students and teachers. For students, the Casebooks offer convenience, referentiality, and portability that make the process of doing research easier. Thus the Casebooks recognize what students already know: that Introduction to Literature is not their only class and the literature research paper is not their only assignment. For instructors, the Casebooks offer a rare combination of flexibility and control in the classroom. For example, teachers may choose to assign one Casebook or more than one; thus, they have the option of having all students in a class write about the same work or having different groups of students, or individual students, write about different works. In addition, instructors may ask students to use only the secondary sources collected in the Casebook, thereby controlling students' use of (and acknowledgment of) sources more closely, or they may encourage students to seek both print and electronic sources beyond those included in the Casebook. By building convenience, structure, and flexibility into each volume, we have designed The Harcourt Casebook Series in Literature to suit a wide variety of teaching styles and research interests. The Casebooks have made the research paper an easier project for us and a less stressful one for our students; we hope they will do the same for you.

Laurie G. Kirszner
Stephen R. Mandell
Series Editors

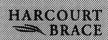

PREFACE

When in the opening lines of "Song of Myself" Whitman loafs and invites his soul, lying at his "ease observing a spear of summer grass," (I.5), his gesture is a familiar one. Readers may easily imagine a friend inviting them to examine the simple beauties of Nature. Later, the invitation is extended, and Whitman claims that he contains within himself all such beauties, that he contains the "kosmos" ("Song of Myself" XXIV). The experience in which Whitman invites his readers to participate may seem, therefore, at the same time too common for serious response, and impossible, or even impious: for how can a man contain the universe, or, from another perspective, how dare a mere man claim to contain the universe? Indeed Whitman is often accused of sacrilege for the arrogance of making this claim. But Whitman does not (or does not primarily) intend to be irreligious. Instead, his claim that he contains the cosmos appears to be a claim to represent the United States itself. He hopes to demonstrate the United States's ideals: the universal welcome of the immigrant and the universal equality of the citizen. In addition, he hopes to define a new poetic style and tradition, a distinctly American literature, a confidently democratic poetry for the democratic nation in which he feels such confidence. He wishes to establish for the newly founded democracy a new foundation for the literary expression of ideas, distinct from the traditions of European—especially British—literature, which he considered stale. With his experimental style and his bold dismissal of previous poetic conventions, Whitman excites both bitter condemnation and elaborate praise. The controversy surrounding Whitman's work, and his life, is ongoing, leaving a number of questions still open about the poet, questions that will be discussed later in this Casebook, in the section entitled "About the Author," and in the critical selections:

> Is Whitman what he makes himself out to be, the first American poetic voice?

How can one characterize Whitman's poetic style? Is it poetic or
antipoetic? Is his style new, or does it recall preliterary or Old English
verse forms, or bardic chant forms?

Is Whitman a spiritual seeker, and if so, of what sort? Conservative?
Derivative of Native American spirituality? Eastern in spiritual
orientation? Or surprisingly modern?

Is Whitman's embrace of diversity and celebration of universal equality
inclusive of African-Americans and women?

Is Whitman homosexual, in the modern sense of the term?

The sources included here attempt to define a range of general interpretive approaches that critics bring to the study of Whitman's work and
life. Because beginning readers often find literary criticism as baffling as the
literature it attempts to interpret, the critical essays in this Casebook have
been chosen to represent a reasonably accessible range of literary theory.
Nevertheless, a brief introduction to theory may be in order.

First, readers should not dismiss the possibility that critical essays can
be accessible. Although some theories seem designed more to obscure than
to illuminate meaning, some become reasonably accessible if the reader can
only keep a few insights in view. Most interpretation attempts to derive or
discover the "intended" meaning of a text. Interpretation may focus upon
what is known of the writer's life or society, upon the historical moment in
which the writing is done, upon the writer's artistic philosophy, or upon a
combination of these. A general interpretive assumption is that a writer's
personal concerns, broad observations about culture, and beliefs about art
will be represented. The introductory material presented in this Casebook,
historical and biographical in nature, itself provides a theoretical basis for
an interpretive approach to Whitman's work, as does the "Preface to the
1855 Edition of *Leaves of Grass*." Even those interpretive theories that begin
from a political position, such as Feminist Theory or Cultural Materialism,
attempt to establish the writer's attitudes or those of the writer's society, as
these are reflected in the work—in these cases attitudes toward women or
toward class conflict.

- Whitman, Walt. "Preface to the 1855 Edition of *Leaves of Grass*."
  Whitman's poetic/artistic manifesto outlines his definitions of the
  concepts poet, poetry, and poetic process, and provides the major
  underpinning for the student research paper in the Casebook.

- Aspiz, Harold. "Sexuality and the Language of Transcendence." Whitman's spiritual vision as that reflects, and is distinct from, his political and sexual ideals, is Aspiz's focus.

- Birmingham, William. "Whitman's Song of the Possible American Self." Birmingham examines Whitman's vision of the American character as it relates to his hopes for America and his assertions about his poetic identity.

- DeLancey, Mark. "Texts, Interpretations, and Whitman's 'Song of Myself.'" DeLancey argues that by bringing oppositions together into himself and into his poetry, Whitman fulfills the purpose of both the writer who is rhetorician and the writer who is interpreter, the purpose of building community.

- Emerson, Ralph Waldo. "Letter to Walt Whitman." The letter represents the immediate response of one of the era's preeminent philosophers and poets. Emerson's exultation over Whitman's achievement fueled Whitman's confidence in the freshness of his poetic voice and his poetry itself.

- Griswold, Rufus W. "Unsigned Review." Griswold's review recognizes the homoerotic in the poetry of Whitman and condemns it, as was typical of the times, in no uncertain terms. Many subsequent writers have responded to the issue of Whitman's "sexual orientation," seeking to establish his homosexuality as historical fact based on his writing or, on the other hand, seeking to "defend" Whitman as heterosexual.

- Jarvis, D. R. "Whitman and Speech-Based Prosody." Jarvis describes Whitman's poetic style as indicative of a "speech-based" poetic philosophy. Whitman's insistent use of a conversational diction reflects his egalitarian political vision.

- Phillips, Dana. "Nineteenth-Century Racial Thought and Whitman's Democratic Ethnography." Phillips explicitly examines Whitman's racial attitudes, arguing that Whitman's construction of an American identity and his elevation of a conformist ideal leave African-American identity in the margins.

- Sarracino, Carmine. "Figures of Transcendence in Whitman's Poetry." Like John Snyder in his 1975 critical biography of Whitman (*The Dear Love of Man: Tragic and Lyric Communion in Walt Whitman*), Sarracino describes Whitman's mysticism in the terms of transcendentalism, the American version of British Romanticism that includes belief in concepts like pantheism (the presence of "God" in all things) and the related notion that all people and things are spiritually connected. The author argues that Whitman seeks to accomplish connection among the Self, the reality surrounding the Self, and the all-uniting "One."

The Bibliography lists many other critical sources for the interpretation of Whitman's work, arranged by topic; these include entries specific to the poems anthologized here, as well as more general Whitman studies, and Internet sites.

ACKNOWLEDGMENTS

In addition to thanking the series editors, Laurie Kirszner and Stephen Mandell, and Harcourt's editors, Claire Brantley and Camille Adkins, I would also like to thank my earliest inspirations: the critics Claude J. Summers and Ted-Larry Pebworth; professors Sheryl Pearson and Melita Schaum, Chris Dahl and Chris R. Vanden Bossche. And my life partner, J. P. Sebastian, for support, encouragement, and love.

CONTENTS

Secondary Sources 37

Introduction

Walt Whitman:
The Singer of the Self
and the Poet of the Cosmos

Whitman the self-consciously American poet, the deliberate creator of a distinctly American poetry, continues to elicit extreme responses among readers, just as his first edition of *Leaves of Grass* did 144 years ago. Whitman's poetry presents the reader with several difficulties, including stylistic and formalistic challenges. Modern readers, who are usually unfamiliar with formal poetic conventions, approach Whitman with an advantage his original audience, with its schooling in the formal elements of traditional poetry, did not possess. But while poetry itself constitutes a significant challenge to many modern readers, Whitman's poetry also puts in the foreground thematic concerns and topics the modern reader may consider too commonplace to serve as the subject matter for poetry. After all, the universal equality he celebrates as a *new* ideal is for our day the virtually universal political ideal. Furthermore, some of Whitman's themes may offend new (as well as not-so-new) readers—especially those who are politically and socially conservative.

CULTURAL TRANSITION AND TURMOIL
IN THE NINETEENTH CENTURY

The nineteenth century delivered many shocks to conservative and liberal minds alike by producing a constant stream of scientific inquiry and discovery, as well as by social, political, and economic upheaval. The comfortable and well-established worldview current throughout Europe and America, based upon a more or less literal interpretation of the Bible, was challenged with increasing seriousness by scientific discovery and theories. These discoveries suggested the "Biblical" worldview's inadequacy or inaccuracy. In fact, this view was contradicted by everything science was in the process of

2

discovering about the formation of the earth, the evolution of humans, and the place of the solar system in the universe. Most shocking to many was the examination of the Bible itself on a scientific basis. Under such scrutiny, its internal inconsistencies and its cultural biases seemed to fail to provide a coherent ethical, moral, and intellectual understanding of the human condition. Such conflicts between objective knowledge and the visions of faith caused upheaval in the community of faith. Believers found themselves having to respond, and feeling the need most often to react, to perceived threats against their faith. Some were no doubt able to adapt the terms of their belief, but many adopted an increasingly militant stance against both those who adapted their beliefs and those who rejected their ideas as irrelevant. Each camp felt driven into extreme positions, and the debate carried on later in the century between proponents and opponents of evolutionary theory degenerated, as it often does now, into uncompromising personal attacks about belief and morality.[1] In short, the foundations and assumptions of Western culture were beginning to be undermined seriously by irreverent radicals, one of whom was Walt Whitman.

THE SHIFT FROM RELIGION TO SCIENCE: WHITMAN'S CONTRIBUTION AND RESPONSE

When Whitman sounds the song of the self in 1855, he is declaring his support, in part, for a new vision of the human condition. For Whitman, anything beyond the self is unnecessary in the human search for the meaning of individual experience. So any outside authority, such as the Bible, tradition, or political history, is rejected by Whitman in favor of the individual's vibrant and ongoing discovery of experience and its meanings. However, it is not merely the old authorities that the nineteenth century questioned and rejected. In fact, "When I Heard the Learn'd Astronomer," included in this Casebook, suggests a rejection of science itself as a means of interpreting reality. In its place, Whitman elevates individualized and experiential contact with reality, and insists upon the individual's power to interpret it. By focusing thus on the individual's immediate perceptual-interpretive functions, Whitman undermines both the old, Biblical authority and the new, scientific authority.

---

[1] For example, see T. H. Huxley's "Agnosticism and Christianity," anthologized in *Prose of the Victorian Period.* Ed. William E. Buckler. Boston: Houghton, 1958.

Even the authority of the great poets is of less importance to Whitman, as a poet, than are his personal encounters with reality, and his personal authority over meaning and over Nature:

Creeds and schools in abeyance,
Retiring back a while sufficed at what they are, but never forgotten,
I harbor for good or bad, I permit to speak at every hazard,
Nature without check with original energy ("Song of Myself" 1.10–13).

These lines demonstrate Whitman's rejection of authority itself in its most general terms ("creeds and schools"). They also anticipate the poet's more explicit rejection of standardized forms of literature held to be the legacy of the "greatest bards" identified in "Had I the Choice." Whitman's publication of his personalized, individualized, and antiauthoritarian vision, therefore, is entirely consistent with the nineteenth-century spirit of discovery, innovation, and revolution. But also consistent is the shock with which he was received.

WHITMAN THE INNOVATOR, OR, EVERYTHING OLD IS NEW AGAIN

Critics typically interpret Whitman's poetic style and persona as the fulfillment of his assertion that "whoever touches this touches a man." He and his poetry are interpreted as intending to convey the spontaneity of the average man of normative tastes and means and to assert the democratic ideal with its broad embrace. The first part of this interpretive portrait is contradicted, however, in much of Whitman's better poetry, by the additions and revisions that the poet made to each edition. The additions of poems, clusters, even books of poems, to each subsequent edition of *Leaves of Grass,* call into question the spontaneity of his initial utterance, or at least its value *as* spontaneous utterance. These revisions, along with many deletions of poems from the *Leaves,* suggest that Whitman underwent ongoing revelation leading to altered utterances; his poems, in other words, were far from the separate and finished spontaneous outpourings of powerful emotion that we would expect from someone so heavily influenced by the Romantic vision of Wordsworth.[2] So Whitman the inspired yet common bard of the masses reveals, in self-conscious literary tinkering with his work, that he is neither

---

[2] Asselineau, Roger. *The Transcendentalist Constant in American Literature.* New York: New York UP, 1980.

spontaneous nor common in his own eyes. Whitman clearly sees himself not as a vessel or a transmitter but as a shaper of the vision he promotes—as an artist, uncommon in sensibility and elevated in role.[3] His artistic self-assurance, along with the "obscenity" of much of his subject matter, drove much of the negative criticism Whitman received, which, in turn, sparked a considerable portion of his revisionist energy.

Just as Whitman asserts in "Had I the Choice," his initial and ongoing purpose is to establish his own poetic uniqueness, his status as poetic innovator, by rejecting the examples of the most recognizable and memorable "names" in the poetry of Western culture: Homer, Shakespeare, and Whitman's contemporary, Tennyson. Much of the poetry Whitman's contemporaries would have read closely resembled the work of British poets and may derive from or imitate it. (Compare, for example, the famous "Thanatopsis," by the American William Cullen Bryant, with the work of William Wordsworth, the preeminent British poet contemporary to Bryant's composition.) In contrast, Whitman's prosaic verse—conversational, noticeably lacking in elaborate poetic images, and presented in the true daily and colloquial language of America—represents an innovation indeed. So dramatic, in fact, was Whitman's departure from convention that some thought his "innovation" indicated lack of talent bordering upon illiteracy.

However, Whitman's chanting style, seemingly so revolutionary to his contemporaries who remained committed to the formal conventions of written poetry—strict meter, rhyme, economy of word, artistry of image—is not nearly as antithetical to traditional formal poetry as it at first appears. For all Poetry (the genre) and poetry (the poems themselves) begin in the primal rhythms of the chanter and of the individual mind, both of which are combining words creatively long before words are actually transcribed into written language. The modern reader (a category that includes Whitman's first readers as well as us) expects to hear formal rhythm and rhyme, and identifies these, solely, with the prosody (the elements and structures involved in formal communication) of poetry.[4] Like Wordsworth before him, Whitman wishes to elevate common speech to the level of the poetic.[5] But *common* is a relative term. If Wordsworth retains the formal requirements

---

[3] Hutchinson, George B. *The Ecstatic Whitman: Literary Shamanism and the Crisis of the Union.* Columbus: Ohio State UP, 1986.

[4] Most often *prosody* is used to refer to poetic elements and structures.

[5] Compare Wordsworth: "The principle object . . . proposed in these Poems was to choose incidents and situations from common life, and to relate or describe them . . . as far as

of poetry in much of his work, using recognizable forms such as sonnet and ode and blank verse, Whitman's innovation is that his prosody itself is "speech-based," and his units of verse are equivalent to his units of meaning; the standard syntactical units of prose—sentence structures—are considered, by Whitman, to be indistinguishable formally from poetry.[6]

WHITMAN AND TRANSCENDENTALISM

Whitman at his best evokes the rolling rhythms of the ancient bard or poet[7] intoning the deeds of the gods, the chanting of the shaman (priest, "medicine man")[8] praising the gods' works; and Whitman reproduces in the reader the hypnotic trance of the primeval fireside listener. Whitman creates the complex images of the wandering creative spirit, too captivating in his vision to drive away and too dangerous in his vision to embrace. In American transcendentalism is found a spiritual belief system similar to those in which such figures—bard and shaman—operated in "primitive" cultures. Hutchinson argues that Whitman aligns himself with the tradition of shamanic ecstasy as a self-conscious prophet. For Hutchinson, Whitman's many mystical tendencies are brought together by his self-identification as shaman. He attempts to absorb into himself multiple divergent phenomena as an expression of his democratic vision; he presents himself as an interpreter of the lessons of nature; and he insists that he is a chanter who magically touches all and is touched by each individual reader.

Whitman's transcendentalist[9] leanings are evident, stylistically, beyond his democratization of poetic language. By democratizing language, he

---

possible in a selection of language really used by men" ("Preface to the Second Edition of the *Lyrical Ballads." English Romantic Writers.* Ed. David Perkins. New York: Harcourt, 1967. 321.); and Whitman's "Preface to the 1855 Edition" statement: "What I experience or portray shall go from my composition without a shred of composition" (*Walt Whitman: Leaves of Grass and Selected Prose.* Ed. Sculley Bradley. New York: Holt, 1949).

6   See Jarvis.

7   Usually identified as "bard" within the tradition of oral transmission of poetry.

8   In spiritual traditions such as American transcendentalism, identified with the belief that Nature is infused with the presence of a Higher Being.

9   American transcendentalism is an essentially pantheistic belief, a belief in the presence of the divine in all people and things. By extension, this universal divinity implies the unity or all-connectedness of all of Nature (including man) with an amorphous deity that Emerson, out of convenience rather than out of conventional piety, called "God."

explicitly rejects the separation of special readers from the masses of humanity. The more mystical portion of Whitman's transcendentalist vision—the notion that not only physical Nature but also all of consciousness is connected by universal divinity—is expressed by him in the creative/transcendent acts of poetry and sex. Whitman achieves transcendence and connection between himself and his reader, and between his reader and the universe, by filling his poetry with the transcendent and transcendence-producing language or imagery of sex.[10] But as already noted, Whitman's transcendentalism has precursors in Wordsworth and Bryant—and, in his more immediate past, in Emerson and Thoreau. The assertion that Whitman represents the first flowering in American literature of the transcendentalist philosophy, and the claim that Whitman creates out of transcendentalist ideas a distinctly *American* poetry, a distinctly *American* idiom, and a distinctly *American* poetic philosophy, may constitute an exaggeration.[11]

THE POLITICAL DIMENSIONS OF WHITMAN'S TRANSCENDENTALISM

Whitman's transcendentalism is evident as well in the democratizing gestures his work makes. The democratic prophet emerges in the overt and covert connection making and culture building of his prose and poetry. DeLancey argues that the writer's purpose and aspiration is to build and to change community. He further asserts that Whitman, by forcing his reader to consider the oppositions "other/self" and "body/soul," demonstrates the connection between such concepts, demonstrates his own connection with his reader, and demonstrates the truth of the assertion he makes, in the opening of "Song of Myself," that "every atom belonging to me as good

---

[10] See Aspiz.

[11] The transcendentalist/Romantic bent on the part of Whitman and his work grounds Asselineau's discussion of Whitman in *The Transcendentalist Constant in American Literature*. Perhaps William Cullen Bryant was this continent's first poetic proponent of transcendentalism in 1811 in "Thanatopsis"; in a more formulated way, Emerson and Thoreau began in the 1840s to popularize the philosophy. Emerson's and Thoreau's poetry, as well, preceded that of Whitman onto the American literary stage. A more serious challenge to the claim for Whitman's preeminence as transcendentalist voice is the fact that Asselineau invariably uses the English Romantic poet Wordsworth's (arguably) greatest poem, published in 1807, the famous "Intimations Ode," as an example of the transcendentalist philosophy.

belongs to you."[12] Sarracino argues that Whitman accomplishes this creation of connection with his reader through structural and linguistic gestures and strategies: Whitman's use of fragmented sentence structure and of ellipses allows the reader to fill in blanks in his poetry, and his circular imagery and insistent repetition of metaphors for the broken line and the circle invite the reader to complete his thought and to step into the visionary space Whitman occupies. Phillips views Whitman's racial politics as the worst of the melting-pot mentality, an attempt to exclude the African-American experience and identity from the "American identity" he seeks to define and celebrate.[13]

WHITMAN'S SOCIOPOLITICAL IDEAL REPRESENTED AS HOMOEROTICISM

The idealism of Whitman's democratic vision endured revisions, war, paralytic stroke, and his heartily cynical observation of corruption later in life. This idealism grounds his universal embrace of disparate phenomena, including those least favored by previous generations of poets (such as common human pursuits), those repudiated by transcendentalists and other "nature" poets (cityscapes, celebrations of industry), and those considered taboo (nakedness, frank sexuality, homosexuality). His bodily and sexual frankness, many argue, *explain* Whitman's "capacious embrace" by situating him on the margins of society. Whitman's outcast status as sexual and homosexual rebel inspires, these critics argue, a compassionate celebration of the outcast or "other." This social and political motivation, other critics note, is at odds with Whitman's desires at other periods of his creative life, characterized by caution, such as in the periods preceding and succeeding

---

[12] In a particularly pithy argument, Michael Moon argues that Whitman is concerned with nothing less than the construction of culture's basic foundations, in his repeated revisions of *Leaves of Grass*. Each edition had as its purpose, Moon argues, specific changes Whitman wished American culture to experience and changes he wanted to make in the ways Americans thought about the dimensions of human life: the body, the "body politic," sex itself, and thought itself.

[13] In a representative feminist reading of Whitman, Maire Mullins argues that Whitman's unique stylistic approach is related to what French feminism calls "feminine writing," which like female sexual response is open-ended and multiply pleasurable (rather than "masculine"—narrow and goal-oriented). Mullins, Maire. "*Leaves of Grass* as a Woman's Book." *Walt Whitman Quarterly Review* 10.4 (1993): 195–208.

the first three editions of *Leaves*.[14] Still other critics argue that his homoerotic desire grounds his democratic vision, that his erotic connections with equals in physical sex express his desire to consider all as political equals.

The thorny questions of Whitman's sexual identity and ideology raise other critical issues in addition to the possibility that his primary poetic and political inspiration was homosexuality itself. On the other end of the spectrum are his denials, in later years, of his homosexuality (to many, transparently disingenuous), denials which for many critics justly expel sexuality altogether from the field of interpretive possibility. A few early critics of Whitman responded with the clearest indications that they understood Whitman to represent that "type" labeled "sodomites" in the age before the category names "homosexual" and "heterosexual" were coined. Such early insights into the sexual tastes of the poet render later denials hollow and account for the confusion and impatience with which modern Gay Studies critics, as well as gay readers, respond to ongoing debate about the orientation of Whitman.[15] Less conservative contemporaneous critics, among them the poet and philosopher Ralph Waldo Emerson, responded with warm regard and excitement (at least at first) to the stylistic and philosophical innovations *Leaves of Grass* represented. Ultimately, the conservative response was the most powerful: Whitman, particularly after the 1860 edition, seems to have spent the bulk of his life returning himself and his work to the closet, excising some of the most vibrant and honest homoerotic poetry of the century.

Milton Hindus presents a broad range of reviews from the first half-century of Whitman reception, two of which are included in this Casebook (Emerson's famous letter of praise and encouragement, and a damning and homophobic attack from the opposite extreme). The latter review illustrates quite plainly the public perception of Whitman as a "sodomite" who is engaged in the presentation, and the celebration, of *Peccatum illud horribile*,

---

[14] Many critics discuss the reasons for Whitman's ambivalent openness, among them Schmidgall and Price. See Schmidgall, Gary. *Walt Whitman: A Gay Life*. New York: Dutton, 1997, and Price, Kenneth M. "Walt Whitman, Free Love, and *The Social Revolutionist*." *American Periodicals* 1.1 (1991): 70–82.

[15] As recently as 1990, for example, Edward Wheat, even as he criticizes the "narrowness" with which homoeroticism is said to be the main theme of the Calamus cluster, proceeds to place the poems, narrowly, into an interpretive niche that recognizes only their political significance. See Wheat, Edward M. "Walt Whitman's Political Poetics: The Therapeutic Function of 'Children of Adam' and 'Calamus.'" *The Midwest Quarterly* 31 (1990): 236–251.

inter Christianos non nominandum ("that sin not to be named among Christian men").[16] Whitman is, then, clearly interpreted, even by the unsympathetic, as "homosexual."[17]

Gary Schmidgall argues against what he claims is a recent tendency in Whitman criticism: the assumption that Whitman's late coyness about his sexual orientation, and his self-censorship in editions of *Leaves* past the third, justify a dismissal or a denial of the facts of Whitman's homosexuality and of its impact on his life and vision. Schmidgall presents biographical evidence, largely taken from Horace Traubel, Whitman's friend and archivist, to support the arguments he bases on the texts of the first three editions. Readers of the Calamus poems, and of any others in which Whitman celebrates his love for men, may as easily rely upon their own insight as upon Schmidgall.[18]

THE CASEBOOK SELECTION OF WHITMAN'S POETRY

The poems included in this Casebook provide a chronological cross section of Whitman's work and introduce a broad selection of Whitman's major themes. In these poems, Whitman signals his clear reliance upon American transcendentalist and British Romantic ideas of universal connectedness and artistic inspiration, as well as upon the transcendentalist/Romantic elevation of the common to the value of the poetic, the artistic, and even the metaphysical. From the range of poetry and the selection of criticism of

---

[16] Hindus, Milton. *Walt Whitman: The Critical Heritage.* London, New York: Routledge, 1971. This phrase, quoted from the Horace Griswold review reprinted in this Casebook, is quite a common identifier for what has come to be called "homosexuality." Amusingly, the phrase, often shortened to *the unnameable,* is an unmistakable synonym for the phenomenon it refuses to name. Since the phrase is only applied to a single phenomenon, it effectively subverts its own intention (to obscure so "horrific" a possibility). The other phrase which attempts to describe the phenomenon is also quite interesting as a brief revelation of the century's belief that sexuality is a function of the combination of body and soul: *anima muliebris in corpore virili inclusa,* which means "a feminine soul trapped in a male body."

[17] John Addington Symonds, along with many other contemporaneous and contemporary critics, on the other hand, identifies Whitman as homosexual in hope of supporting political empowerment for that by then newly named category of persons.

[18] See for example "For You O Democracy" in this Casebook. Schmidgall's arguments are, on the whole, inevitably successful, but occasionally slip into inadequate support and hollow logical poses rather than remaining on solid logical ground.

Whitman's work collected here, a few central issues may emerge to introduce the reader to the Whitman corpus and to the field of Whitman studies:

- Whitman embraced as quintessentially American the democratic ideal at a time when the ideals of the American democracy were threatened.
- Whitman applied the democratic ideal to his poetry, both in his choice of subject matter "to sing" and in his universally accessible chanting form (initially perceived as antipoetic).
- Whitman rediscovered a primitive or pure poetic form and claimed it for his creation of a distinctly "American" poetry.
- Whitman's spiritual vision reflected both the democratic ideal and the ideals of "aboriginal" religions, expressing a transcendentalist pantheism rather than a theistic or monotheistic, mainstream vision.
- Whitman's sexual identity, itself culturally transgressive, may account for his embrace of broadly diverse phenomena.

WORKS CONSULTED

Aspiz, Harold. "Sexuality and the Language of Transcendence." *Walt Whitman Quarterly Review* 5.2 (1987): 1–7.

Assilineau, Roger. *The Transcendentalist Constant in American Literature.* New York: New York UP, 1980.

Birmingham, William. "Whitman's Song of the Possible American Self." *Cross Currents* 43 (1993): 341–357.

Bradley, Sculley, ed. *Walt Whitman:* Leaves of Grass *and Selected Prose.* New York: Holt, 1962.

DeLancey, Mark. "Texts, Interpretations, and Whitman's 'Song of Myself.'" *American Literature* 61 (1989): 359–381.

Hindus, Milton. *Walt Whitman: The Critical Heritage.* New York: Routledge, 1971.

Hutchinson, George B. *The Ecstatic Whitman: Literary Shamanism and the Crisis of the Union.* Columbus: Ohio State UP, 1986.

Huxley, Thomas Henry. "Agnosticism and Christianity." *Prose of the Victorian Period.* Ed. William E. Buckler. New York: Houghton, 1958. 537–541.

Jarvis, D. R. "Whitman and Speech-Based Prosody." *Walt Whitman Review* 27.2 (1981): 51–62.

Kucich, John. *Repression in Victorian Fiction: Charlotte Bronte, George Eliot, and Charles Dickens.* Berkeley: U of California P, 1987.

Moon, Michael. *Disseminating Whitman: Revision and Corporeality in* Leaves of Grass. Cambridge: Harvard UP, 1991.

Mullins, Maire. "*Leaves of Grass* as a 'Woman's Book.'" *Walt Whitman Quarterly Review* 10.4 (1993): 195–208.

Phillips, Dana. "Nineteenth-Century Racial Thought and Whitman's 'Democratic Ethnology of the Future.'" *Nineteenth-Century Literature* 49 (1994): 289–320.

Price, Kenneth M. "Walt Whitman, Free Love, and *The Social Revolutionist.*" *American Periodicals* 1.1 (1991): 70–82.

Sarracino, Carmine. "Figures of Transcendence in Whitman's Poetry." *Walt Whitman Quarterly Review* 5.1 (1987): 1–11.

Schmidgall, Gary. *Walt Whitman: A Gay Life.* London, New York: Dutton/Penguin, 1997.

Snyder, John. *The Dear Love of Man: Tragic and Lyric Communion in Walt Whitman.* Paris: Mouton, 1975.

Wheat, Edward M. "Walt Whitman's Political Poetics: The Therapeutic Function of 'Children of Adam' and 'Calamus.'" *The Midwest Quarterly* 31 (1990): 236–251.

Wordsworth, William. "Preface to the Second Edition of the Lyrical Ballads." *English Romantic Writers.* Ed. David Perkins. New York: Harcourt, 1967. 320–331.

Zehr, Janet S. "The Act of Remembering in 'Out of the Cradle Endlessly Rocking.'" *Walt Whitman Quarterly Review* 1.2 (1983): 21–25.

Literature

About the Author

Walt Whitman (1819–1892) was born when the republic was still in its first fifty years, when the promise of the American ideal of universal equality was still relatively new. This ideal was, significantly, as yet substantially unrealized by and for African Americans, women, Native Americans, and other minorities. Perhaps more significantly, Whitman was born virtually at the moment American identity began to crystallize, with the final repulsion by the United States of British dominance of North America in the War of 1812. By the time he himself was fifty years of age, the republic had faced and survived a devastating challenge to its very existence, the American Civil War. Yet even after the war, when the legal structure was in place to extend suffrage to African-American males, in practice the great American ideal of universal equality remained elusive. Women were more than fifty years away from gaining the vote; many African Americans were a century away from actual voting rights; and Native Americans as well as many immigrant minorities were disempowered, as they remain even now.

Whitman was born on the largely rural Long Island, the beaches of which he so often celebrates and, in his poetic persona, inhabits. Early in his life, his family moved to Brooklyn, where for only a brief six years Whitman was formally educated. His uneducated parents exposed Whitman to various ideologies that figure later in his thought and work. They were firm adherents to the democratic political ideals of the founding fathers, as well as close friends with the Quaker Elias Hicks. From the first influence, undoubtedly, derives Whitman's democratic zeal; the second influence accounts for his confidence in the inner revelation of divine truths, and for later transcendentalist assertions about the god within. Whitman celebrates his humble genetic legacy and his American identity at the same time as he honors his earthiness and the influences of his parents, when he proclaims, in the opening lines of "Song of Myself," that he has been "form'd from this soil, this air, / Born here of parents born here from parents the same, and their parents the same."

At the age of thirteen he ended his academic career and became a printer's apprentice. This early professional choice no doubt smoothed Whitman's later career path, especially his movement among the fields of printing, journalism, and publishing. Whitman's adolescence and young adulthood saw a swift kaleidoscope of teaching and newspaper jobs, culminating in the editorship of the Brooklyn Eagle in 1846. The rapid shifts among Whitman's careers during his adolescence, usually a time of experimentation both professional and sexual, may elicit speculation about the relationship between Whitman's political and sexual orientations and his restlessness. His ardent democratic principles, forged during this time, did eventually cause him some conflict, precipitating at least one firing—the loss of the Brooklyn Eagle editorship in January 1848. (Later, the "indecency" of Leaves of Grass cost him his job at the Department of the Interior.) Any of his experimentations—professional, sexual, political—may illustrate the early expression of the mature Whitman's central sexual and political tendencies: his embrace of the "transgressive" or marginal and his celebration of diversity.

THE PUBLICATION OF LEAVES OF GRASS

The publication of Whitman's first edition of Leaves of Grass shocked and delighted his readers. Ringing the death knell of poetic decorum, and, some said, of decency, Whitman's poetry provoked his conservative audience to the baldest insults. Whitman's background in printing and publishing accounts for the ease with which he published his own first edition and for the bold shamelessness with which he promoted himself and all the editions of his poetry. He printed and distributed the first edition at his own expense. (Whitman mythology has it that he actually set some of the type for it himself.) The omission of his name from the title page of that first edition, apparently a gesture of humility, is revealed as a ploy by his self-identification within the poem "Song of Myself," by the anonymous, glowing reviews he wrote and submitted for the volume, by his commercial use of Emerson's congratulatory letter in (and on the cover of) the second edition, and by his assertion of his own innovatory style and function, in the preface to the first edition.[1] For the rest of his life, Whitman continued to exercise much control over the publication of *Leaves of Grass,* revising and enlarging it through the additions of several large clusters of poems, including "Children of Adam" and "Calamus" in 1860, and "Drum Taps," published separately in 1865 and incorporated into the 1867 edition of *Leaves.* Whitman also attempted to exercise control over the reception of *Leaves* itself, and of himself as a poet, as is evidenced by his early writing of anonymous reviews, by his later excision from *Leaves* of his most explicit verses, and by contributions to biographies of his own life.

Whitman's poetic voice found him, after a professional false start in journalism, in the decade immediately preceding the Civil War, when the country stood poised (in Lincoln's later words) "to test if this nation, or any nation . . . conceived and . . . dedicated [to the ideals of liberty and universal equality] can long endure." Whitman's political vision, established so clearly in the embrace of all realities upon which his poetry, and especially his catalogues, insist, is already expansive in the decade before his first edition of *Leaves* appears. In the 1840s, a full ten years before his poetic manifesto of democratic idealism, Whitman involved himself in the abolitionist movement. The owner of the *Brooklyn Eagle* fired him over his stance against the extension of slavery to the new territories. And in the last years of that decade, Whitman contributed to the abolitionist *Freemen* newspaper in New York. As is inevitably the case with a democratic national vision, the conflict between the personal pursuit of life, liberty, and happiness, and the social pressures and necessities of the equality ideal and of national identity—freedom versus conformity—creates an irresolvable tension.[2] Whitman's vision, as well, exhibits the stress of the seemingly opposed positions of individuality and equality. The inherent danger of his individualist ideal is an almost animal self-absorption and lawlessness "which would be corrosive of democracy or any other political system."[3] The

---

[1] See Hindus, Milton. *Walt Whitman: The Critical Heritage.* New York: Routledge, 1971. Hindus includes examples of Whitman's anonymous self-reviews. And see Whitman's preface in this Casebook.

[2] Whitman's commitment to racial equality has recently been questioned by Dana Phillips on precisely this ground: the argument that Whitman specifies a "singular culture . . . and . . . common racial identity" for citizens of the United States (Phillips 116).

[3] Wheat, Edward M. "Walt Whitman's Political Poetics: The Therapeutic Function of 'Children of Adam' and 'Calamus.'" *The Midwest Quarterly* 31 (1990): 236–251.

inherent danger to individuality of (a homogenizing) equality, on the other hand, is mindless conformity.

Whitman's inner conflict over the claims of individualism and those of equality must have been intensified during the Civil War, when the conflict of individual freedoms (of African Americans) against the claims of the slave states was echoed on the national level by the conflict between individual states and the republic. But Whitman's response to this conflict, after his brother was wounded in 1862, was characteristically a humane rather than political one. He symbolically embraced the woundedness of the nation, by embracing the wounded themselves, devoting his time during the rest of the war to volunteer nursing in Washington, D.C., hospitals. His experiences during and after the war inspired what was later added, as the third great cluster of additional poems, to the growing Leaves of Grass: "Drum Taps" (published as a separate collection in May 1865 and incorporated into Leaves in 1867). A few months after the publication of "Drum Taps," Whitman published, in September 1865, one of his greatest and most classically formal poems, the elegy to Lincoln "When Lilacs Last in the Dooryard Bloom'd."

Whitman's final years in Washington, from 1865 to 1873, saw the solidification of his place in the history of American letters. At the end of June 1865 Whitman was fired from the Department of the Interior because its secretary considered Leaves of Grass obscene. (He was hired by the attorney general's office the next day due to the influence of his friends.) At the beginning of the following year a pamphlet entitled "The Good Gray Poet" was published by William Douglas O'Connor in defense of Whitman's character and work. Its title is a descriptive phrase with which Whitman's name has ever since been associated. British literary critic William Rossetti published an article on Whitman in the London Chronicle in the middle of 1867, and the next year brought out an English edition of Whitman's poems (Poems of Walt Whitman). The first critical biography of Whitman, to which he contributed heavily, as he did to later biographies written during his lifetime, appeared in 1867. (Whitman's concern for his place in the history of letters caused him always to contribute actively to his own poetic and literary reputation.)

Whitman was also learning, during this sojourn in the nation's capital, that the ideal he celebrated was in practice a heavily tarnished one. In 1871, he published a vigorous attack on American society and its economic vision in "Democratic Vistas," a far-reaching and angry prose piece. As he had in his "Preface to the 1855 Edition of Leaves of Grass" (reprinted in this

Casebook), Whitman here elevates the poet as prophet or conscience of democracy.

Only a few years of uninhibited vigor remained for Whitman in Washington after the war, despite his energetic emotional recovery from the tragedies and traumas of 1865. In 1873, Whitman suffered a stroke which partially paralyzed him, and was moved to the home of the brother whose injury had brought him to Washington in the first place. There, in Camden, New Jersey, Whitman lived the duration of his life, ever revising and editing his completed work and adding to his corpus important late poems and even more important prose works. "Specimen Days," his notes from the Civil War years, appeared in 1882. In 1888, Whitman prefaced the collection of poems *November Boughs* with "A Backward Glance O'er Travel'd Roads," a final statement on *Leaves* as well as on literature in general and on his spiritual vision. Surrounded in his final years of life by admiring friends, Whitman oversaw the final "deathbed" edition of his collected works (1892), and died March 26, 1892, just short of his seventy-third birthday.

The Poems

"Song of Myself" appeared in the first edition of 1855 and was last edited by Whitman in 1881. The first two sections (lines 1-37) represent a fraction of the poem's sixty-five pages. Whitman was not exaggerating when he asked the reader to "Stop this day and night with me," nor when he promised that the reader would then "possess the good of the earth and sun" and "shall listen to all sides and filter them from your self." His embrace of diverse phenomena for poetic celebration is, indeed, wide ranging; and his assurance that he need not look beyond his own embrace, his own person, to find a "kosmos," is proved by his inclusion of that cosmos in his song of the "self."

"Had I the Choice" (undated) and "When I Heard the Learn'd Astronomer" (1865) briefly express the individualist's vision. In each poem, the speaker asserts the primacy of direct experiential encounter with reality and rejects authority, literary or scientific, in the creation of art or the understanding of the cosmos. "Out of the Cradle Endlessly Rocking" (1859) reinforces this position, and clearly aligns Whitman with the second-generation English Romantic poet Keats, in Keats's romance with death as a transitional state and a source of inspiration.[1] "For You O Democracy" (1860) is an early idealistic expression of Whitman's political ideal with clear homoerotic dimensions: a nation of comrades whose "manly love" (1.9) Whitman proposes to use to "make the continent indissoluble" (1.1). "A Noiseless Patient Spider" (1862–63) provides a natural metaphor for the transcendent urges Whitman himself experiences. "Cavalry Crossing a Ford" (1865) hints at such a transcendence as well, in the ambiguous combination of images of injury, Union-army identity, and African-American racial identity, as well as in its central image, the ford itself. "The Dalliance of the Eagles"

---

[1] Compare "Out of the Cradle Endlessly Rocking" with Keats's "Ode to a Nightingale" and "Ode on a Grecian Urn."

(1880) celebrates raw, natural sexuality. "The Base of All Metaphysics" (1871) presents Whitman's spiritual philosophy in its simplest form, elevating "cohesive" love above the authoritarian religious forms that, in Whitman's view, obscure rather than reveal truth. Whitman's "Preface to the 1855 edition of *Leaves of Grass*" (included in the Secondary Sources section of the Casebook) represents the poet's first aesthetic and political manifesto, and is the primary basis for the argument presented by the sample student research paper: a comparison of Whitman's stated aesthetic philosophy with his poetic practice of it.

from

Song of Myself
(1855)

1

I celebrate myself, and sing myself,
And what I assume you shall assume,
For every atom belonging to me as good belongs to you.

I loafe and invite my soul,
5   I lean and loafe at my ease observing a spear of summer grass.

My tongue, every atom of my blood, form'd from this soil, this air,
Born here of parents born here from parents the same, and their parents
      the same,
I, now thirty-seven years old in perfect health begin,
Hoping to cease not till death.

10 Creeds and schools in abeyance,
Retiring back a while sufficed at what they are, but never forgotten,
I harbor for good or bad, I permit to speak at every hazard,
Nature without check with original energy.

2

Houses and rooms are full of perfumes, the shelves are crowded with
      perfumes,
15 I breathe the fragrance myself and know it and like it,
The distillation would intoxicate me also, but I shall not let it.

The atmosphere is not a perfume, it has no taste of the distillation, it is
   odorless,
It is for my mouth forever, I am in love with it,
I will go to the bank by the wood and become undisguised and naked,
20   I am mad for it to be in contact with me.

The smoke of my own breath,
Echoes, ripples, buzz'd whispers, love-root, silk-thread, crotch and vine,
My respiration and inspiration, the beating of my heart, the passing of blood
   and air through my lungs,
The sniff of green leaves and dry leaves, and of the shore and dark-color'd
   sea-rocks, and of hay in the barn,
25   The sound of the belch'd words of my voice loos'd to the eddies of the wind,
A few light kisses, a few embraces, a reaching around of arms,
The play of shine and shade on the trees as the supple boughs wag,
The delight alone or in the rush of the streets, or along the fields and
   hill-sides,
The feeling of health, the full-noon trill, the song of me rising from bed
   and meeting the sun.

30   Have you reckon'd a thousand acres much? have you reckon'd the earth
   much?
Have you practis'd so long to learn to read?
Have you felt so proud to get at the meaning of poems?

Stop this day and night with me and you shall possess the origin of all poems,
You shall possess the good of the earth and sun, (there are millions of
   suns left,)
35   You shall no longer take things at second or third hand, nor look through
   the eyes of the dead, nor feed on the spectres in books,
You shall not look through my eyes either, nor take things from me,
You shall listen to all sides and filter them from your self.

DISCUSSION QUESTIONS

1. Sarracino points out that the first and last words of the entire poem
    "Song of Myself" are, respectively, "I" and "you." The same is true of
    the Casebook's selection from the poem, sections 1 and 2: It begins with
    the phrase "I celebrate myself" and ends with "filter them from your
    self." What might this suggest about Whitman's ideas of his relation
    to his readers?

2. Of what significance is the "spear of grass" Whitman's speaker is observing?

3. What do you think Whitman's purpose might be in establishing the continuous presence of generations of his family "born here"?

4. What is Whitman's purpose, in this selection of "Song of Myself," in describing both the domestic scene and the "bank by the wood"?

Out of the Cradle Endlessly Rocking
(1881)

Out of the cradle endlessly rocking,
Out of the mocking-bird's throat, the musical shuttle,
Out of the Ninth-month[1] midnight,
Over the sterile sands and the fields beyond, where the child leaving his bed
    wandered alone, bareheaded, barefoot,
5   Down from the showered halo,
Up from the mystic play of shadows twining and twisting as if they were alive,
Out from the patches of briers and blackberries,
From the memories of the bird that chanted to me,
From your memories sad brother, from the fitful risings and fallings I heard,
10 From under that yellow half-moon late-risen and swollen as if
    with tears,
From those beginning notes of yearning and love there in the mist,
From the thousand responses of my heart never to cease,
From the myriad thence-aroused words,
From the word stronger and more delicious than any,
15 From such as now they start the scene revisiting,
As a flock, twittering, rising, or overhead passing,
Borne hither, ere all eludes me, hurriedly,
A man, yet by these tears a little boy again,
Throwing myself on the sand confronting the waves,
20 I, chanter of pains and joys, uniter of here and hereafter,
Taking all hints to use them, but swiftly leaping beyond them,
A reminiscence sing.

---

[1] September, in Quaker usage.

Once Paumanok,[2]
When the lilac-scent was in the air and Fifth-month[3] grass was growing,
25   Up this seashore in some briers,
Two feathered guests from Alabama, two together,
And their nest, and four light-green eggs spotted with brown,
And every day the he-bird to and fro near at hand,
And every day the she-bird crouched on her nest, silent, with bright eyes,
30   And every day I, a curious boy, never too close, never disturbing them,
Cautiously peering, absorbing, translating.

Shine! Shine! Shine!
Pour down your warmth, great sun!
While we bask, we two together.

35   *Two together!*
Winds blow south, or winds blow north,
Day come white, or night come black,

Home, or rivers and mountains from home,
Singing all time, minding no time,
40   *While we two keep together.*

Till of a sudden,
Maybe killed, unknown to her mate,
One forenoon the she-bird crouched not on the nest,
Nor returned that afternoon, nor the next,
45   Nor ever appeared again.

And thenceforward all summer in the sound of the sea,
And at night under the full of the moon in calmer weather,
Over the hoarse surging of the sea,
Or flitting from brier to brier by day,
50   I saw, I heard at intervals the remaining one, the he-bird,
The solitary guest from Alabama.

---

[2] Pronounced *paw-mah'-nok.* The Native American name for Long Island, where Whitman grew up.

[3] May.

Blow! blow! blow!
Blow up sea-winds along Paumanok's shore;
I wait and I wait till you blow my mate to me.

55 Yes, when the stars glistened,
All night long on the prong of a moss-scalloped stake,
Down almost amid the slapping waves,
Sat the lone singer wonderful causing tears.

He called on his mate,
60 He poured forth the meanings which I of all men know.

Yes my brother I know,
The rest might not, but I have treasured every note,
For more than once dimly down to the beach gliding,
Silent, avoiding the moonbeams, blending myself with the shadows
65 Recalling now the obscure shapes, the echoes, the sounds and sights
        after their sorts,
The white arms out in the breakers tirelessly tossing,
I, with bare feet, a child, the wind wafting my hair,
Listened long and long.

Listened to keep, to sing, now translating the notes,
70 Following you my brother.

Soothe! soothe! soothe!
Close on its wave soothes the wave behind,
And again another behind embracing and lapping, every one close,
But my love soothes not me, not me.

75 *Low hangs the moon, it rose late,*
It is lagging— O I think it is heavy with love, with love.

O madly the sea pushes upon the land,
With love, with love.

O night! Do I not see my love fluttering out among the breakers?
80 *What is that little black thing I see there in the white?*

Loud! loud! loud!
Loud I call to you, my love!

High and clear I shoot my voice over the waves,
Surely you must know who is here, is here,
85 *You must know who I am, my love.*

Low-hanging moon!
What is that dusky spot in your brown yellow?
O it is the shape, the shape of my mate!
O moon do not keep her from me any longer.

90 *Land! land! O land!*
Whichever way I turn, O I think you could give me my mate back again
        if you only would,
For I am almost sure I see her dimly whichever way I look.

O rising stars!
Perhaps the one I want so much will rise, will rise with some of you.

95 *O throat! O trembling throat!*
Sound clearer through the atmosphere!
Pierce the woods, the earth,
Somewhere listening to catch you must be the one I want.

Shake out carols!
100 *Solitary here, the night's carols!*
Carols of lonesome love! death's carols!
Carols under that lagging, yellow, waning moon!
O under that moon where she droops almost down into the sea!
O reckless despairing carols.

105 *But soft! sink low!*
Soft! let me just murmur,
And do you wait a moment you husky-noised sea,
For somewhere I believe I heard my mate responding to me,
So faint, I must be still, be still to listen,
100 *But not altogether still, for then she might not come immediately to me.*

Hither my love!
Here I am! here!
With this just-sustained note I announce myself to you,
This gentle call is for you my love, for you.

115 *Do not be decoyed elsewhere,*
    That is the whistle of the wind, it is not my voice,
    That is the fluttering, the fluttering of the spray,
    Those are the shadows of leaves.

    O darkness! O in vain!
120 *O I am very sick and sorrowful.*

    O brown halo in the sky near the moon, drooping upon the sea!
    O troubled reflection in the sea!

    O throat! O throbbing heart!
    And I singing uselessly, uselessly all the night.

    O past! O happy life! O songs of joy!
125 *In the air, in the woods, over fields,*
    Loved! loved! loved! loved! loved!

    But my mate no more, no more with me!
    We two together no more.

130 The aria sinking,
    All else continuing, the stars shining,
    The winds blowing, the notes of the bird continuous echoing,
    With angry moans the fierce old mother incessantly moaning,
    On the sands of Paumanok's shore gray and rustling,
135 The yellow half-moon enlarged, sagging down, drooping, the face of the sea
        almost touching,
    The boy ecstatic, with his bare feet the waves, with his hair the atmosphere
        dallying,
    The love in the heart long pent, now loose, now at last tumultuously bursting,
    The aria's meaning, the ears, the soul, swiftly depositing,
    The strange tears down the cheeks coursing,
140 The colloquy there, the trio, each uttering,
    The undertone, the savage old mother incessantly crying,
    To the boy's soul's questions sullenly timing, some drowned secret hissing,
    To the outsetting bard.

    Demon or bird! (said the boy's soul,)
145 Is it indeed toward your mate you sing? or is it really to me?

For I, that was a child, my tongue's use sleeping, now I have heard you,
Now in a moment I know what I am for, I awake,
And already a thousand singers, a thousand songs, clearer, louder and
  more sorrowful than yours,
A thousand warbling echoes have started to life within me, never to die.

150 O you singer solitary, singing by yourself, projecting me,
  O solitary me listening, never more shall I cease perpetuating you,
  Never more shall I escape, never more the reverberations,
  Never more the cries of unsatisfied love be absent from me,
  Never again leave me to be the peaceful child I was before what there in
    the night,
155 By the sea under the yellow and sagging moon,
  The messenger there aroused, the fire, the sweet hell within,
  The unknown want, the destiny of me.

  O give me the clue! (it lurks in the night here somewhere,)
  O if I am to have so much, let me have more!

160 A word then, (for I will conquer it,)
  The word final, superior to all,
  Subtle, sent up—what is it?—I listen;
  Are you whispering it, and have been all the time, you sea-waves?
  Is that it from your liquid rims and wet sands?

165 Whereto answering, the sea,
  Delaying not, hurrying not,
  Whispered me through the night, and very plainly before daybreak,
  Lisped to me the low and delicious word death,
  And again death, death, death, death,
170 Hissing melodious, neither like the bird nor like my aroused child's heart,
  But edging near as privately for me rustling at my feet,
  Creeping thence steadily up to my ears and laving me softly all over,
  Death, death, death, death, death.

  Which I do not forget,
175 But fuse the song of my dusky demon and brother,
  That he sang to me in the moonlight on Paumanok's gray beach,
  With the thousand responsive songs at random,
  My own songs awaked from that hour,

And with them the key, the word up from the waves,
180 The word of the sweetest song and all songs,
That strong and delicious word which, creeping to my feet,
(Or like some old crone rocking the cradle, swathed in sweet garments,
        bending aside,)
The sea whispered me.

DISCUSSION QUESTIONS

1. What thematic idea might be suggested by the endlessness of the cradle rocking? By the waves the speaker confronts?

2. What might be significant (in terms of Whitman's idea of the identity of the poet) about the confusion the speaker experiences between himself as a man reminiscing and himself made a boy by his tears?

3. The speaker lists many implied sources here for the reminiscence he sings. Can you categorize these sources?

4. What is the significance of the loss that the speaker of this poem recounts, and of the word he hears the sea whisper, at this moment? Why would the result of this experience be the transformation of a boy into a poet, as Whitman implies is the case here?

5. How are the loss and the word whispered by the sea related to the endless rocking and the ceaseless waves?

6. What immediately obvious comparisons (for example, about the identity of the poet) can be drawn between this poem and the excerpt from "Song of Myself"?

When I Heard the Learn'd
Astronomer
(1865)

When I heard the learn'd astronomer,
When the proofs, the figures, were ranged in columns before me,
When I was shown the charts and diagrams, to add, divide, and
        measure them,
5 When I sitting heard the astronomer where he lectured with much
        applause in the lecture-room,
How soon unaccountable I became tired and sick,

Till rising and gliding out I wander'd off by myself,
In the mystical moist night-air, and from time to time,
10 Look'd up in perfect silence at the stars.

DISCUSSION QUESTIONS

1. What types of experiencing or knowing are contrasted in this poem?
2. What claim does Whitman make for the value of knowing by direct experience when he describes the night air as "mystical"?

A Noiseless Patient Spider
(1881)

A noiseless patient spider,
I mark'd where on a little promontory it stood isolated,
Mark'd how to explore the vacant vast surrounding,
It launch'd forth filament, filament, filament, out of itself,
5 Ever unreeling them, ever tirelessly speeding them.

And you O my soul where you stand,
Surrounded, detached, in measureless oceans of space,
Ceaselessly musing, venturing, throwing, seeking the spheres to
     connect them,
Till the bridge you will need be form'd, till the ductile anchor hold,
10 Till the gossamer thread you fling catch somewhere, O my soul.

DISCUSSION QUESTIONS

1. What is the spider's way of experiencing "reality"?
2. Which qualities of the spider, unstated but clear, make the analogy between the spider and the soul work?
3. Which qualities do not work for this analogy?

Had I the Choice

Had I the choice to tally greatest bards,
To limn their portraits, stately, beautiful, and emulate at will,
Homer with all his wars and warriors—Hector, Achilles, Ajax,

Or Shakespeare's woe-entangled Hamlet, Lear, Othello—Tennyson's
    fair ladies,
5   Meter or wit the best, or choice conceit to wield in perfect rhyme,
       delight of singers;
These, these, O sea, all these I'd gladly barter,
Would you the undulation of one wave, its trick to me transfer,
Or breathe one breath of yours upon my verse,
And leave its odor there.

DISCUSSION QUESTIONS

1. In the speaker's view, what is the best source of inspiration for the poet?

2. What comparative worth does Whitman assign to the formally recognized
    elements of poetry and the movement and the odor (and the unspecified
    gesture, the "trick") of the sea?

3. What does Whitman imply about himself by both emulating and
    rejecting the poets he names? What does he imply about their value
    as sources of inspiration and of poetic patterns?

Cavalry Crossing a Ford
(1865)

A line in long array where they wind betwixt green islands,
They take a serpentine course, their arms flash in the sun—hark to the
    musical clank,
Behold the silvery river, in it the splashing horses loitering stop to drink,
Behold the brown-faced men, each group, each person a picture, the
negligent rest on the saddles,
5   Some emerge on the opposite bank, others are just entering the ford—while,
Scarlet and blue and snowy white,
The guidon flags flutter gayly in the wind.

DISCUSSION QUESTIONS

1. What dramatic tension does the short descriptive piece "Cavalry Crossing
    a Ford" present?

2. What appears to be important, thematically, to Whitman in this image of
    men in a "line in long array"?

The Dalliance of the Eagles
(1880, 1881)

Skirting the river road, (my forenoon walk, my rest,)
Skyward in air a sudden muffled sound, the dalliance of the eagles,
The rushing amorous contact high in space together,
The clinching interlocking claws, a living, fierce, gyrating wheel,
5   Four beating wings, two beaks, a swirling mass tight grappling,
In tumbling turning clustering loops, straight downward falling,
Till o'er the river pois'd, the twain yet one, a moment's lull,
A motionless still balance in the air, then parting, talons loosing,
Upward again on slow-firm pinions slanting, their separate diverse flight,
10   She hers, he his, pursuing.

DISCUSSION QUESTIONS

1. What might the speaker mean by implying that his morning walk is also his "rest"?

2. Why does Whitman here depict the fierce passion as well as the moral neutrality of the eagles' mating?

For You O Democracy
(1860, 1881)

Come, I will make the continent indissoluble,
I will make the most splendid race the sun ever shone upon,
I will make divine magnetic lands,
     With the love of comrades,
5   With the life-long love of comrades.

I will plant companionship thick as trees along all the rivers of America,
     and along the shores of the great lakes, and all over the prairies,
I will make inseparable cities with their arms about each other's necks,

     By the love of comrades,
     By the manly love of comrades.

10   For you these from me, O Democracy, to serve you ma femme!
For you, for you I am trilling these songs.

DISCUSSION QUESTIONS

1. What part in the creation of a continent-spanning country does the speaker envision for himself?

2. What might the speaker mean by "manly love"?

3. Of what relative importance, to this speaker and to his democracy-enhancing project, are male-male and male-female relationships?

The Base of All Metaphysics
(1871)

And now gentlemen,
A word I give to remain in your memories and minds,
As base and finalè too for all metaphysics.

(So to the students the old professor,
At the close of his crowded course.)

Having studied the new and antique, the Greek and Germanic systems,
Kant having studied and stated, Fichte and Schelling and Hegel,
Stated the lore of Plato, and Socrates greater than Plato,
And greater than Socrates sought and stated, Christ divine having
    studied long,
I see reminiscent to-day those Greek and Germanic systems,
See the philosophies all, Christian churches and tenets see,
Yet underneath Socrates clearly see, and underneath Christ the divine I see,
The dear love of man for his comrade, the attraction of friend to friend,
Of the well-married husband and wife, of children and parents,
Of city for city and land for land.

DISCUSSION QUESTIONS

1. What change occurs in the image of the learned man between the poems "When I Heard the Learn'd Astronomer" and "The Base of All Metaphysics"?

2. What, according to Whitman, *is* the basis of all metaphysics (philosophical and spiritual inquiry)?

Research Topics

The Sexual Vision of Walt Whitman

1. The issue of Whitman's sexual "vision" continues to be debated, in large part because of the trouble he took to obscure himself behind the wide sexual embrace his poems represent, thereby revealing his ambivalence toward his own sexual vision. This ambivalence, according to Kenneth Price (see the Bibliography), is in fact a powerful creative force for Whitman. Other writers, too (John Kucich, for example, in *Repression in Victorian Fiction*), have traced the artistic productivity of the repression/sublimation mechanism described by Freud. What evidence of "productive repression" can you find in the poems included here?

The Political Vision of Walt Whitman

2. Whitman's democratic ideal, the elevation of the individual and the universal equality of all people and phenomena, is at the same time consistent with the antiauthoritarian attitude of the nineteenth century and dangerous to any political system, as Edward M. Wheat argues (see Works Consulted). In what ways does Whitman align himself with one or the other of these opposite poles of the American vision— individualism versus equality— or interpose himself between them?

3. What political or social vision seems inherent in the poems collected here? Are Mark DeLancey and William Birmingham correct in suggesting that Whitman's primary political agenda is to build community? How do the Casebook's selections from "Song of Myself" and "The Noiseless Patient Spider" fit such an interpretation of Whitman's purpose?

SEXUALITY AS TRANSCENDENCE IN WHITMAN

4. Whitman seeks transcendence in two ways, according to Harold Aspiz. Identify evidence in the poems collected in the Casebook that Whitman is elevating sex and poetic composition themselves to the status of the transcendental.

Whitman as a Prophet

5. As George Hutchinson argues (see Works Consulted), Whitman aligns himself with shamanic, "pre-institutionalized" forms of "religious" or

spiritual experience. Shamans of native traditions concern themselves with individual and group relationships to the spiritual. Furthermore, shamans aid in maintaining such relationships when either the individual or the group undertakes some task, such as a vision quest, a hunting expedition, or a war. Of what relevance might such observations be to an understanding of "Cavalry Crossing a Ford" or to Whitman's vision of the poet himself as that is outlined in the 1855 Preface?

Whitman as a Prophet of Democracy

6. Whitman positions himself between the conflicting poles of the American political experiment—radical individualism versus universal equality. He may attempt to absorb these opposites and to "redeem" the conflict; or he may envision (as Birmingham maintains) a balancing act in which he "raises egocentricity to impossible heights on the one hand and affirms the inherently relational nature of the self on the other." Describe Whitman's democratic vision as you perceive it to be represented in each of the poems.

Whitman's Prosody

7. Whitman's irregular line length, irregular meter, and absence of rhyme, all distinctive features of the poems included in this Casebook, force the reader to evaluate the value of Whitman's poetry *as* poetry. D. R. Jarvis and Carmine Sarracino address the issue of Whitman's "literariness," focusing on two formal distinctions of Whitman's poetry: his free verse style and his formal/metaphorical figures of transcendence. How do the units of meaning (roughly speaking, the sentences) as well as the subject matter of "Cavalry Crossing a Ford" (or any of the other poems collected in the Casebook) illustrate what Jarvis designates "speech-based prosody" and demonstrate Whitman's use of "broken line" or "circular" images of transcendence?

Whitman's Critical Reception, Then and Now

8. Milton Hindus collects evidence of the critical conflicts swirling around Whitman's initial publications, and around Whitman himself (see Emerson's letter to Whitman and the Griswold review). These criticisms of Whitman had to do with style, conformity to poetic, sexual, and political expectations, and the self-promotion in which Whitman is engaged. Choose a selection of the poems included here, and respond to them from these perspectives. How do Whitman's stylistic choices strike you? How original are his style and choice of subject matter (the sea, the

stars, migrating birds, spiders, human experience)? What agenda might Whitman have in rejecting the example of the "greatest bards" (Homer, Shakespeare, and Tennyson), as he asserts he wishes to do in "Had I the Choice"?

Whitman the Kosmos, a Transcendentalist Vision

9. Whitman's claim, in the selection from "Song of Myself," that "every atom belonging to me as good belongs to you," expresses concretely the spiritual (and political) vision propounded by transcendentalist philosophers Ralph Waldo Emerson, Henry David Thoreau, and Bronson Alcott. Using the text of "The Oversoul" by Emerson or "Civil Disobedience" by Thoreau, examine the extent to which Whitman may be identified among the transcendentalists.

Whitman and Race Relations

10. Dana Phillips argues that Whitman resolves the inherent conflict between individualism and equality (the two seemingly opposed primary ideals of American democracy) by elevating a homogeneous ideal American identity, thereby sublimating the individual differences, especially the ethnic and racial differences that outline individualism itself, in favor of equality. In the limited selection of Whitman's poetry presented in this Casebook, find evidence for or against the position Phillips adopts.

Whitman the Feminist

11. What evidence can you find in Whitman's poetry (or in his Preface) that Whitman entertained feminist ideals: the equality of the sexes, the suspicion of gender expectations, the rejection of heterosexism?

Secondary Sources

WALT WHITMAN
SCULLEY BRADLEY, ED.

Preface to 1855 Edition
"Leaves of Grass"
(1962)*

America does not repel the past or what it has produced under its forms or amid other politics or the idea of castes or the old religions . . . accepts the lesson with calmness . . . is not so impatient as has been supposed that the slough still sticks to opinions and manners and literature while the life which served its requirements has passed into the new life of the new forms . . . perceives that the corpse is slowly borne from the eating and sleeping rooms of the house . . . perceives that it waits a little while in the door . . . that it was fittest for its days . . . that its action has descended to the stalwart and wellshaped heir who approaches . . . and that he shall be fittest for his days.

The Americans of all nations at any time upon the earth have probably the fullest poetical nature. The United States themselves are essentially the greatest poem. In the history of the earth hitherto the largest and most stirring appear tame and orderly to their ampler largeness and stir. Here at last is something in the doings of man that corresponds with the broadcast doings of the day and night. Here is not merely a nation but a teeming nation of nations. Here is action untied from strings necessarily blind to particulars and details magnificently moving in vast masses. Here is the hospitality which forever indicates heroes. . . . Here are the roughs and beards and space and ruggedness and nonchalance that the soul loves. Here the performance disdaining the trivial unapproached in the tremendous

---

* Note that some of the articles in this section do not use current MLA documentation style. See the Appendix for new MLA format.

audacity of its crowds and groupings and the push of its perspective spreads with crampless and flowing breadth and showers its prolific and splendid extravagance. One sees it must indeed own the riches of the summer and winter, and need never be bankrupt while corn grows from the ground or the orchards drop apples or the bays contain fish or men beget children upon women.

Other states indicate themselves in their deputies . . . but the genius of the United States is not best or most in its executives or legislatures, nor in its ambassadors or authors or colleges or churches or parlors, nor even in its newspapers or inventors . . . but always most in the common people. Their manners speech dress friendships—the freshness and candor of their physiognomy—the picturesque looseness of their carriage . . . their deathless attachment to freedom—their aversion to anything indecorous or soft or mean—the practical acknowledgment of the citizens of one state by the citizens of all other states—the fierceness of their roused resentment— their curiosity and welcome of novelty—their self-esteem and wonderful sympathy—their susceptibility to a slight—the air they have of persons who never knew how it felt to stand in the presence of superiors—the fluency of their speech—their delight in music, the sure symptom of manly tenderness and native elegance of soul . . . their good temper and openhandedness—the terrible significance of their elections—the President's taking off his hat to them not they to him—these too are unrhymed poetry. It awaits the gigantic and generous treatment worthy of it.

The largeness of nature or the nation were monstrous without a corresponding largeness and generosity of the spirit of the citizen. Not nature nor swarming states nor streets and steamships nor prosperous business nor farms nor capital nor learning may suffice for the ideal of man . . . nor suffice the poet. No reminiscences may suffice either. A live nation can always cut a deep mark and can have the best authority the cheapest . . . namely from its own soul. This is the sum of the profitable uses of individuals or states and of present action and grandeur and of the subjects of poets.—As if it were necessary to trot back generation after generation to the eastern records! As if the opening of the western continent by discovery and what has transpired since in North and South America were less than the small theatre of the antique or the aimless sleepwalking of the middle ages! The pride of the United States leaves the wealth and finesse of the cities and all returns of commerce and agriculture and all the magnitude of geography or shows of exterior victory to enjoy the breed of fullsized men or one fullsized man unconquerable and simple.

The American poets are to enclose old and new for America is the race of races. Of them a bard is to be commensurate with a people. To him the other continents arrive as contributions . . . he gives them reception for their sake and his own sake. His spirit responds to his country's spirit . . . he incarnates its geography and natural life and rivers and lakes. Mississippi with annual freshets and changing chutes, Missouri and Columbia and Ohio and Saint Lawrence with the falls and beautiful masculine Hudson, do not embouchure where they spend themselves more than they embouchure into him. The blue breadth over the inland sea of Virginia and Maryland and the sea off Massachusetts and Maine and over Manhattan bay and over Champlain and Erie and over Ontario and Huron and Michigan and Superior, and over the Texan and Mexican and Floridian and Cuban seas and over the seas off California and Oregon, is not tallied by the blue breadth of the waters below more than the breadth of above and below is tallied by him. When the long Atlantic coast stretches longer and the Pacific coast stretches longer he easily stretches with them north or south. He spans between them also from east to west and reflects what is between them. On him rise solid growths that offset the growths of pine and cedar and hemlock and liveoak and locust and chestnut and cypress and hickory and limetree and cottonwood and tuliptree and cactus and wildvine and tamarind and persimmon . . . and tangles as tangled as any canebreak or swamp . . . and forests coated with transparent ice and icicles hanging from the boughs and crackling in the wind . . . and sides and peaks of mountains . . . and pasturage sweet and free as savannah or upland or prairie . . . with flights and songs and screams that answer those of the wildpigeon and highhold and orchard-oriole and coot and surf-duck and redshouldered-hawk and fishhawk and white-ibis and Indian-hen and cat-owl and water-pheasant and qua-bird and pied-sheldrake and blackbird and mockingbird and buzzard and condor and night-heron and eagle. To him the hereditary countenance descends both mother's and father's. To him enter the essences of the real things and past and present events—of the enormous diversity of temperature and agriculture and mines—the tribes of red aborigines—the weatherbeaten vessels entering new ports or making landings on rocky coasts—the first settlements north or south—the rapid stature and muscle—the haughty defiance of '76, and the war and peace and formation of the constitution . . . the union always surrounded by blatherers and always calm and impregnable—the perpetual coming of immigrants—the wharfhem'd cities and superior marine—the unsurveyed interior—the loghouses and clearings and wild animals and hunters and trappers . . . the free commerce—the fisheries and whaling and gold-digging—the endless gestation of new states—the convening of Congress every December, the members duly coming up from all climates and the uttermost parts . . . the noble character of the young mechanics and of all free American workmen and workwomen . . . the general ardor and friendliness and enterprise—the perfect equality of the female with the male . . . the large amativeness—the fluid movement of the population—the factories and mercantile life and laborsaving machinery—the Yankee swap—the New-York firemen and the target excursion—the southern plantation life—the character of the northeast and of the northwest and southwest—slavery and the tremulous spreading of hands to protect it, and the stern opposition to it which shall never cease till it ceases or the speaking of tongues and the moving of lips cease. For such the expression of the American poet is to be transcendent and new. It is to be indirect and not direct or descriptive or epic. Its quality goes through these to much more. Let the age and wars of other nations be chanted and their eras and characters be illustrated and that finish the verse. Not so the great psalm of the republic. Here the theme is creative and has vista. Here comes one among the wellbeloved stonecutters and plans with decision and science and sees the solid and beautiful forms of the future where there are now no solid forms.

Of all nations the United States with veins full of poetical stuff most need poets and will doubtless have the greatest and use them the greatest. Their Presidents shall not be their common referee so much as their poets shall. Of all mankind the great poet is the equable man. Not in him but off from him things are grotesque or eccentric or fail of their sanity. Nothing out of its place is good and nothing in its place is bad. He bestows on every object or quality its fit proportions neither more nor less. He is the arbiter of the diverse and he is the key. He is the equalizer of his age and land . . . he supplies what wants supplying and checks what wants checking. If peace is the routine out of him speaks the spirit of peace, large, rich, thrifty, building vast and populous cities, encouraging agriculture and the arts and commerce—lighting the study of man, the soul, immortality—federal, state or municipal government, marriage, health, freetrade, intertravel by land and sea . . . nothing too close, nothing too far off . . . the stars not too far off. In war he is the most deadly force of the war. Who recruits him recruits horse and foot . . . he can make every word he speaks draw blood. Whatever stagnates in the flat of custom or obedience or legislation he never stagnates. Obedience does not master him, he masters it. High up out of reach he stands turning a concentrated light . . . he turns the pivot with his finger . . . he baffles the swiftest runners as he stands and easily overtakes and envelops them. The time straying toward infidelity and confections and persiflage he withholds by his steady faith . . . he spreads out his dishes . . . he offers the sweet firmfibred meat that grows men and women. His brain is the ultimate brain. He is no arguer . . . he is judgment. He judges not as the judge judges but as the sun falling around a helpless thing. As he sees the farthest he has the most faith. His thoughts are the hymns of the praise of things. In the talk on the soul and eternity and God off of his equal plane he is silent. He sees eternity less like a play with a prologue and denouement . . . he sees eternity in men and women . . . he does not see men and women as dreams or dots. Faith is the antiseptic of the soul . . . it pervades the common people and preserves them . . . they never give up believing and expecting and trusting. There is that indescribable freshness and unconsciousness about an illiterate person that humbles and mocks the power of the noblest expressive genius. The poet sees for a certainty how one not a great artist may be just as sacred as the greatest artist. . . . The power to destroy or remould is freely used by him but never the power of attack. What is past is past. If he does not expose superior models and prove himself by every step he takes he is not what is wanted. The presence of the greatest poet conquers . . . not parleying or struggling or any prepared attempts. Now he has passed that way see after him! there is not left any vestige of despair or misanthropy or cunning or exclusiveness or the ignominy of a nativity or color or delusion of hell or the necessity of hell . . . and no man thenceforward shall be degraded for ignorance or weakness or sin.

The greatest poet hardly knows pettiness or triviality. If he breathes into any thing that was before thought small it dilates with the grandeur and life of the universe. He is a seer . . . he is individual . . . he is complete in himself . . . the others are as good as he, only he sees it and they do not. He is not one of the chorus . . . he does not stop for any regulations . . . he is the president of regulation. What the eyesight does to the rest he does to the rest. Who knows the curious mystery of the eyesight? The other senses corroborate themselves, but this is removed from any proof but its own and foreruns the identities of the spiritual world. A single glance of it mocks all the investigations of man and all the instruments and books of the earth and all reasoning. What is marvelous? what is unlikely? what is impossible or baseless or vague? after you have once just opened the space of a peachpit and given audience to far and near and to the sunset and had all things enter with electric swiftness softly and duly without confusion or jostling or jam.

The land and sea, the animals, fishes and birds, the sky of heaven and the orbs, the forests mountains and rivers, are not small themes . . . but folks expect of the poet to indicate more than the beauty and dignity which always attach to dumb real objects . . . they expect him to indicate the path between reality and their souls. Men and women perceive the beauty well enough . . . probably as well as he. The passionate tenacity of hunters, wood-men, early risers, cultivators of gardens and orchards and fields, the love of healthy women for the manly form, seafaring persons, drivers of horses, the passion for light and the open air, all is an old varied sign of the unfailing perception of beauty and of a residence of the poetic in outdoor people. They can never be assisted by poets to perceive . . . some may but they never can. The poetic quality is not marshaled in rhyme or uniformity or abstract addresses to things nor in melancholy complaints or good precepts, but is the life of these and much else and is in the soul. The profit of rhyme is that it drops seeds of a sweeter and more luxuriant rhyme, and of uniformity that it conveys itself into its own roots in the ground out of sight. The rhyme and uniformity of perfect poems show the free growth of metrical laws and bud from them as unerringly and loosely as lilacs or roses on a bush, and take shapes as compact as the shapes of chestnuts and oranges and melons and pears, and shed the perfume impalpable to form. The fluency and or-naments of the finest poems or music or orations or recitations are not independent but dependent. All beauty comes from beautiful blood and a beautiful brain. If the greatnesses are in conjunction in a man or woman it is enough . . . the fact will prevail through the universe . . . but the gaggery and gilt of a million years will not prevail. Who troubles himself about his ornaments or fluency is lost. This is what you shall do: Love the earth and sun and the animals, despise riches, give alms to every one that asks, stand up for the stupid and crazy, devote your income and labor to others, hate tyrants, argue not concerning God, have patience and indulgence toward the people, take off your hat to nothing known or unknown or to any man or number of men, go freely with powerful uneducated persons and with the young and with the mothers of families, read these leaves in the open air every season of every year of your life, re-examine all you have been told at school or church or in any book, dismiss whatever insults your own soul, and your very flesh shall be a great poem and have the richest fluency not only in its words but in the silent lines of its lips and face and between the lashes of your eyes and in every motion and joint of your body. . . . The poet shall not spend his time in unneeded work. He shall know that the ground is always ready plowed and manured . . . others may not know it but he shall. He shall go directly to the creation. His trust shall master the trust of everything he touches . . . and shall master all attachment.

The known universe has one complete lover and that is the greatest poet. He consumes an eternal passion and is indifferent which chance hap-pens and which possible contingency of fortune or misfortune and per-suades daily and hourly his delicious pay. What balks or breaks others is fuel for his burning progress to contact and amorous joy. Other proportions of the reception of pleasure dwindle to nothing to his proportions. All expected from heaven or from the highest he is rapport with in the sight of the daybreak or a scene of the winterwoods or the presence of children playing or with his arm round the neck of a man or woman. His love above all love has leisure and expanse . . . he leaves room ahead of himself. He is no irresolute or suspicious lover . . . he is sure . . . he scorns intervals. His experience and the showers and thrills are not for nothing. Nothing can jar him . . . suffering and darkness cannot—death and fear cannot. To him complaint and jealousy and envy are corpses buried and rotten in the earth . . . he saw them buried. The sea is not surer of the shore or the shore of the sea than he is of the fruition of his love and of all perfection and beauty.

The fruition of beauty is no chance of hit or miss . . . it is inevitable as life . . . it is exact and plumb as gravitation. From the eyesight proceeds another eyesight and from the hearing proceeds another hearing and from the voice proceeds another voice eternally curious of the harmony of things with man. To these respond perfections not only in the committees that were supposed to stand for the rest but in the rest themselves just the same. These understand the law of perfection in masses and floods . . . that its finish is to each for itself and onward from itself . . . that it is profuse and impartial . . . that there is not a minute of the light or dark nor an acre of the earth or sea without it—nor any direction of the sky nor any trade or employment nor any turn of events. This is the reason that about the proper expression of beauty there is precision and balance . . . one part does not need to be thrust above another. The best singer is not the one who has the most lithe and powerful organ . . . the pleasure of poems is not in them that take the handsomest measure and similes and sound.

Without effort and without exposing in the least how it is done the greatest poet brings the spirit of any or all events and passions and scenes and persons some more and some less to bear on your individual character as you hear or read. To do this well is to compete with the laws that pursue and follow time. What is the purpose must surely be there and the clue of it must be there . . . and the faintest indication is the indication of the best and then becomes the clearest indication. Past and present and future are not disjoined but joined. The greatest poet forms the consistence of what is to be from what has been and is. He drags the dead out of their coffins and stands them again on their feet . . . he says to the past, Rise and walk before me that I may realize you. He learns the lesson . . . he places himself where the future become present. The greatest poet does not only dazzle his rays over character and scenes and passions . . . he finally ascends and finishes all . . . he exhibits the pinnacles that no man can tell what they are for or what is beyond . . . he glows a moment on the extremest verge. He is most wonderful in his last half-hidden smile or frown . . . by that flash of the moment of parting the one that sees it shall be encouraged or terrified afterwards for many years. The greatest poet does not moralize or make applications of morals . . . he knows the soul. The soul has that measureless pride which consists in never acknowledging any lessons but its own. But it has sympathy as measureless as its pride and the one balances the other and neither can stretch too far while it stretches in company with the other. The inmost secrets of art sleep with the twain. The greatest poet has lain close betwixt both and they are vital in his style and thoughts.

The art of art, the glory of expression and the sunshine of the light of letters is simplicity. Nothing is better than simplicity . . . nothing can make up for excess or for the lack of definiteness. To carry on the heave of impulse and pierce intellectual depths and give all subjects their articulations are powers neither common nor very uncommon. But to speak in literature with the perfect rectitude and insouciance of the movements of animals and the unimpeachableness of the sentiment of trees in the woods and grass by the roadside is the flawless triumph of art. If you have looked on him who has achieved it you have looked on one of the masters of the artists of all nations and times. You shall not contemplate the flight of the graygull over the bay or the mettlesome action of the blood horse or the tall leaning of sunflowers on their stalk or the appearance of the sun journeying through heaven or the appearance of the moon afterward with any more satisfaction than you shall contemplate him. The greatest poet has less a marked style and is more the channel of thoughts and things without increase or diminution, and is the free channel of himself. He swears to his art, I will not be meddlesome, I will not have in my writing any elegance or effect or originality to hang in the way between me and the rest like curtains. I will have nothing hang in the way, not the richest curtains. What I tell I tell for precisely what it is. Let who may exalt or startle or fascinate or sooth I will have purposes as health or heat or snow has and be as regardless of observation. What I experience or portray shall go from my composition without a shred of my composition. You shall stand by my side and look in the mirror with me.

The old red blood and stainless gentility of great poets will be proved by their unconstraint. A heroic person walks at his ease through and out of that custom or precedent or authority that suits him not. Of the traits of the brotherhood of writers savans musicians inventors and artists nothing is finer than silent defiance advancing from new free forms. In the need of poems philosophy politics mechanism science behaviour, the craft of art, an appropriate native grand-opera, shipcraft, or any craft, he is greatest forever and forever who contributes the greatest original practical example. The cleanest expression is that which finds no sphere worthy of itself and makes one.

The messages of great poets to each man and woman are, Come to us on equal terms, Only then can you understand us, We are no better than you, What we enclose you enclose, What we enjoy you may enjoy. Did you suppose there could be only one Supreme? We affirm there can be unnumbered Supremes, and that one does not countervail another any more than one eyesight countervails another . . . and that men can be good or grand only of the consciousness of their supremacy within them. What do you think is the grandeur of storms and dismemberments and the deadliest battles and wrecks and the wildest fury of the elements and the power of the sea and the motion of nature and of the throes of human desires and dignity and hate and love? It is that something in the soul which says, Rage on, Whirl on, I tread master here and everywhere, Master of the spasms of the sky and of the shatter of the sea, Master of nature and passion and death, And of all terror and all pain.

The American bards shall be marked for generosity and affection and for encouraging competitors. . . . They shall be kosmos . . . without monopoly or secresy . . . glad to pass any thing to any one . . . hungry for equals night and day. They shall not be careful of riches and privilege . . . they shall be riches and privilege . . . they shall perceive who the most affluent man is. The most affluent man is he that confronts all the shows he sees by equivalents out of the stronger wealth of himself. The American bard shall delineate no class of persons nor one or two out of the strata of interests nor love most nor truth most nor the soul most nor the body most . . . and not be for the eastern states more than the western or the northern states more than the southern.

Exact science and its practical movements are no checks on the greatest poet but always his encouragement and support. The outset and remembrance are there . . . there are the arms that lifted him first and brace him best . . . there he returns after all his goings and comings. The sailor and traveler . . . the atomist chemist astronomer geologist phrenologist spiritualist mathematician historian and lexicographer are not poets, but they are the lawgivers of poets and their construction underlies the structure of every perfect poem. No matter what rises or is uttered they sent the seed of the conception of it . . . of them and by them stand the visible proofs of souls . . . always of their fatherstuff must be begotten the sinewy races of bards. If there shall be love and content between the father and the son and if the greatness of the son is the exuding of the greatness of the father there shall be love between the poet and the man of demonstrable science. In the beauty of poems are the tuft and final applause of science.

Great is the faith of the flush of knowledge and of the investigation of the depths of qualities and things. Cleaving and circling here swells the soul of the poet yet is president of itself always. The depths are fathomless and therefore calm. The innocence and nakedness are resumed . . . they are neither modest nor immodest. The whole theory of the special and supernatural and all that was twined with it or educed out of it departs as a dream. What has ever happened . . . what happens and whatever may or shall happen, the vital laws enclose all . . . they are sufficient for any case and for all cases . . . none to be hurried or retarded . . . any miracle of affairs or persons inadmissible in the vast clear scheme where every motion and every spear of grass and the frames and spirits of men and women and all that concerns them are unspeakably perfect miracles all referring to all and each distinct and in its place. It is also not consistent with the reality of the soul to admit that there is anything in the known universe more divine than men and women.

Men and women and the earth and all upon it are simply to be taken as they are, and the investigation of their past and present and future shall be unintermitted and shall be done with perfect candor. Upon this basis philosophy speculates ever looking toward the poet, ever regarding the eternal tendencies of all toward happiness never inconsistent with what is clear to the senses and to the soul. For the eternal of all toward happiness make the only point of sane philosophy. Whatever comprehends less than that . . . whatever is less than the laws of light and of astronomical motion . . . or less than the laws that follow the thief the liar the glutton and the drunkard through this life and doubtless afterward . . . or less than vast stretches of time or the slow formation of density or the patient upheaving of strata—is of no acount. Whatever would put God in a poem or system of philosophy as contending against some being or influence, is also of no account. Sanity and ensemble characterise the great master . . . spoilt in one principle all is spoilt. The great master has nothing to do with miracles. He sees health for himself in being one of the mass . . . he sees the hiatus in singular eminence. To the perfect shape comes common ground. To be under the general law is great for that is to correspond with it. The master knows that he is unspeakably great and that all are unspeakably great . . . that nothing for instance is greater than to conceive children and bring them up well . . . that to be is just as great as to perceive or tell.

In the make of the great masters the idea of political liberty is indispensable. Liberty takes the adherence of heroes wherever men and women exist . . . but never takes any adherence or welcome from the rest more than from poets. They are the voice and exposition of liberty. They out of ages are worthy the grand idea . . . to them it is confided and they must sustain it. Nothing has precedence of it and nothing can warp or degrade it. The attitude of great poets is to cheer up slaves and horrify despots. The turn of their necks, the sound of their feet, the motions of their wrists, are full of hazard to the one and hope to the other. Come nigh them awhile and though they neither speak or advise you shall learn the faithful American lesson. Liberty is poorly served by men whose good intent is quelled from one failure or two failures or any number of failures, or from the casual indifference or ingratitude of the people, or from the sharp show of the rushes of power, or the bringing to bear soldiers and cannon or any penal statutes. Liberty relies upon itself, invites no one, promises nothing, sits in calmness and light, is positive and composed, and knows no discouragement. The battle rages with many a loud alarm and frequent advance and retreat . . . the enemy triumphs . . . the prison, the handcuffs, the iron necklace and anklet, the scafford, garrote and leadballs do their work . . . the cause is asleep . . . the strong throats are choked with their own blood . . . the young men drop their eyelashes toward the ground when they pass each other . . . and is liberty gone out of that place? No never. When liberty goes it is not the first to go nor the second nor third to go . . . it waits for all the rest to go . . . it is the last. . . . When the memories of the old martyrs are faded utterly away . . . when the large names of patriots are laughed at in the public halls from the lips of the orators . . . when the boys are no more christened after the same but christened after tyrants and traitors instead . . . when the laws of the free are grudgingly permitted and laws for informers and blood-money are sweet to the taste of the people . . . when I and you walk abroad upon the earth stung with compassion at the sight of numberless brothers answering our equal friendship and calling no man master—and when we are elated with noble joy at the sight of slaves . . . when the soul retires in the cool communion of the night and surveys its experience and has much extasy over the word and deed that put back a helpless innocent person into the gripe of the gripers or into any cruel inferiority . . . when those in all parts of these states who could easier realize the true American character but do not yet—when the swarms of cringers, suckers, doughfaces, lice of politics, planners of sly involutions for their own preferment to city offices or state legislatures or the judiciary or congress of the presidency, obtain a response of love and natural deference from the people whether they get the offices or no . . . when it is better to be a bound booby and rogue in office at a high salary than the poorest free mechanic or farmer with his hat unmoved from his head and firm eyes and a candid and generous heart . . . and when servility by town or state or the federal government or any oppression on a large scale or small scale can be tried on without its own punishment following duly after in exact proportion against the smallest chance of escape . . . or rather when all life and all the souls of men and women are discharged from any part of the earth—then only shall the instinct of liberty be discharged from that part of the earth.

As the attributes of the poets of the kosmos concentre in the real body and soul and in the pleasure of things they possess the superiority of genuineness over all fiction and romance. As they emit themselves facts are showered over with light . . . the daylight is lit with more volatile light . . . also the deep between the setting and rising sun goes deeper many fold. Each precise object or condition or combination or process exhibits a beauty . . . the multiplication table its—old age its—the carpenter's trade its—the grand-opera its . . . the hugehulled cleanshaped New-York clipper at sea under steam or full sail gleams with unmatched beauty . . . the American circles and large harmonies of government gleam with theirs . . . and the commonest definite intentions and actions with theirs. The poets of the kosmos advance through all interpositions and coverings and turmoils and stratagems to first principles. They are of use . . . they dissolve poverty from its need and riches from its conceit. You large proprietor they say shall not realize or perceive more than any one else. The owner of the library is not he who holds a legal title to it having bought and paid for it. Any one and every one is owner of the library who can read the same through all the varieties of tongues and subjects and styles, and in whom they enter with ease and take residence and force toward paternity and maternity, and make supple and powerful and rich and large. . . . These American states strong and healthy and accomplished shall receive no pleasure from violations of natural models and must not permit them. In paintings or mouldings or carvings in mineral or wood, or in the illustrations of books or newspapers, or in any comic or tragic prints, or in the patterns of women stuffs or anything to beautify rooms or furniture or costumes, or to put upon cornices or monuments or on the prows or sterns of ships, or to put anywhere before the human eye indoors or out, that which distorts honest shapes or which creates unearthly beings or places or contingencies is a nuisance and revolt. Of the human form especially it is so great it must never be made ridiculous. Of ornaments to a work nothing outre can be allowed . . . but those ornaments can be allowed that conform to the perfect facts of the open air and that flow out of the nature of the work and come irrepressibly from it and are necessary to the completion of the work. Most works are most beautiful without ornament. . . . Exaggerations will be revenged in human physiology. Clean and vigorous children are jetted and conceived only in those communities where the models of natural forms are public every day. . . . Great genius and the people of these states must never be demeaned to romances. As soon as histories are properly told there is no more need of romances.

The great poets are also to be known by the absence in them of tricks and by the justification of perfect personal candor. Then folks echo a new cheap joy and a divine voice leaping from their brains: How beautiful is candor! All faults may be forgiven of him who has perfect candor. Henceforth let no man of us lie, for we have seen that openness wins the inner and outer world and that there is no single exception, and that never since our earth gathered itself in a mass have deceit or subterfuge or prevarication attracted its smallest particle or the faintest tinge of a shade—and that through the enveloping wealth and rank of a state or the whole republic of states a sneak or sly person shall be discovered and despised . . . and that the soul has never been once fooled and never can be fooled . . . and thrift without the loving nod of the soul is only a foetid puff . . . and there never grew up in any of the continents of the globe nor upon any planet or satellite or star, nor upon the asteroids, nor in any part of ethereal space, nor in the midst of density, nor under the fluid wet of the sea, nor in that condition which precedes the birth of babes, nor at any time during the changes of life, nor in that condition that follows what we term death, nor in any stretch of abeyance or action afterward of vitality, nor in any process of formation or reformation anywhere, a being whose instinct hated the truth.

Extreme caution or prudence, the soundest organic health, large hope and comparison and fondness for women and children, large alimentiveness and destructiveness and causality, with a perfect sense of the oneness of nature and the propriety of the same spirit applied to human affairs . . . these are called up of the float of the brain of the world to be parts of the greatest poet from his birth out of his mother's womb and from her birth out of her mother's. Caution seldom goes far enough. It has been thought that the prudent citizen was the citizen who applied himself to solid gains and did well for himself and his family and completed a lawful life without debt or crime. The greatest poet sees and admits these economies as he sees the economies of food and sleep, but has higher notions of prudence than to think he gives much when he gives a few slight attentions at the latch of the gate. The premises of the prudence of life are not the hospitality of it or the ripeness and harvest of it. Beyond the independence of a little sum laid aside for burial-money, and of a few clapboards around and shingles overhead on a lot of American soil owned, and the easy dollars that supply the year's plain clothing and meals, the melancholy prudence of the abandonment of such a great being as a man is to the toss and pallor of years of moneymaking with all their scorching days and icy nights and all their stifling deceits and underhanded dodgings, or infinitesimals of parlors, or shameless stuffing while others starve . . . and all the loss of the bloom and odor of the earth and of the flowers and atmosphere and of the sea and of the true taste of the women and men you pass or have to do with in youth or middle age, and the issuing sickness and desperate revolt at the close of a life without elevation or naivete, and the ghastly chatter of a death without serenity or majesty, is the great fraud upon modern civilization and forethought, blotching the surface and system which civilization undeniably drafts, and moistening with tears the immense features it spreads and spreads with such velocity before the reached kisses of the soul. . . . Still the right explanation remains to be made about prudence. The prudence of the mere wealth and respectability of the most esteemed life appears too faint for the eye to observe at all when little and large alike drop quietly aside at the thought of the prudence suitable for immortality. What is wisdom that fills the thinness of a year or seventy or eighty years to wisdom spaced out by ages and coming back at a certain time with strong reinforcements and rich presents and the clear faces of wedding-guests as far as you can look in every direction running gaily toward you? Only the soul is of itself . . . all else has reference to what ensues. All that a person does or thinks is of consequence. Not a move can a man or woman make that affects him or her in a way or a month or any part of the direct lifetime or the hour of death but the same affects him or her onward afterward through the indirect lifetime. The indirect is always as great and real as the direct. The spirit receives from the body just as much as it gives to the body. Not one name of word or deed . . . not of venereal sores or discolorations . . . not the privacy of the onanist . . . not of the putrid veins of gluttons or rum-drinkers . . . not peculation or cunning or betrayal or murder . . . no serpentine poison of those that seduce women . . . not the foolish yielding of women . . . not prostitution . . . not of any depravity of young men . . . not of the attainment of gain by discreditable means . . . not any nastiness of appetite . . . not any harshness of officers to men or judges to prisoners or fathers to sons or sons to fathers or of husbands to wives or bosses to their boys . . . not of greedy looks or malignant wishes . . . nor any of the wiles practised by people upon themselves . . . ever is or ever can be stamped on the programme but it is duly realized and returned, and that returned in further performances . . . and they returned again. Nor can the push of charity or personal force ever be any thing else than the profoundest reason, whether it bring arguments to hand or no. No specification is necessary . . . to add or subtract or divide is in vain. Little or big, learned or unlearned, white or black, legal or illegal, sick or well, from the first inspiration down the windpipe to the last expiration out of it, all that a male or female does that is vigorous and benevolent and clean is so much sure profit to him or her in the unshakable order of the universe and through the whole scope of it forever. If the savage or felon is wise it is well . . . if the greatest poet or savan is wise it is simply the same . . . if the President or chief justice is wise it is the same . . . if the young mechanic or farmer is wise it is no more or less . . . if the prostitute is wise it is no more nor less. The interest will come round . . . all will come round. All the best actions of war and peace . . . all help given to relatives and strangers and the poor and old and sorrowful and young children and widows and the sick, and to all shunned persons . . . all furtherance of fugitives and of the escape of slaves . . . all the self-denial that stood steady and aloof on wrecks and saw others take the seats of the boats . . . all offering of substance or life for the good old cause, or for a friend's sake or opinion's sake . . . all pains of enthusiasts scoffed at by their neighbors . . . all honest men baffled in strifes recorded or unrecorded . . . all the grandeur and good of the few ancient nations whose fragments of annals we inherit . . . and all the good of the hundreds of far mightier and more ancient nations unknown to us by name or date or location . . . all that was ever manfully begun, whether it succeeded or not . . . all that has at any time been well suggested out of the divine heart of man or by the divinity of his mouth or by the shaping of his great hands . . . and all that is well thought or done this day on any part of the surface of the globe . . . or on any of the wandering stars or fixed stars by those there as we are here . . . or that is henceforth to be well thought or done by you whoever you are, or by any one—these singly and wholly inured at their time and inure now and will inure always to the identities from which they sprung or shall spring. . . . Did you guess any of them lived only its moment? The world does not so exist . . . no parts palpable or impalpable so exist . . . no result exists now without being from its long antecedent result, and that from its antecedent, and so backward without the farthest mentionable spot coming a bit nearer to the beginning than any other spot. . . . Whatever satisfies the soul is truth. The prudence of the greatest poet answers at last the craving and glut of the soul, is not contemptuous of less ways of prudence if they conform to its ways, puts off nothing, permits no let-up for its own case or any case, has no particular Sabbath or judgment-day, divides not the living from the dead or the righteous from the unrighteous, is satisfied with the present, matches every thought or act by its correlative, knows no possible forgiveness or deputed atonement . . . knows that the young man who composedly periled his life and lost it has done exceeding well for himself, while the man who has not periled his life and retains it to old age in riches and ease has perhaps achieved nothing for himself worth mentioning . . . and that only that person has no great prudence to learn who has learnt to prefer real longlived things, and favors body and soul the same, and perceives the indirect assuredly following the direct, and what evil or good he does leaping onward and waiting to meet him again—and who in his spirit in any emergency whatever neither hurries or avoids death.

The direct trial of him who would be the greatest poet is today. If he does not flood himself with the immediate age as with vast oceanic tides . . . and if he does not attract his own land body and soul to himself and hang on its neck with incomparable love and plunge his semitic muscle into its merits and demerits . . . and if he be not himself the age transfigured . . . and if to him is not opened the eternity which gives similitude to all periods and locations and processes and animate and inanimate forms, and which is the bond of time, and rises up from its inconceivable vagueness and infiniteness in the swimming shape of today, and is held by the ductile anchors of life, and makes the present spot the passage from what was to what shall be, and commits itself to the representation of this wave of an hour and this one of the sixty beautiful children of the wave—let him merge in the general run and wait his development. . . . Still the final test of poems or any character or work remains. The prescient poet projects himself centuries ahead and judges performer or performance after the changes of time. Does it live through them? Does it still hold on untired? Will the same style and the direction of genius to similar points be satisfactory now? Has no new discovery in science or arrival at superior planes of thought and judgment and behaviour fixed him or his so that either can be looked down upon? Have the marches of tens and hundreds and thousands of years made willing detours to the right hand and the left hand for his sake? Is he beloved long and long after he is buried? Does the young man think often of him? and do the middle-aged and the old think of him?

A great poem is for ages and ages in common and for all degrees and complexions and all departments and sects and for a woman as much as a man and a man as much as a woman. A great poem is no finish to a man or woman but rather a beginning. Has any one fancied he could sit at last under some due authority and rest satisfied with explanations and realize and be content and full? To no such terminus does the greatest poet bring . . . he brings neither cessation or sheltered fatness and ease. The touch of him tells in action. Whom he takes he takes with firm sure grasp into live regions previously unattained . . . thenceforward is no rest . . . they see the space and ineffable sheen that turn the old spots and lights into dead vacuums. The companion of him beholds the birth and progress of stars and learns one of the meanings. Now there shall be a man cohered out of tumult and chaos . . . the elder encourages the younger and shows him how . . . they too shall launch off fearlessly together till the new world fits an orbit for itself and looks unabashed on the lesser orbits of the stars and sweeps through the ceaseless rings and shall never be quiet again.

There will soon be no more priests. Their work is done. They may wait awhile . . . perhaps a generation or two . . . dropping off by degrees. A superior breed shall take their place . . . the gangs of kosmos and prophets en masse shall take their place. A new order shall arise and they shall be the priests of man, and every man shall be his own priest. The churches built under their umbrage shall be the churches of men and women. Through the divinity of themselves shall the kosmos and the new breed of poets be interpreters of men and women and of all events and things. They shall find their inspiration in real objects today, symptoms of the past and future . . . They shall not deign to defend immortality or God or the perfection of things or liberty or the exquisite beauty and reality of the soul. They shall arise in America and be responded to from the remainder of the earth.

The English language befriends the grand American expansion . . . it is brawny enough and limber and full enough. On the tough stock of a race who through all change of circumstances was never without the idea of political liberty, which is the animus of all liberty, it has attracted the terms of daintier and gayer and subtler and more elegant tongues. It is the powerful language of resistance . . . it is the dialect of common sense. It is the speech of the proud and melancholy races and of all who aspire. It is the chosen tongue to express growth faith self-esteem freedom justice equality friendliness amplitude prudence decision and courage. It is the medium that shall well nigh express the inexpressible.

No great literature nor any like style of behaviour or oratory or social intercourse or household arrangements or public institutions or the treatment by bosses of employed people, nor executive detail or detail of the army or navy, nor spirit of legislation or courts or police or tuition or architecture or songs or amusements or the costumes of young men, can long elude the jealous and passionate instinct of American standards. Whether or no the sign appears from the mouths of the people, it throbs a live interrogation in every freeman's and freewoman's heart after that which passes by or this built to remain. Is it uniform with my country? Are its disposals without ignominious distinctions? Is it for the evergrowing communes of brothers and lovers, large, well-united, proud beyond the old models, generous beyond all models? Is it something grown fresh out of the fields or drawn from the sea for use to me today here? I know that what answers for me an American must answer for any individual or nation that serves for a part of my materials. Does this answer? or is it without reference to universal needs? or sprung of the needs of the less developed society of special ranks? or old needs of pleasure overlaid by modern science and forms? Does this acknowledge liberty with audible and absolute acknowledgment, and set slavery at naught for life and death? Will it help breed one goodshaped and wellhung man, and a woman to be his perfect and independent mate? Does it improve manners? Is it for the nursing of the young of the republic? Does it solve readily with the sweet milk of the nipples of the breasts of the mother of many children? Has it too the old ever-fresh forbearance and impartiality? Does it look with the same love on the last born and those hardening toward stature, and on the errant, and on those who disdain all strength of assault outside of their own?

The poems distilled from other poems will probably pass away. The coward will surely pass away. The expectation of the vital and great can only be satisfied by the demeanor of the vital and great. The swarms of the polished deprecating and reflectors and the polite float off and leave no remembrance. America prepares with composure and goodwill for the visitors that have sent word. It is not intellect that is to be their warrant and welcome. The talented, the artist, the ingenious, the editor, the statesman, the erudite . . . they are not unappreciated . . . they fall in their place and do their work. The soul of the nation also does its work. No disguise can pass on it . . . no disguise can conceal from it. It rejects none, it permits all. Only toward as good as itself and toward the like of itself will it advance halfway. An individual is as superb as a nation when he has the qualities which make a superb nation. The soul of the largest and wealthiest and proudest nation may well go half-way to meet that of its poets. The signs are effectual. There is no fear of mistake. If the one is true the other is true. The proof of a poet is that his country absorbs him as affectionately as he has absorbed it.

HAROLD ASPIZ

Sexuality and the Language
of Transcendence
(1987)

The Romantics generally believed that poetry originates in ecstasy and is a manifestation of the creative urge. Whitman's unique contribution to this Romantic premise is his exploration of sexuality as a concomitant and an analogue of spiritual transcendence. Whitman perceived both sexuality and poetry as creative acts that express human love, the higher consciousness, and the search for the primal Word that can unlock the world's mystery. As the poems reach for an epiphany, for holiness, the Whitman persona's ascension into the mystic, transcendent state seems to be launched by the springboard of the tensioned physical senses. Holiness, as one critic points out, "is always something ecstatic . . . an intimation that the senses report too little, that something ought to order our lives, according to an apprehension of perfect harmony, unity, etc."[1] And as Agnieszka Salska observes, "seen as a progression toward a moment of contact, an illumination, or reconciliation, [Whitman's] poems resemble religious meditations as they strive to attain a state of grace, though grace may come in shockingly secular guises—as sexual (even homosexual) union or as a political vision of perfect domesticity. The visionary climax of a Whitman poem," she adds, "constitutes the structural climax as well."[2]

Inborn in each person, Whitman seems to say, coexist the sexual urge and the urge to transcend. These two ennobling urges nurture one another; the mightiest sexual drives lead the persona to an intimation of the transcendent state. But one way of interpreting Whitman's sexual utterances is that the two states—sexual and spiritual elevation—may not be equal. Sexuality in Whitman's poems is not usually an end in itself, for the sexual state is anterior to and generally less sustained than the transcendent state. In fact, most depictions of sexual arousal in *Leaves of Grass* are structured to culminate in a state of spiritual and visionary elevation.

Sexuality in *Leaves of Grass* is expressed as a nexus of metaphors— verbal constructs related to the persona's craving for transcendence. Inasmuch as metaphors are generally capable of being translated into other metaphors,[3] Whitman's sexual and transcendental utterances often form sets of interacting and interchangeable constructs. To Whitman, sexuality is an essential element in his role as poet, a "maker," or "vates." ("The Vates," he noted, "were priests and physiologists.")[4] The persona portrays a maker in both senses of that word: a horny maker/begetter of a new world vision, if not of a new world, and a vatic, creative maker/poet who seeks the primal Word to interpret it and to confer a gift of it on mankind. These roles involve the classical patterns of transcendence: intense passion, irrationality, and insights into the divinity of the most diverse phenomena. Both sexual exaltation and spiritual transcendence partake of what Louis Zukofsky has called the essential "fire and light Power" of the creative process.[5]

Most of Whitman's sexual utterances, in the poems, form part of an elaborate pattern in which the fleshly, sexual passion is transcended or merged into the sublime or spiritual. His language of sexuality becomes involved in his language of transcendence in two ways: first, the "public" language addressed to his readers and the "En-Masse" as part of a eugenics-related program for the purification of a new, perfected race, and second, the self-dramatizing utterance of the Whitman persona as a sexually charged mystic creator and speaker who replicates the rapturous state of primal creation in language that is animistic, totemic, ritualistic, and symbolic.

Whitman's public language is not inconsistent with a transcendentalist view which strabismically focused one eye on the North Star and the other on some glittering reformist cause. As I have pointed out elsewhere, an array of American reformers and scientists in Whitman's day believed that the new eugenics—programmed marriage and programmed parenting, often including the sort of earth-shaking copulations and rapturous sex idealized in "A Woman Waits for Me," "I Sing the Body Electric," and "Song of the Broad-Axe"—could help usher in the millennium.[6] In these poems and in some of his self-written anonymous reviews, Whitman idealizes the persona in terms of the eugenic ideal as the champion American breeder to be matched with prize female stock. As the ideological mainstay of phrenology, whose lore was so important to Whitman's development, the new eugenics was a chief source of the public stance toward sexuality in Whitman's poems. The public Whitman, whose *Democratic Vistas* proclaims that "parentage must consider itself in advance,"[7] depicted the marriage bed, with its athletic copulations between splendidly matched specimens, as a launching pad for a new breed of spiritualized Americans. "Spontaneous Me" praises "the great chastity of paternity to match the great chastity of maternity." Like John Humphrey Noyes, the much-scandalized leader of the Oneida Community and the Perfectionists, who resided in Brooklyn during the formative years of *Leaves of Grass* (1849–1854),[8] the public Whitman sought to inculcate a spiritually centered sexual self-control and to establish new, purer sexual *mores* as initiatory steps toward a new spiritual order. The

Adamic Whitman persona in the early editions of *Leaves of Grass*—"Lusty, phallic, with potent original loins, perfectly sweet" ("Ages and Ages Returning at Intervals")—is a vigorous, horny, fatherly, pedagogical, and spiritual being who refracts much of the ideology and language of sexual reform, which mingled the physically superb, the pleasurable, and the mystical. Even the sexual ecstasy depicted in the poems mirrors the reformists' notion that sexual ecstasy is eugenically desirable and, ultimately, spiritual.

In terms of the poems' elements of mystic sexuality, it need not matter, of course, whether the implied sexual acts are heterosexual, homosexual, masturbatory, or the free play of the persona's sexual fantasy. Those expressions of sexuality which operate outside heterosexual contexts are equally analogues of the Whitman persona's universal, spiritual love and his transcendent craving. The "adhesive" love of the "Calamus" poems, as Clayton Eshelman points out, involves a blending of the sexual and the spiritual—beyond sex itself.[9] Similarly, Whitman requires his readers to interpret the imagery of masturbation or of sexual fantasy as expressed in "The Sleepers," "Native Moments," parts of "Song of Myself," and "Spontaneous Me" as manifestations, or analogues, of the same transcendent reaching for mystical experience inherent in the heterosexual sexual/creative act. (The "masturbation of the brain" is what Horatio Greenough had called Emerson's creative process.)[10] "Spontaneous Me," that Dionysian hymn to the persona's autoerotic sexual arousal, may be read as a totemic act in which the persona bestows the reader with his "bunch"—a term suggesting both a poetic bouquet or garland and the persona's phallus, the ultimate totem of his inexhaustible creativity. In this poem and others, the persona's sexual and mystic penetration of nature itself, his mingling with, and his insemination of, nature are rituals of transcendence.

A brief canvass of the references of sexuality in "Song of Myself" confirms that the poem's sexual episodes are generally juxtaposed to, and integral with, episodes of transcendence. From the outset—"I celebrate myself, and sing myself"—the poem lays down the theme of transcendence, of the persona's participation in the universal divinity, of his desire to "possess the origin of all poems." Enraptured by his "luscious" masculine self, and meditating on the "electrical" and "procreant urge of the world," the persona experiences his first epiphany as he beds down with God, "the hugging and loving bed-fellow," who secretly bestows on him the bread of life. After singing a hymn of praise to his "I am," his spiritual essence, the persona records his sexually charged union with his spiritual self, or with some spiritual element of the oversoul, one "transparent summer morning" as the "I am" settled its "head athwart my hips and gently turn'd over upon me, / And parted the shirt from my bosom-bone, and plunged your tongue to my bare-stript heart, / And reach'd till you felt my beard, and reach'd till you held my feet." Significantly, this erotic experience is followed by the persona's transcendent awareness of "the peace and knowledge that pass all the argument of the earth," his first inkling of a clue to the universe ("a kelson of the creation is love"), his discovery of divinity in places great and small, and his first intimation of the word or symbol, in Section 6, that may serve to unlock the mystery ("A child said *What is the grass?*"). He is now launched into the astonishing series of visions of city and country—visions that would be inaccessible to anyone untouched by the divine afflatus—climaxed by the massive kaleidoscopic catalogue of sights and sounds of Section 15.

The middle sections of "Song of Myself" exhibit a series of sexual arousals by which the persona transcends further and becomes more profoundly visionary. He becomes as one of the gods, reading the souls of women and men, and is aware of his divine selfhood. As the first stage of his transcendence was marked by his having been presented with the bread of life by his divine bed-fellow, so the second stage is marked by the bread-of-life imagery (Section 19) in which the persona sits like a guest at God's table:

This is the meal equally set, this is the meat for natural hunger.

Like an Emersonian hero, the persona beholds emblems everywhere and accepts his duty to interpret them for the world:

To me the converging objects of the universe perpetually flow,
All are written to me, and I must get what the writing means.

To catapult him into a still higher transcendent state for greater visionary excursions, the persona undergoes the most astonishing sexual experiences in the entire poem: his titanic matings with the female earth and the female sea and the empyrean universe. These passages are analogues to the striking moments in Sections 14 and 15 of "By Blue Ontario's Shore" in which the nationalistic and superhuman persona seemingly copulates with the personified North American continent—with the entire geographic entity—in order to beget the wished-for breed of superb domestic heroes. (It must have been passages like these that moved Emerson to remark in 1857, in a lovely Victorian euphemism, on "Our wild Whitman, with real imagination but choked by Titanic abdomen."[11] Abdomen indeed!) With lyrical intensity, Section 21 of "Song of Myself" suggests that by coupling as an equal with the "voluptuous cool-breath'd earth" ("Thruster holding me tight and that I hold tight! / We hurt each other as the bridegroom and bride hurt each other")[12] and by being cushioned and lulled by the sea ("Dash me with amorous wet, I can repay you") the persona has become "integral"—that is Whitman's word—with the sea and the earth and has acquired a cosmic force of his own. And in Section 24 his spermatic essence becomes a striking metaphor for his transcendence and for the potential transcendence of the "many long dumb voices" as his phallic self ejects heavenward the "threads that connect the stars—and of wombs and of the father-stuff"—that is, the persona's semen. Doting on himself and on his marvelous universe, he exclaims:

> Something I cannot see puts upward libidinous prongs,
> Seas of bright juice suffuse heaven.

And with these spermatic "prongs," the semen that contemporary scientists claimed was the most refined distillation of the brain, the spinal cortex, and the soul, the persona takes hold of heaven, stains the white radiance of eternity with his own sexual/spiritual being.

By his superhuman copulation with, and his ritual impregnation of, the earth, the sea, and the stars, the persona has ritually become equal to nature. And as repayment for his caresses nature has granted him the prizes of vision, language, and wisdom. Now he can read the laws of nature and can perceive the dialectical balance in the universe; now he can speak "the password primeval," that is, the divine word from the beginning of time. He has become transcendentally lucid. "Speech," he declares in Section 25, "is the twin of my vision."

The persona's transcendent flight is triggered by other sexual stimuli. Listening to the world's sounds, he hears "the train'd soprano" whose voice (in the 1855 version) "convulses me like the climax of my love-grip."[13] Exploring the world of "Blind loving wrestling touch, sheath'd, hooded sharp-tooth'd touch!" the persona soon beholds (in Section 29):

> Sprouts take and accumulate, stand by the curb prolific and vital,
> Landscapes projected masculine, full-sized and golden.

Those vital "sprouts," the product of his own spermatic essence, or his spermatic imagination, may be interpreted, in terms of Whitman's public voice, as the idealized poetic race who will inhabit the golden landscapes of the future, unified by the "omnific" lesson of love, or, more abstractly, as the persona's poetic utterances—his own creative/spermatic essence translated into words.

Intensely stimulated, the persona launches into the most sustained stretch of lyrical, visionary, and transcendent poetry in all of *Leaves of Grass*. In the final third of the poem, he confirms the universal emblem ("I believe a leaf of grass is no less than the journey-work of the stars"); he radiates emblems, seeing the phenomena of the universe as "emblems of myself"; he transcends space, time, and causality in the massive catalogues of Section 33, where he is "afoot with my vision," the co-sufferer of all who have died or agonized; he is the healer of bodies and souls, who resurrects corpses; and, superbly, he is the "replenished" superman. He is the "friendly and flowing savage" whose electrical "emanations" manifest his divine power, the divinity who, like a patriarchal god, is "This day . . . jetting the stuff of far more arrogant republics"—countless numbers of those "prolific and vital" sprouts produced by his divine spermatic self. After "outbidding" all the gods of the past and "Accepting the rough deific sketches to fill out better in myself," in Section 40, he proclaims his inexorable transcendence, in suggestive physiological terms, as a sublime begetter and inseminator of the latent female life force, swearing a fearsome oath upon his "life-lumps!"—the spermatic core of his masculine being:

> . . . waiting my time to be one of the supremes,
> The day getting ready for me when I shall do as much good as the best,
>   and be as prodigious,
> By my life-lumps! becoming already a creator,
> Putting myself here and now to the ambush'd womb of the shadows.[14]

It is worth recapitulating here that the persona's partners in the heroic copulations in "Song of Myself" have been the earth, the sea, the heavens, and that mysterious, seemingly disembodied, archetypal shadowy womb rather than any discernibly real women or men, however abstract or idealized. As a godlike creature, the persona is surely free to choose his sexual partners. Yet the choice of such vague and exalted lovers highlights the symbolic and metaphorical quality of the ostensible sex acts and underscores the hypothesis that the poem's awesome drama of sex is in essence a drama of spiritual transcendence.

In this most exalted state, the Christ-like persona offers the bread of life to the blind (those "with dimes on eyes walking") and to those who never attend "the feast." He continues his upward journey on the stairs leading to the godhead. And as he is nearly suffocated by his lover-disciples, we are made aware that we are in the presence of a god who has mastered "the best of time and space, and who was never measured and never will be measured," and who now confers the bread of life in his own divine right ("Sit awhile, dear son, / Here are biscuits to eat and here is milk to drink"). No longer is he a Daniel who has to "get what the writing means": he is one who finds "letters from God dropt in the street," and recognizes that "every one is sign'd by God's name."

The poem's final epiphany brings the persona to us as a disembodied spirit in the air and beneath our footsoles. In the hauntingly proto-Roethkean harrowing of hell in Section 49, he undergoes the ultimate experience. Couched between two sexually charged French words—accoucheur" (the term by which many professional obstetricians in Whitman's day preferred to be called) and "debouch" (with its suggestions of both verbal utterance and birthing)—the persona descends into the primal ooze and undergoes the entire cycle of death, decay, and spiritual rebirth. "Unless the individual survives the mutation of matter" and thus achieves immortality, said Whitman's friend Daniel G. Brinton, "the universe is pointless." [15]

If the ultimate quest of the transcendentalists was to decipher and reveal the sensory and supersensory emblems of the universe and to survive "the mutation of matter," surely Whitman's triumphant and sexually charged persona succeeds in doing so and shows that the universe is not purposeless. And his quest has succeeded, in large measure, because of his essential sexuality and his capacity for sexual ecstasy.

NOTES

[1]   Bernard Avishai, "Sacred and Secular," *The Nation* 13 April 1985, 434.

[2]   Agnieszka Salska, *Walt Whitman and Emily Dickinson: Poetry of the Central Consciousness* (Philadelphia: University of Pennsylvania Press, 1985), 115.

[3]   Karsten Harris, "The Many Uses of Metaphor," *Critical History,* 5 (Autumn 1978), 170–171.

[4]   Walt Whitman, *Notebooks and Unpublished Prose Manuscripts,* ed. Edward F. Grier (New York: New York University Press, 1984), 5:1899.

[5]   "Reading and Talking," in *The Voice That is Great Within Us: American Poetry of the Twentieth Century,* ed. Hayden Carruth (New York: Bantam, 1971), 253.

[6]   Harold Aspiz, *Walt Whitman and the Body Beautiful* (Urbana: University of Illinois Press, 1980), 183–209. Excellent sources on nineteenth-century sexual reformism are Taylor Stoehr's *Free Love in America: A Documentary History* (New York: AMS Press, 1979), and Hal D. Sears's *The Sex Radicals: Free Love in High Victorian America* (Lawrence: The Regents Press of Kansas, 1977).

[7]   In *Prose Works 1892,* ed. Floyd Stovall (New York: New York University Press, 1964), 2:397.

[8]   Lawrence Foster, *Religion and Sexuality: Three American Communal Experiments of the Nineteenth Century* (New York: Oxford University Press, 1981), 108.

[9]   Cited in Scott Giantvalley, "Recent Whitman Studies and Homosexuality," *The Cabiron and Gay Books Bulletin,* no. 12 (Spring/Summer, 1985), 16.

[10] Erik Ingvar Thurin, *Emerson as Priest of Pan: A Study in the Metaphysics of Sex* (Lawrence: The Regents Press of Kansas, 1981), 205–206.

[11] *Letters of Ralph Waldo Emerson*, ed. Ralph Rusk (New York: Columbia University Press, 1939), 5:87.

[12] *Leaves of Grass: A Facsimile of the First Edition* (San Francisco: Chandler, 1968), 27.

[13] *Facsimile*, 32.

[14] The "ambush'd womb" is confusing. Of course, Whitman may simply have meant hidden. But "ambush'd" generally implies hidden (in the woods) to spring an assault—the wrong word in this context. He may have intended something like "embouch'd," by analogy with "embouchure" (Section 49), meaning the entry of a river to the sea—a suggestive sexual image. The poet who twice called a Tibetan priest a "llama" was not linguistically infallible.

[15] Brinton in *Walt Whitman Fellowship Papers*, 3 (May 1897), 34 (verso of a numbered sheet).

WILLIAM BIRMINGHAM

Whitman's Song of the Possible American Self
(1993)

My suggestion is this: religious Americans might profit spiritually from a committed reading of Walt Whitman's "Song of Myself." By a committed reading I mean one in which, having suspended disbelief, readers allow themselves to experience the text as meaningful aesthetic event, bringing to bear only later their critical faith practice.

Whitman, I should warn, was a great poet of experience and the possibilities it contains, but a terrible philosopher. A stanza from the last poem in the first edition (1855) of *Leaves of Grass* only slightly exaggerates how badly he often wrote when a philosophical mood came upon him:

> Great is justice;
> Justice is not settled by legislators and laws . . . it is in the soul,
> It cannot be varied by statutes any more than love or pride or the attraction
>   of gravity can,
> It is immutable . . . it does not depend on majorities . . . majorities or what
>   not come at last before the same passionless and exact tribunal. (144)

The ungainly and demotic "what not" instances, however, one of Whitman's great gifts to later poets—license to replace conventionally poetic English with the language and rhythms of common American speech.

Examples from two minor African-American poets may clarify the effect of this democratization of language. (Other groups and other poets could as easily be used.) Three or four decades before Whitman's birth in 1819, Phyllis Wheatley, doing her best to work in a language foreign both to her African and to her American heritage, writes that her love of freedom springs from having been "snatch'd from *Afric's* happy seat" and concludes, "Such, such my case. And can I then but pray / Others may never feel tyrannic sway?" (Randall 38). However valid Wheatley's generous sentiment, the language rings untrue. (Its falseness brings to the poem an aura of cultural imperialism that may, paradoxically, enhance its effectiveness.) Three decades after Whitman's death in 1892, the congregation in James Weldon Johnson's "Listen, Lord—A Prayer" prays that the minister "Who breaks the bread of life this morning" be kept "out of the gunshot of the devil":

> Wash him with hyssop inside and out,
> Hang him up and drain him dry of sin.
> Pin his ear to the wisdom post,
> And make his words sledge hammers of truth —
> Beating on the iron heart of sin. (Randall, 41–42)

Johnson is not writing dialect poetry, yet his language rises from within the congregation's experience, capturing the black Baptist sacramentalization of the sermon. He can do so because the tradition Whitman began opened up poetry to the varieties of American language. Literary language no longer reigns. Or, better, every language feeds the poetic imagination.

I cite the African-American tradition because it has been marginalized by our culture as a whole, and Whitman's aesthetic vision—not only of language but of the possible American self—comprehends those relegated to society's edge. In her preface to *Passion*—I continue to draw on the African-American tradition—June Jordan, alluding obliquely to Whitman's homosexuality, speaks of him as "the one white father who shares the systematic disadvantages of his heterogeneous offspring trapped inside a closet that is, in reality, as huge as the continental spread of North and South America" (x) and ultimately asserts that "[a]gainst self-hatred," which is what those at the margins are so often taught, "there is Whitman" (xxiii). At its best, Whitman's poetic vision affirms, against self-hatred, a possible American self that is inclusive rather than exclusive, trusting rather than suspicious, egalitarian rather than hierarchical, relational rather than individualistic.

Whitman's inclusive vision of the possible self will surely appeal to those at home with contextual theology, though it is in other ways disquieting to the religious mind. It discovers the transcendent, if at all, in the immanent—in the spirit (but not the Spirit) with whose grandeur the world is charged. In "Song of Myself," the self experiences the divine not as Other but as merged with the cosmos, with which the self merges as well. Further—and this limitation is secular as well as religious—that cosmos seems closed to evil and to tragedy. There is more here than facile optimism, however; "Song of Myself" offers not an ideal self, realized or to come, but a delineation of what the empirical American self and its world may become if it follows the trajectory of the best in its democratic experience. If taken as optimism from below, this bears a close resemblance to hope.

"Song of Myself" is a single poem that Whitman in editions after the first divided into separate songs. Since the poem works better for me if I ignore the divisions, I shall use the first edition as I attempt to share my experience of the American self that the poem portrays. The poem's hero is "Walt Whitman," whom I will call "Walt." This Walt is no more Walt Whitman than the Dante who "saw the Highest Light [. . .] raised so far above / the minds of mortals" was Dante Alighieri, supporter of Emperor Henry VII. And no less, unless we take the products of imagination to be unreal.

The opening lines are familiar:

I celebrate myself,
And what I assume you shall assume,
For every atom belonging to me as good belongs to you. (27)

The third line is crucial: as I am, so are you; to celebrate myself is to celebrate you. Of equal importance is a kind of a-telic passivity, with soul here used—much as in African-American speech—to name the integrated self alive in matter and spirit to the present moment:

I loafe and invite my soul,
I lean and loafe at my ease . . . observing a spear of summer grass.

There is nothing less or more important than either a blade of grass or the air around us:

The atmosphere is not a perfume . . . it has no taste of the distillation . . .
    it is odorless,
It is for my mouth forever . . . I am in love with it,
I will go to the bank by the wood and become undisguised and naked,
I am mad for it to be in contact with me.

Walt's recurrent obsessions with health and nakedness are often, as here, distracting, and sometimes risible. Clothed or not, the self rejoices in the air, the simple air, and the vitality it makes possible:

> The smoke of my own breath,
> Echos, ripples, and buzzed whispers . . . loveroot, silkthread, crotch and vine,
> My respiration and inspiration . . . the beating of my heart . . . the passing of
> blood and air through my lungs,
> The sniff of green leaves and dry leaves, and of the shore and darkcolored
> sea-rocks, and of hay in the barn,
> The sound of the belched words of my own voice . . . words loosed to the
> eddies of the wind,
> [. . .] the song of me rising from bed and meeting the sun.

The self exercises presence, to the common grass and air, to itself. Both presence and the present—"There was never any more inception than there is now [. . .] Nor any more heaven or hell than there is now"—orient the self toward the future. (Hegel provides the linguistic frame for Walt's insight but is not, as the last sentence indicates, its source.)

> Urge and urge and urge,
> Always the procreant urge of the world.
>
> Out of the dimness opposite equals advance. . . . Always substance and
> increase,
> Always a knit of identity . . . always distinction . . . always a breed of life.
>
> To elaborate is no avail. . . . Learned and unlearned feel that it is so. (28)

"I and this mystery"—the mystery of self, situated in time and place and present to itself—"I and this mystery here I stand":

> Clear and sweet is my soul . . . and clear and sweet is all that is not my soul.
>
> Lack one lacks both . . . and the unseen is proved by the seen,
> Till that becomes unseen and receives proof in its turn. (29)

Internal to Walt's soul is all that is not itself; exclusion would empty his soul's existence. "I am satisfied. . . . I see, dance, laugh, sing; / As God comes a loving bedfellow and sleeps at my side," who, when he departs, "leaves for me baskets [. . .] bulging the house with their plenty." Walt will not "scream at my eyes" that they should calculate the contents' market value but will continue to gaze "after and down the road" at the one who left "close on the peep of the day."

Walt will not be distracted by questions of the curious, or even

> The real or fancied indifference of some man or woman I love,
> The sickness of one of my folks—or of myself . . . or lack or loss of
>   money . . . or depressions or exaltations,
> These come to me days and nights and go from me again,
> But they are not the Me myself. (29–30)

All mockings and arguments are in the past; now, "I witness and wait."

Walt witnesses, waits, and remembers. He believes, he says, in his soul, experienced though unseen; and "the other I am must not abase itself to you, / And you must not be abased to the other." What he remembers is this: experiencing the union of self and soul, which he expresses through the metaphor of oral intercourse, and the awareness to which that union led. "Loafe with me on the grass . . . loose the stop from your throat," he says, "Not words, not music or rhyme I want . . . not custom or lecture, not even the best, / Only the lull I like, the hum of your valved voice."

> I mind how we lay in June, such a transparent summer morning;
> You settled your head athwart my hips and gently turned over upon me,
> And parted the shirt from my bosom-bone, and plunged your tongue to my
>   barestript heart,
> And reached till you felt my beard, and reached till you held my feet.
>
> Swiftly arose and spread around me the peace and joy and knowledge that
>   pass all the art and argument of the earth;
> And I know that the hand of God is the elderhand of my own [. . .] (30–31)

It is tempting, in an age when the confessional poetry of Robert Lowell and Sylvia Plath is so greatly admired, to center on autobiographical questions: is this heterosexual? homosexual? is it based on an actual, not an imagined event, with the soul an unnamed lover? I assume that Whitman's imagination is here remembering and re-creating an act of homosexual love, but that is beside the point I wish to make: in an erotic transport, Walt experiences the ensouled self and in peace and joy now perceives

> [. . .] that the hand of God is the elderhand of my own,
> And I know that the spirit of God is the eldest brother of my own,
> And that all the men ever born are also my brothers . . . and the women
>   my sisters and lovers
> And that a kelson of the creation is love;
> And limitless are leaves stiff or drooping in the fields,

And brown ants in the little wells beneath them,
And mossy scabs of the wormfence, and heaped stones, and elder and mullen
and pokeweed.

Walt's self, now integrated, experiences a divine presence that relates it intimately to humankind and the realization of the binding power of love, which embraces the trees and ants, the moss and weeds—in other words, the cosmos from the immanent God to the disregarded elements of life.

Recurrent throughout the rest of "Song of Myself" are epiphanic images that disclose the mystery—and the incalculable worth—of each element of the cosmos. The common grass is a symbol for them all:

A child said, What is the grass? fetching it to me with full hands:
How could I answer the child. . . . I do not know what it is any more than he.

Walt guesses. The grass may represent his "disposition, out of hopeful green stuff woven." Or may be "itself a child . . . the produced babe of the vegetation." Or—"Growing among black folks as among white, / Kanuck, Tuckahoe, Congressman, Cuff"—it may be "a uniform hieroglyphic" bespeaking the singleness of humankind. It may be all those things, and more; "[. . .] now it seems to me the beautiful uncut hair of graves," the symbol of unity through time, and of death's meaningfulness:

Tenderly will I use you curling grass,
It may be you transpire from the breasts of young men,
It may be if I had known them I would have loved them,
It may be you are from old people and from women, and from offspring taken
soon out of their mothers' laps,
And here you are the mother's laps.

This grass, "dark to be from the white heads of old mothers, / Darker than the colorless beards of old men, / Dark to come from under the faint red roofs of mouths," is "so many uttering tongues," (32) speaking what the dead are, what they have become:

They are alive and well somewhere;
The smallest sprout shows there is really no death,
And if there ever was it led forward life [. . .]

All goes onward and outward . . . and nothing collapses,
And to die is different from what any one supposed, and luckier.

Whitman, biographers have pointed out, seems to have feared death mightily. Walt, perhaps because his self has already died once through ensoulment, conceives it as leading forward life; a philosopher distinguishing Walt from Heidegger, might say that he sees the human person as a being-for-life, a life at whose end "nothing collapses" and all is explosively good—not the self, but part of the self:

> I pass death with the dying, and birth with the new-washed babe . . . and am
>   not contained between my hat and my boots,
> And peruse manifold objects, no two alike, and every one good,
> The earth good, and the stars good, and their adjuncts all good.

As "the mate and companion of people, all just as immortal and fathomless as myself" (33), Walt rejects no one:

> For me all that have been boys and love women,
> For me the man that is proud and knows how it feels to be slighted,
> For me the sweetheart and the old maid . . . for me mothers and the mothers
>   of mothers,
> For me lips that have smiled, eyes that have shed tears [. . .]

When next he asks, "Who need be afraid of the merge?" he has entered treacherous terrain. "Undrape," he cries, ". . . you are not guilty to me, nor stale nor discarded [. . .]" He can "see through the broadcloth and gingham"; he is "[. . .] acquisitive, tireless . . . and can never be shaken away." At this point in the poem, there is no need to dread "the merge"—the process by which others may enter and touch the heart of one's being. Later, Walt himself is its victim. Yet without merging in the sense that Whitman uses it—Buber's I-thou is a possible analogy—the self is closed off. Walt's self is indiscriminate in its embrace:

> The little one sleeps in its cradle,
> I lift the gauze and look a long time, and silently brush away flies with my
>   hand.
>
> The youngster and the redfaced girl turn aside up the bushy hill,
> I peeringly view them from the top.
>
> The suicide sprawls on the bloody floor of the bedroom.
> It is so . . . I witnessed the corpse . . . there the pistol had fallen.

Thus begins one of the catalogues, close to random in their order, that fill Whitman's poetry. Here, Walt recalls in all its wondrous and overwhelming variety what the open self admits as *thou*. The city:

> The blab of the pave . . . the tires of carts and stuff of bootsoles and talk of
>   promenaders,

The heavy omnibus, the driver with his interrogating thumb, the dank of the
    shod horses on the granite floor,
The carnival of sleighs, the clinking and shouted jokes and pelts of snowballs;
The hurrahs for popular favorites . . . the fury of roused mobs,
The flap of the curtained litter—the sick man inside [. . .]
The impassive stones that receive and return so many echoes,
The souls moving along . . . are they invisible while the least atom of the
    stones is visible? (33–34)

The country:

The big doors of the country-barn stand open and ready,
The dried grass of the harvest-time loads the slow-drawn wagon,
The clear light plays on the brown gray and green intertinged,
The armfuls are packed to the sagging mow:
I am there. . . . I help. . . .

Walt encounters a runaway slave, who "came to my house and stopped
outside":

Through the swung half-door of the kitchen I saw him limpsey and weak,
And went where he sat on a log, and led him in and assured him,
And brought water and filled a tub for his sweated body and bruised feet
    [. . .] (35)

He experiences the gently erotic fantasy of a young woman—"Twenty-eight
years of womanly life, and all so lonesome" (36)—as she watches from behind the window blinds, young men, one for each of her years, swimming
close to the shore. She pictures herself joining them:

Dancing and laughing along the beach came the twenty-ninth bather,
The rest did not see her, but she saw them and loved them.

The beards of the young men glistened with wet, it ran from their long hair,
Little streams passed all over their bodies.

An unseen hand also passed over their bodies,
It descended tremblingly from their temples and ribs.

And the young men "do not know who puffs and declines with pendant and
bending arch."
    Walt, let me recall, is not Whitman in my reading, but Whitman's pos-
sible and often enough realized self. The young woman's fantasy may indeed, as some have suggested, derive ultimately from Whitman's putative

desire for anonymous sex. Certainly, Whitman shared prejudices against blacks common among Northern whites of his day (a fact made all the less forgivable by his awareness of how he might regard them, how the self of "Song of Myself"—and, later, "I Sing the Body Electric"—did regard them). Whatever the bare facts, Whitman imagines through Walt possibilities—a woman's erotic moment, a white man's moral opportunity to wash a black man's feet—that bring the future into the present.

Walt turns now to the recollection of workers, He delights in the butcher-boy's street dance, "his shuffle and breakdown," and the rhythmic cooperation of blacksmiths ringing an anvil:

> The lithe sheer of their waists plays even with their massive arms,
> Overhand the hammers roll—overhand so slow—overhand so sure,
> They do not hasten, each man hits in his place. (37)

He admires the mastery of the teamster who "holds firmly the reins of his four horses":

> The negro that drives the huge dray of the stoneyard . . . steady and tall he
>   stands poised on one leg on the stringpiece [. . .]
> His glance is calm and commanding . . . he tosses the slouch of his hat away
>   from his forehead,
> The sun falls on his crispy hair and moustache . . . falls on the black of his
>   polished and perfect limbs.

Walt's self is "the caresser of life wherever moving:" a team of oxen ("What is that you express in your eyes?"); the wood-drake and wood-duck which, frightened by his tread, "rise together [. . .] slowly circle around. / . . . I believe in those winged purposes [. . .]"; the wild gander's "Ya-honk!" which "The pert may suppose [is] meaningless, but I listen closer, / I find its purpose and place up there toward the November sky." Meaning animates living creation if the self is present to it, accepts union with it: "What is commonest and cheapest and nearest and easiest is Me." The possible self rejects otherness through opposition.

Whitman's was, to borrow the aesthetic theologian John Dixon's term, a horizontal imagination, polar to the vertical, hierarchical imagination dominant in Western culture. (Dixon notes that the Reformation belief in the priesthood of all believers was the product of the horizontal imagination, but as decades passed, the pulpit rose higher and higher, creating in Protestant church architecture a visual hierarchy that implicitly denied the belief.) The horizontal imagination is democratic; it prizes each reality for what it is, not for the height of the step it occupies on the stairway to the heavens. When Walt proclaims "Every kind for itself and its own [. . .] he is not insisting on the superiority of human to beast but stating his primary affinity with the human. In "Song of Myself," we next find a catalog more than three pages long in which Walt through anamnesis summons up in wild disorder epiphanic images, mostly one to a line, of the human: a prostitute "draggles her shawl," the "President holds a cabinet council [. . .] surrounded by the great secretaries," matrons walk on the piazza arms entwined, the "crew of the fish-smack pack repeated layers of halibut in the hold." No person is better than the others, none worse; all are there—and valued. They "tend inward" to Walt and he outward to them:

> The pure contralto sings in the organ loft,
> The carpenter dresses his plank . . . the tongue of his foreplane whistles its
>   wild ascending lisp,
> The married and unmarried children ride home to their thanksgiving dinner,
> The pilot seizes the king-pin, he heaves down with a strong arm [. . .]
> The spinning-girl retreats and advances to the hum of the big wheel,
> The farmer stops by the bars of a Sunday and looks at the oats and rye,
> The lunatic is carried at last to the asylum a confirmed case,
> He will never sleep any more as he did in the cot in his mother's bedroom
>   [. . .]
> The deckhands make fast the steamboat, the plank is thrown for the
>   shoregoing passengers,
> The young sister holds out the skein, the elder sister winds it off in a ball and
>   stops now and then for the knots [. . .]
> Patriarchs sit at supper with sons and grandsons and great grandsons around
>   them,
> In walls of adobe, in canvass tents, rest hunters and trappers after their day's
>   sport,
> The city sleeps and the country sleeps,
> The living sleep for their time . . . the dead sleep for their time,
> The old husband sleeps by his wife and the young husband sleeps by his wife;
> And these one and all tend inward to me, and I tend outward to them,
> And such as it is to be of these more or less I am. (39–42)

The last line offers a useful ambiguity: "to be of these" can mean both "to belong to these" and "to be made up of these." That ambiguity persists:

> I am of old and young, of the foolish as much as the wise,
> Regardless of others, ever regardful of others,
> Maternal as well as paternal, a child as well as a man [. . .]

Walt is of "the great nation, the nation of many of many nations" and is

> Of every hue and trade and rank, of every caste and religion,
> Not merely of the New World but of Africa Europe or Asia. . . . a wandering
>   savage,
> A farmer, mechanic, or artist . . . a gentleman, sailor, lover or quaker,
> A prisoner, fancy-man, rowdy, lawyer, physician or priest. (43)

"I resist anything better than my own diversity [. . .]" The diversity springs from the inward and outward movements of the relational self, which is "at home" with and "comrade of" the human. To this Walt adds the claim, which might justly have terrified Whitman in later years ("Only Emily Dickinson was as formidably alone" (143), Paul Zweig says in commenting on Whitman's lack of literary friendships):

> These are the thoughts of all men in all ages and lands, they are not original
>   with me,
> If they are not yours as much as mine they are nothing or next to nothing
>   [. . .]

I find—others do not—an undertone of anxiety in the lines that follow; there is a rush of recapitulation and a braggadocio that betrays unsureness. These thoughts, Walt says, like the grass and air, are common; they are for the illiterate and the learned, for the powerful and the powerless, for the victors and the vanquished, and he feels at one with them all. His thoughts are like a "meal pleasantly set [. . .] meat and drink for natural hunger" (44), and "like the press of a bashful hand." He is not trying to astonish any more than the daylight does. "Who goes there!" he asks, "hankering, gross, mystical nude?" (45). He does not echo the "snivel" that "life is a suck and a sell." Instead of whimpering, he cocks his hat as he pleases. Shall he pray? There's no need, for he has "found no sweeter fat than sticks" to his own bones. He knows that he is "solid and sound," that he is deathless and august—"I do not trouble my spirit to vindicate itself or be understood [. . .]" (46). He does not care whether he is acknowledged today or in a thousand years, since "One world is aware, and by far the largest to me, and that is myself [. . .]" Walt laughs at "what you call dissolution." And I am convinced that he has been weeping—in loneliness. He reminds me of Teilhard de Chardin, as he searched fruitlessly for permission from his superiors to publish *The Phenomenon of Man,* writing to his brother that "it is here in Rome that we find the Christic pole of the earth" (299). The willfulness is sad.

Now the tone changes, growing peaceful:

I am the poet of the body,
And I am the poet of the soul.

The pleasures of heaven are with me, and the pains of hell are with me,
The first I graft and increase upon myself. . . . the latter I translate into a
    new tongue.

I am the poet of the woman the same as the man,
And I say it is as great to be a woman as to be a man [. . .]

No longer frenetic, in the rhythms of irenic eros, Walt now "walks with the
tender and growing night":

Press close barebosomed night! Press close magnetic nourishing night!
Night of south winds! Night of the large few stars!
Still nodding night! Mad naked summer night! (47)

He is lover to the earth "of the slumbering and liquid trees [. . .] of the
mountains misty-topt [. . .] of the vitreous pour of the full moon just
tinged with blue!" And to the sea: "Cushion me soft . . . rock me in billowy
drowse [. . .] I am integral with you" (48). And they are lovers to him, and
any humans who know them.

Walt Whitman, an American, one of the roughs, a kosmos,
Disorderly fleshy and sensual. . . . eating drinking and breeding,
No sentimentalist. . . . no stander above men and women or apart from
    them . . . no more modest than immodest. (50)

Walt has just praised "materialism" and the "exact demonstration" of positive science, which discloses facts which "are useful and real." But "they are
not my dwelling. . . . I enter by them to an area of the dwelling" (49). His is
the materialism of life. As "one of the roughs," he is free from the laws of
polite society which at the time may have been ready to acknowledge
scientific facts about the body but despised its carnality. He is a fleshly
"kosmos" who would speak for all those voices that are dumb—"the interminable generations of slaves of prostitutes and deformed persons [. . .]
of the diseased and the despairing [. . .] of the threads that connect the
stars—and of wombs and of the fatherstuff [. . .] of the rights of them the
others are down upon [. . .]" (50)

Whoever degrades another degrades me . . . and whatever is done or said
    returns at last to me,
And whatever I do or say I also return.

Through Walt, "forbidden voices" will be heard. He moves from the visually incongruous ideal of keeping "as delicate around the bowels as around the head and heart" (51) to celebration of his body—"translucent mould of me." If he worships anything,

> Breast that presses against other breasts it shall be you,
> My brain it shall be your occult convolutions,
> Root of washed sweet-flag, timorous pond-snipe, nest of guarded duplicate
> eggs, it shall be you,
> Mixed tussled hair of head and beard and brawn it shall be you [. . .]
> Hands I have taken, face I have kissed, mortal I have ever touched, it shall
> be you.

The last line, in which bodies truly touched become integral to the body-self that Walt worships, diminishes the autoeroticism for which this passage has been praised and blamed.

Walt turns from "the flesh and its appetites" to the "miracles" of seeing, hearing, and feeling. The tension grows when he comes to hearing: "Speech is the twin of my vision" and "provokes me forever, / It says sarcastically, Walt, you understand enough . . . why don't you let it out then?" (53) Not all things can be articulated—buds wait "in gloom protected by frost," and some of what he knows he must now refuse to speech. "Writing and talking do not prove me,"

> I think I will do nothing for a long time but listen,
> And accrue what I hear into myself . . . and let sounds contribute toward me.

And he hears "the bravura of birds . . . the bustle of growing wheat . . . gossip of flames [. . .] the recitative of fish-pedlars and fruit-pedlars . . . the loud laugh of workpeople at their meals [. . .]" He hears "the violincello or man's hearts' complaint, / And hear the keyed cornet or else the echo of sunset." The opera's music plunges him to "the farthest down horror" and raises him up "again to feel the puzzle of puzzles, / And that we call Being" (55).

And what is being? "If nothing lay more developed," Walt answers, "the quahaug and its callous shell were enough." Unlike the clam,

> I have instant conductors all over me whether I pass or stop,
> They seize every object and lead it harmlessly through me.
> I merely stir, press, feel with my fingers and am happy,
> To touch my person to some one else's is about as much as I can stand.

When Walt for the second time meditates on touch, there is nothing of the unitive touch of that "transparent summer morning." Touch, "quivering me to a new identity," is nightmare:

> My flesh and blood playing out lightning, to strike what is hardly different
> from myself [. . .]
> Immodestly sliding the fellow-sense away,
> They bribed to swap off with touch, and go and graze at the edges of
> me [. . .]
> Fetching the rest of the herd around to enjoy them awhile,
> Then all uniting to stand on a headland and worry me.
>
> The sentries desert every other part of me,
> They have left me helpless to a red marauder [. . .]
> I am given up by traitors;
> I talk wildly. . . . I have lost my wits . . . I and nobody else am the greatest
> traitor,
> I went myself first to the headland [. . .] (55–56)

Sensitivity to touch permeates Whitman's poetry, as does the desire to "merge"—to accept unity with all that is not himself. The clam with its shell is miracle enough, but evolution has brought the human into being. Walt's open self, with its "instant conductors" develops out of trust in the not-self it allows to become part of it. And, inevitably, that trust will meet betrayal by "prurient provokers [. . .] / Behaving licentious toward me" (55); touch becomes invasion. Yet:

> All truths wait in all things,
> They neither hasten their own delivery nor resist it,
> They do not need the obstetric forceps of the surgeon,
> The insignificant is as big to me as any,
> What is less or more than a touch? (56)

Through touch Walt may suffer betrayal, but through touch, especially through the images brought forth by memory and imagination, the delight of the cosmos enters the self. And so, he can say,

> I believe a leaf of grass is no less than the journeywork of the stars,
> And the pismire is equally perfect, and a grain of sand and the egg of a
> wren, [. . .]
> And the narrowest hinge of my hand puts to scorn all machinery,
> And the cow crunching with depressed head surpasses any statue, [. . .]
> And I could come every afternoon of my life to look at the farmer's girl
> boiling her iron tea-kettle and baking shortcake.

Through imagination that seeks all and lets all in, Walt is "afoot with my vision," without "ties and ballasts." He is

> By the city's quadrangular houses . . . in log-huts, or camping with
>   lumbermen, [. . .]
> Where the black bear is searching for roots or honey . . . where the beaver
>   pats the mud with his paddle-tail; [. . .]
> Over the sharp-peaked farmhouse with its scalloped scum and slender shoots
>   from the gutters,
> Over the western persimmon . . . over the longleaved corn and the delicate
>   blueflowered flax; [. . .]
> Where the cheese-cloth hangs in the kitchen, and andirons straddle the
>   hearth-slab, and cobwebs fall in festoons from the rafters;
> Where triphammers crash . . . where the press is whirling its cylinders;
> Approaching Manhattan, up by the long-stretching island,
> Under Niagara, the cataract failing like a veil [. . .]
> Through the salt-lick or orange glade . . . or under conical firs;
> Through the gymnasium . . . through the curtained saloon . . . through the
>   office or public hall [. . .]
> Speeding with tailed meteors . . . throwing fire-balls like the rest,
> Carrying the crescent child that carries its own full mother in its belly;
> Storming enjoying planning loving cautioning,
> Backing and filling, appearing and disappearing,
> I tread day and night such roads. (59–63)

Walt's identification through imagination extends to the heroic suffering of "The mother condemned for a witch and burnt with dry wood, and her children gazing on" (65), "The hounded slave that flags in the race and leans by the fence, blowing and covered with sweat," "[. . .] the mashed fireman with breastbone broken. . . ." He does "not ask the wounded person how he feels. . . . I myself become the wounded person." He experiences through imagination and recounts the story of the wounds and deaths suffered at the Alamo and during the sea-battle between the British *Serapis* and John Paul Jones's *Bon Homme Richard*. "I become any presence of humanity here" (70).

Walt has "heard what was said of the universe"—what was said of Kronos and Zeus, "of Osiris and Isis and Belus and Brahma and Adonai" (74) and will limn them all, "In my portfolio placing Manito loose, and Allah on a leaf, and the crucifix engraved [. . .]" but discovers "as much or more in a framer framing a house, / Putting higher claims for him there with his rolled-up sleeves, driving the mallet and chisel." The Egyptians may have divinized the bull and held the scarab an ikon of the sun god, but the natural is of more account than the supernatural, with

> The bull and the bug never worshipped half enough,
> Dung and dirt more admirable than was dreamed.

Walt's "Magnifying and applying" does not turn the bull and the bug into gods; by letting them remain themselves in all their complex and ultimately cosmic significance, he allows their sacred truths to emerge. It is not a question of despising the supernatural; his faith, Walt says, is the "greatest of faiths," because it "encloses all worship ancient and modern" (77), but is also "the least of faiths," because it centers on what is there, the thing itself in all its interrelationships. Each man and woman, like Walt, can perceive that "Immense have been the preparations for me, / Faithful and friendly the arms that have helped me. [. . .] All forces have been steadily employed to complete and delight me, / Now I stand on this spot with my soul" (80).

> I have said that the soul is not more than the body,
> And I have said that the body is not more than the soul,
> And nothing, not God, is greater to one than one's-self is,
> And whoever walks a furlong without sympathy walks to his own funeral,
>   dressed in his shroud,
> And I or you pocketless of a dime may purchase the pick of the earth,
> And to glance with an eye or show a bean in its pod confounds the learning
>   of all times,
> And there is no trade or employment but the young man following it may
>   become a hero,
> And there is no object so soft but it makes a hub for the wheeled universe,
> And any man or woman shall stand cool and supercilious before a million
>   universes. (84–85)

There is no need to be "curious" about God; traces of the divine are everywhere:

> I see something of God each hour of the twenty-four, and each moment then,
> In the faces of men and women I see God, and in my own face in the
>   glass [. . .]

Death and the "bitter hug of mortality" leave Walt unalarmed for death is another birth:

> And as to you corpse I think you are good manure, but that does not
>   offend me,

I smell the white roses sweetscented and growing,
I reach to the leafy lips. . . . I reach to the polished breasts of melons. (86)

And "There is that in me. . . . I do not know what it is . . . [. . .] it is without a name. . . . it is a word unsaid:

Do you see O my brothers and sisters?
It is not chaos or death . . . it is form and union and plan . . . it is eternal
  life . . . it is happiness. (87)

If this seems to contradict what he has said, "Very well then . . . myself; / I am large. . . . I contain multitudes."

"The last scud of day [. . .] coaxes me to the vapor and the dusk," Walt says to the reader:

I bequeath myself to the dirt to grow from the grass I love,
If you want me again look for me under your bootsoles. [. . .]
Failing to fetch me at first keep encouraged,
Missing me one place search another,
I stop some where waiting for you.

"Song of Myself" is the story-song of the possible American self, Walt's own and that of his compatriots. For religious believers, the poem will not be, as it was for Whitman, their foundational story—the sacred vision through which creation is understood. My foundational story—incarnation, teaching and healing, suffering and death, resurrection, communion within God and with God (through community as well as alone) and among the panoply of God's creation—conditions how I have read Whitman's poem and sets limits on the extent to which I can participate in it with willing belief. The same will and should be true for others who bring to Whitman's text their own foundational stories.

Stories do not preclude one another, however. Graham Greene's *Brighton Rock*, which performed a mythic role in my life when I was twenty, did not forestall my simultaneously profiting from Jane Austen's wisdom. When I outgrew the nearly manichean dilemma of *Brighton Rock* and, briefly, found Kafka's myth a key to understanding, I had no need to reject Greene. Without lessening my ability to profit from the creation stories of the Seven Days and the Gospel of John, the religious convergence that marks our day has enabled me to discover contrary yet valid meanings in the Rig Veda's Hymn of Creation. Among the more salubrious demands of our age may be its requirement that we participate in sacred stories not our own. Our fundamental stories now remain incomplete unless we confront them with the fundamental stories of others, including the stories of those who like Whitman embrace all religions and the stories of those who embrace none.

Leaves of Grass, more than any of the other seminal works published during the half-decade of 1850–1855, addresses America as a geographical and cultural totality in the process of self-creation. The Union was threatened; Whitman envisions unity present. Greed was manifest; he supposes heroes "pocketless of a dime" and originates delight in the common grass and air. American individualism was raw; he raises egocentricity to impossible heights on the one hand and affirms the inherently relational nature of the self on the other. Democracy was, given the depredations of slavery and the deprivations of women, unrealized; he imagines equality of dignity and respect. He loves and finds hope in both city and countryside.

The angel, however, is in the details, what Zweig calls "the unvarnished, shaggy particulars of the everyday world." Whitman perceives, Zweig says, "a sexual prodding from within life to produce more and better life" (136–137). In "Song of Myself," Walt witnesses the particulars and waits, observing with ear and touch as well as eye—trusting in the inner capacity of each thing to make itself new. One essential element is patience. Those who loiter instead of rushing by see the "butcher-boy [put] off his killing clothes" and dance "his shuffle and breakdown" (36). Another is compassion, which Walt exercises without the pity that reduces sufferers to their pain, whether it is the "child that peeped in at the door and then drew back and was never seen again" or a man "in the poorhouse tubercled by rum" (78). But the most important is trust. To readers, Walt says:

> [. . .] each man and woman of you I lead upon a knoll,
> My left hand hooks you round the waist,
> My right hand points to landscapes of continents, and a plain public road.

> Not I, not any one else can travel that road for you,
> You must travel it for yourself. (82)

REFERENCES

Dixon, John W. "Hierarchy and Laity." *Christian Century,* October 25, 1967. 1353–58.

Jordan, June. *Passion: New Poems, 1977–1980.* Boston: Beacon Press, 1980.

Randall, Dudley, ed. *The Black Poets.* New York: Bantam Books, 1971.

Teilhard de Chardin, Pierre. *Letters from a Traveler.* New York: Harper & Brothers, 1962.

Whitman, Walt. *Complete Poetry and Collected Prose,* selected by Justin Kaplan. New York: Library of America, 1982.

Zweig, Paul. *Walt Whitman: The Making of the Poet.* New York: Basic Books, 1984.

MARK DeLancey

Texts, Interpretations, and Whitman's "Song of Myself"
(1989)

Aristotle tells us that the rhetorician must be able to argue both sides of a question.[1] The poets have responded to this demand all along. In the *Odyssey,* the suitors speak for the opposition, as do Satan and his crew in *Paradise Lost.* In Westerns, the opposition wears the black hats. Shorter forms such as the lyric often signify wrongheaded argument with a simple negative. "Thy trivial harp," Emerson complains in the first lines of "Merlin," "will never please / Nor fill my craving ear." Against the harpist, the black-hats, or Satan the author develops his case, and that they merit rebuttal presupposes that their views are forces in the community he addresses. The community to be formed by persuasion is always yet to be, and if the author speaks for the future, the opposition parties speak for conventional experience. The nature of the rhetorician's task demands that he aspire to a modernity beyond the horizon of the familiar. But if the author is committed to the new, we may ask how he escapes the old while compelling the assent of his listeners, who would not need to be persuaded did not the author assume that they were committed to the world he abandons. How does the author propose to achieve modernity? How does the audience, committed to the old world, gain access to the new? The idea of observing both sides of a question suggests an answer.

I. The Question of Difference

Experience is many-sided. By observing two sides of a question, an author hopes to arrive at an answer that reconciles different and conflicting experiences. Thus he achieves something new. As Cleanth Brooks suggests, a text dramatizes a conflict of familiar "attitudes."[2] "His analysis of Donne's "Canonization," for example, charts the clash and reconciliation of two conventional views of love, Petrarchan and Christian (10–17). "In a unified poem," he says, "the poet has 'come to terms' with his experience" (p. 189). He comes to terms with an experience of a world constituted by modes of discourse that have solicited or won his assent.

To argue two sides of a question, in this view, is not simply to argue pro and con. It is to deliberate on a question answered differently by two modes of familiar discourse. A difference within experience, and by extension a rift within the community, drives the author to question the community's self-understanding and to affirm a new understanding. He argues both sides of the question to embrace and to bridge the difference that makes change available to him and his community. The coherence of a poem, what Brooks calls its "real meaning," "lies in the unification of attitudes into a hierarchy subordinated to a total and governing attitude" (p. 189). To achieve this unity, which can authentically reconcile two sides of the question, and thus compel the reader's agreement, only if those two sides and their differences are preserved intact, the author must do justice to both. Each side speaks as a half of a new whole. Both belong to the opposition party, and wear the black hats, if they resist change. If they consent to change, both belong to the author's party and wear the white hats. If the community consents to the new understanding affirmed by the author, its understanding of experience changes.

Brooks thus very nearly closes ranks with Deconstruction. To say, as the deconstructers do, that a text emerges from a play of differences in the language system is to say that it emerges from historical difference—from differences among established discourses. Historical difference gives rise to the possibility of the traditional task, shared by the texts of Deconstruction itself, of compelling agreement by arguing both sides of a question. The text "decenters" the historical community, "deconstructs" the edifice of habit and common sense, and defeats opposition to change by observing the differences within familiar experience. Because any reconciling (or "effacing") of differences creates new differences, the decentering of experience is perpetual. Familiar experience and the new experience made available by a given text put one another in question. It then falls to yet another text to resolve the new question.[3]

Though he emphasizes the author's achievement, Brooks would not deny that it relies on a "deconstruction" of familiar experience. Nor would he deny that the decentering of experience is perpetual. The deconstructers, however, are less inclined than Brooks to concede that the author and in turn the audience achieve understanding. J. Hillis Miller insists that

> the critic's attempt to untwist the elements in the texts he interprets only twists them up again in another place and leaves always an element of opacity, or an added opacity, as yet unraveled. The critic is caught in his own version of the interminable repetitions which determine the poet's career. The critic experiences this as his failure to get his poet right in a final decisive formulation which would allow him to have done with that poet, once and for all. Though each poet is different, each contains his own form of undecidability.

This might be defined by saying that the critic can never show decisively whether or not the work of the writer is "decidable," whether or not it is capable of being definitively interpreted. The critic cannot unscramble the tangle of lines of meaning, comb its threads out so they shine clearly side by side. He can only retrace the text, set its elements in motion once more, in that experience of the failure of determinable reading which is decisive here.[4]

Meaning is indeterminate because any understanding questions, and is reciprocally questioned by, any understanding already achieved. Caught in "interminable repetitions" of the act of questioning, author and critic alike are condemned to a world whose meanings are always questionable.

This difference between Brooks and Miller is important because it reveals a blind spot in their assumptions. Both assume that an author's characteristic act of questioning consists in, or at least coincides with, a questioning of meaning: having put meaning in question, a text is the place where one tries (successfully or unsuccessfully) to interpret, to understand. Brooks and Miller thus fail to observe a primary difference: one may question a truth affirmed by an author, and one may question an interpreter's understanding of what an author affirms. Just as there is a diversity of answers, and one truth competes with another, there is a diversity of interpretations of a given answer.

The end of rhetoric is agreement in the sphere of truth. Persuasion, that is to say, begins in a difference that puts truth in question. What troubles an author is that the answers affirmed by his community differ: the text emerges from a difference that renders truth questionable and to that extent indeterminate. By observing both sides of the question, the author hopes to reconcile the difference and put the question of truth to rest. Only by affirming and transcending difference can the author determine what he considers to be the truth and secure the agreement of his community. "Truth," in this sense, is not "absolute" truth, though it may appear so if the difference resolved appears to embrace all possible experience. It is a settling of differences between accepted truths. Authors who claim to have nothing to do with "truth" make a negligible exception to the general rule, given this sense of the term. If they do not put the truths of my experience in question, they do not address questions important to me. If they give reasons for denying these truths, or the possibility of truth in general, they give me reason to think they speak the truth. If they give no reasons, I have no reason to listen.

The end of interpretation, by contrast, can only be agreement in the sphere of meaning. Interpretation begins in a difference that puts meaning in question. What troubles the interpreter is that a given text evidently means different things to different interpreters and indeed to himself. Hence to the interpreter, a text emerges from a difference that renders its meanings questionable and indeterminate. By observing both sides of the question, the interpreter hopes to reconcile the difference and put the question of meaning to rest. In this sense, "meaning," like "truth," is a provisional solution to a problem. By transcending difference in the sphere of meaning, the interpreter determines meaning and secures the agreement of his community. But after an interpreter has determined the meaning of a text, and hence too of the truth that it affirms, that meaning and that truth may be put in question by other meanings and other truths.

Brooks and Miller arrive at contradictory conclusions because their premise, which denies the difference between texts and interpretations, is self-contradictory. How the difference reasserts itself in their conclusions is a question I address later, when I explore the reason behind the nearly universal tendency to deny it. But first I want to illustrate the difference by looking at Whitman's rhetoric in "Song of Myself."

II. *Whitman and the Rhetoric of Democracy*

"Song of Myself" opens with the speaker inviting the audience to embrace him:

> I celebrate myself, and sing myself,
> And what I assume you shall assume,
> Every atom belonging to me as good belongs to you.
>
> I loafe and invite my soul,
> I lean and loafe at my case observing a spear of summer grass.[5]

The "soul" that he invites is also the audience that he addresses as "you." In the embrace of his reader and soul, the words on the page—the poet's "atoms," his body—will awaken to life. Since the soul will then assume the poet's atoms, reader and writer will share one living body and one embodied soul.

The poet thus speaks as a body estranged from its soul. The soul cannot attend to Whitman's ample body—will not read "Leaves of Grass"—because the community, confined to "houses and rooms" and intoxicated by the "perfumes" of "creeds and schools," has its nose stuck in other books. When the reader does come to him, soul and body reunite, and the poet comes to himself. Leaving the library, and becoming "undisguised and naked" at the "bank by the wood," Whitman comes to himself, and literally to his senses, by embracing the pure, unintoxicating "atmosphere" ("I am mad for it to be in contact with me").

On the one side are the "houses and rooms," their shelves crowded with intoxicating books. On the other is the pure "atmosphere" of the out-of-doors. The two sides voice different rhetorical appeals. The library expresses its seductiveness in images of containment. The schools and creeds bring nature indoors by distilling out its essences. This rhetoric of refinement invites the soul to take all of Nature into itself—to become a delirious vessel of Nature's wine, which can then be poured out for other bacchants. The rhetoric of the atmosphere, by contrast, invites all things to lose themselves in its currents. As it speaks through him, the atmosphere drowns the poet's voice ("The smoke of my own breath, / Echoes, ripples, buzz'd whispers") in a sea of voices indistinguishable from his own. In an orgiastic abandonment of identity, he complies with the persuasions of a rhetoric that urges him to identify himself with all that he is not.

Each side lacks what the other claims as its virtue. If the one, for all its intoxicants, stands accused of too much refinement, the other, for all its massive sobriety, stands accused of "buzzing," of saying everything and nothing. But the poet, who has come to the wood from the library, combines them both in himself. As he dissolves in the atmosphere, and then falls asleep, the alienated halves of his experience reunite. The poet awakens revitalized, and the two streams of his experience blend together in a "full-noon trill, the song of me rising from bed and meeting the sun."

This song of mature mid-day does not reveal its central commitment until Section 5, when the poet finally confronts his soul and reader face to face. Pointedly, the poet asks his lover to "loose the stop from your throat," to free his voice from the self-imposed and repressive checks of the schools. He does not want "music" or "lecture," just the "hum" that has been bottled up inside.

The soul accepts the body's renewed invitation, and a memory revives.

> I mind how once we lay such a transparent summer morning,
> How you settled your head athwart my hips and turn'd gently over upon me,
> And parted the shirt from my bosom-bone, and plung'd your tongue to my
>   bare-stript heart,
> And reach'd till you felt my beard, and reach'd till you held my feet.

"Swiftly arose and spread around me," the poet continues, "the peace and knowledge that pass all the argument of the earth." Then, changing to the present tense, he announces what the recollection teaches: "And I know. . . ." Here are the two sides of Whitman's experience and the whole conceived in their embrace: the present of the living soul, which, loosing the stop from its throat, reanimates the past; the past itself, a transparent summer morning in which soul and body once embraced; and the past regained as present truth.

The past recalled by the poet is the dawn of the sense of his immortality, when the soul first embraced the body and its transient world. Borne into the bodily eye by the transient light that rises and spreads across the landscape, the "argument of the earth" is in effect taken up and resolved by the soul, whose light, rising and spreading over the landscape of mortality, immortalizes it as transcendent peace and knowledge. The transient light, the earth in its arms, and the things of day dematerialize in the embrace of the soul's eternal light. "I mind how once we lay such a transparent summer morning." Transparency is their achievement. Each pervading the other, body and soul sing together a poem of early knowledge and rising peace, which dissolves all things in the transparency it creates.

Considered as one side of a controversy in which familiar attitudes are put in question, this moment suggests to me Wordsworth's "Ode," in particular the relation between the "celestial light" and "the light of common day." To Wordsworth—Wordsworth-the-child, that is—"every common sight . . . did seem / Apparelled in celestial light, / The glory and the freshness of a dream."[6] The common *seems* celestial. The child's "dream" effectively denies commonplace nature and divorces him from it. The real, however, quickly reasserts itself as this priest of nature watches the light he thought celestial "die away, / And fade into the light of common day." But because the common light, measured against the "vision splendid," must appear demonic, the child in his heaven-born freedom puts himself at strife with his blessedness. He falls into a demonic universe of death until, halted in his flight "like a guilty Thing surprised," the life within his dying embers remembers and gathers him and his faded moments back to its breast.

Just as the light of the soul embraces Whitman and immortalizes the transient report of the senses, an interior light immortalizes Wordsworth's passing moments. The heart's affections and recollections—the "master light of all our seeing"—"make / Our noisy years seem moments in the being / Of the eternal Silence; truths that wake, / To perish never." This inextinguishable light explains why the common at first "seems" celestial and at the same time authorizes (though on different grounds) the dream of nature's priest as a truth. The "immortal sea / Which brought us hither" reclaims all things. "In a moment"—in all moments at once given and taken by eternal, "celestial" life—the soul can "travel thither, / And see the Children sport upon the shore, And hear the mighty waters rolling evermore."

The *transparency* of Whitman's vision points to a different Wordsworthian experience.

> Five years have past; five summers, with the length
> Of five long winters! and again I hear
> These waters, rolling from their mountain springs
> With a soft inland murmur.— Once again
> Do I behold these steep and lofty cliffs,
> That on a wild secluded scene impress
> Thoughts of more deep seclusion; and connect
> The landscape with the quiet of the sky.
> The day is come when I again repose
> Here, under this dark sycamore, and view
> These plots of cottage-ground, these orchard-tufts,
> Which at this season, with their unripe fruits,
> Are clad in one green hue, and lose themselves
> 'Mid groves and copses. Once again I see
> These hedge-rows, hardly hedge-rows, little lines
> Of sportive wood run wild: these pastoral farms,
> Green to the very door; and wreaths of smoke
> Sent up, in silence from among the trees!
> With some uncertain notice, as might seem
> Of vagrant dwellers in the houseless woods,
> Or of some Hermit's cave, where by his fire
> The Hermit sits alone.[7]

It is summer, and it is morning. The poet listens to the inland murmur because he cannot yet see. He records what he hears, pauses, and then, as dawn begins to break, beholds the steep and lofty cliffs: "The day is come."

Casting their shadow, with the sun rising behind them, on a secluded scene, the cliffs impress thoughts of yet deeper seclusion. The poet's thoughts are in effect a shadow impressed on the scene by cliffs blocking out the sun. But the shadow bears witness to the light, and thus the cliffs "connect" the landscape with the quiet of the sky. Running wild like the lines of sportive wood, Wordsworth's syntax also permits "I" as the subject of "connect": "Once again do I behold . . . and connect." The "I" or self, then, is like the cliff that both blocks out the sun and connects the darkened landscape with the quiet of the sky. The subject and the landscape are one in their power to sever and connect, and this power now begins to "connect" things formerly severed, the subject and his landscape chief among them. In this day and this scene the poet sees what he saw before: past and present merge. Orchard tufts, clad in one green hue, lose themselves amid groves and copses. The lines of hedge-rows run wild, the green threatens to swallow the farmhouses, and the smoke of breakfast fires drifts away into the light.

This act of connecting is a rhetorical gesture. Subject and object are wedded, so to speak, by a copula that urges each, as it flickers in the moment of syntactical distinction, to lose itself in the other. Different things become one being, which speaks through them to identify each with all. This "power that rolls through all things"—a "something far more deeply interfused"—lends them a transient identity that dissolves immediately in a oneness. Though the superficial (i.e., syntactical) differences between them are preserved, all things die into the living whole.

The wreaths of smoke commemorate this death. Carrying a double valency like that of the cliffs, the smoke suggests to Wordsworth the two sides of his own divided experience—the dark seclusion that he shares with the Hermit in his cave and the community with nature, and with one another, that he shares with the vagrants. When he acknowledges, as the sun rises from behind the cliffs and spreads its light across the landscape, the power that rolls through all things, the divided halves of his experience unite, consume themselves in one another, and dissolve like the smoke rising and spreading into the transparency of the sky.

Whitman's coupling of soul and body achieves the same transparency, and achieves it by the same means, as though he were assenting to a Wordsworthian rhetoric of unity. The poet's "body"—everything that belongs to transient sensory experience—dies into, and is immortalized by, the soul's transparent light. Whitman's problem, the primary problem addressed not only by "Song of Myself" but by his poetry as a whole, is that the soul that embraced him on that summer morning has gone on to a new incarnation in the present-day American schools. Its rhetorical program is now one of internalization. The soul now bottles intoxicating perfumes distilled from nature.

Though he reproaches the schools, landing a glancing blow at their effeminacy, for distilling "perfumes" out of life, Whitman says he "likes" their "fragrance" (l. 15). He "likes" the "lull" and "hum" of the schools' "valvéd voice" (l. 86). The experience of the schools is his own present experience, and it moves between an act of (feminine and "feudal") refinement—of bringing the outside inside in the form of intoxicating essences—and an act of pouring out, in drunken song, what has been contained. This new commitment of the soul to self-containment suggests the rhetorical program of Emerson.

"The Supreme Being," Emerson writes in "Nature," "does not build up nature around us, but puts it forth through us, as the life of the tree puts forth new branches and leaves through the pores of the old."[8] Nature is God's word—"a projection of God in the unconscious" (I, 64–65)—and "the present expositor of the divine mind" (I, 65). But since God pours forth his Word through man, and exclusively through him, nature is equally human history and the expositor of man's own divinity:

> Man is the dwarf of himself. Once he was permeated and dissolved by spirit. He filled nature with his overflowing currents. Out of him sprang the sun and moon; from man the sun, from woman the moon. The laws of his mind, the periods of his actions externized themselves into day and night, into the year and the seasons. But, having made for himself this huge shell, his waters retired; he no longer fills the veins and veinlets; he is shrunk to a drop. He sees that the structure still fits him, but fits him colossally. Say, rather, once it fitted him, now it corresponds to him from far and on high. He adores timidly his own work. Now is man the follower of the sun, and woman the follower of the moon. Yet sometimes he starts in his slumber, and wonders at himself and his house, and muses strangely at the resemblance betwixt him and it. He perceives that if his law is still paramount, if still he have elemental power, if his word is sterling yet in nature, it is not conscious power, it is not interior but superior to his will. It is instinct. (I, 71–72)

The spirit that contained and permeated nature has withdrawn itself, becoming unconscious instinct. Man's creation, a shell now containing his drop of conscious power, lies dead around him as what Emerson calls the "Not Me."

Emerson's rhetoric hopes to persuade his community that what man creates, which is the Not Me because it constitutes a fixed past resisting present power, waits to be drunk in by the spirit that poured it forth. Man "thinks his fate alien," but "the soul contains the event that shall befall it, for the event is only the actualization of its thoughts" (VI, 40). The soul is a vessel and its acts both realize and take the stamp of the nature it contains. Man "shall see that nature is the opposite of the soul, answering to it part for part. One is seal and one is print. Its beauty is the beauty of his own mind. Its laws are the laws of his own mind. Nature then becomes the measure of his own attainments. So much of nature as he is ignorant of, so much of his own mind does he not yet possess" (I, 86–87). Piercing the husk of the world, the spirit abstracts its essence, and the circuit of conscious life expands. The act of comprehending, made available by an influx of unconscious power, lends actuality to that which is comprehended. Thus the fully comprehending spirit—the transparent eyeball of "Nature"—contains, pours out, and is the world that it sees.

When Whitman characterizes the schools' project of absolute self-containment as "intoxicating," he borrows Emerson's vocabulary. The god invoked by Emerson in "Bacchus" is the alienated god within, the capricious god of "instinct." The Not Me is his vineyard, and a draught of wine, "Food which teach and reason can," assimilates the communicant to his own alienated powers, whereupon he "May float at pleasure through all natures" and "unlock / Every crypt of every rock" (IX, 125–26).

Emerson's prayer is thus a prayer to become Bacchus, and then something more than Bacchus, as he reclaims from the Not Me the power to distill and drink in the essence of original godhead that he once yielded to it.

> Pour, Bacchus! the remembering wine;
> Retrieve the loss of me and mine!
> Vine for vine be antidote,
> And the grape requite the lote!
> Haste to cure the old despair,—
> Reason in Nature's lotus drenched,
> The memory of ages quenched. (IX, 127)

Reason sleeps, drenched in the lotus of the Not Me, but when the antidote takes effect, reason reawakens to discover itself in a Nature renewed.

> Let the wine repair what this undid;
> And where the infection slid,
> A dazzling memory revive;
> Refresh the faded tints,
> Recut the aged prints,
> And write my old adventures with the pen
> Which on the first day drew,
> Upon the tablets blue,
> The dancing Pleiads and eternal men. (IX, 127)

His essence abstracted from the written record of the Not Me, and placed again within the circuit of the spirit, the Man that hardened into the material forms of the Not Me awakens once more as Man. His alienated and dormant essence again becomes actual thought, which is to say a thought-in-act, and the spirit writes again its old adventures.

Whitman's complaint, to return to Section 5 of "Song of Myself," is that the soul, in its Emersonian incarnation, abases the body: "I believe in you my soul, the other I am must not abase itself to you, / And you must not be abased to the other." Distilling the thought or essence out of the Not Me, Emersonian intellectuality devalues the body of nature, and the body of nature reciprocates by drenching Reason in the lote. To neutralize their "stupendous antagonism" (VI, 22), as Emerson in "Fate" calls the interplay of spirit and nature, Whitman adopts the Wordsworthian attitude of repose beneath the sycamore and loafs on the grass. In this repose, the transient body merges with the quiet of the sky, and all things, as they sink in the depths of the sea of being, are made one. The problem is that a state in which all things are one, and in which they lose themselves like smoke in the light, cannot be an object of thought, except as Being again materializes in individual beings. Of each single "truth" the whole is predicated. The being that dwells in such peace is everything and nothing—a "huge first Nothing" (l. 1153) as Whitman calls it when he looks back upon the depths out of which he has risen—and can neither think, nor be thought, nor listen, nor speak.

Whitman's solution is to reunite the alienated halves of his experience. Past and present redefine one another. Embraced by the Emersonian soul, the transparent summer morning of Wordsworthian oneness awakens as a memory. The soul unstops its throat, pours back into the past the essences it lacks, and thus transforms Wordsworth's "sea" into a mass of equal but thinkable entities comprehended by the soul. Under the pressure of Wordsworthian unity, the soul in turn is made one with the sea whose parts it embraces as its own knowable form and body.

The rhetorical resources of the Wordsworthian and Emersonian experiences thus speak simultaneously in an emerging Whitmanian modernity:

> And I know that the hand of God is the promise of my own,
> And I know that the spirit of God is the brother of my own,
> And that all the men ever born are also my brothers, and the women my
> sisters and lovers,
> And that a kelson of the creation is love,
> And limitless are leaves stiff or drooping in the fields,
> And brown ants in the little wells beneath them,
> And mossy scabs of the worm fence, heap'd stones, cider, mullein and
> poke-weed.

This is the rhetoric of Whitmanian democracy. The speaker is one with God, and with the other members of the community, but he *knows* each one, and every blade of grass, as a self-contained part of a whole constituted by the parts that it comprehends. In contrast with Emerson's rhetoric of internalization and Wordsworth's of unity, Whitman's rhetoric is one of harmony. Diverse individuals, the atoms of a spiritual whole, compose a community whose soul, which embraces each member equally, and which therefore communicates the experience of each to all, expresses itself in a harmony of voices.

III. *Argument and Representation*

The achievement of "modernity" begins with the poet's commitment to two contradictory truths. Whitman addresses himself, as the voice and "body" of the Wordsworthian past, to the soul of the Emersonian present. A substitution has occurred. For its conventional or historically established object, the Wordsworthian subject substitutes a new object. Instead of addressing the Wordsworthian soul whose redemptive power identifies each with all, the Wordsworthian subject addresses the Emersonian soul whose similarly redemptive power contains all. We may say that Whitman predicates the Emersonian subject of the Wordsworthian subject. The two subjects, so joined, put one another in question because the proposition is unconventional—the conventional of course corresponding to the discourses of the "past" and "present" (as Whitman understands them). Whitman's questioning of conventional experience is thus founded on a trope, an unconventional combination of conventional elements.

The trope behaves like a complex simile. In the simile "men are [like] birds," what I. A. Richards would call the vehicle ("birds") suggests properties that literally or conventionally belong to the tenor ("men").[9] The nature of this suggestiveness implies that the trope arises from the substitution of an unconventional predicate—"birds," "whose own conventional predicates are thus provisionally eclipsed—for the conventional predicates of "men," which are likewise eclipsed. While the trope may suggest any number of predicates, and we recover them only by a kind of guesswork, our conventional understanding of the two terms limits the possibilities. Each suggestion puts all other suggestions in question, and we select from the alternatives only those predicates that common sense or familiar experience tells us can be predicated of "men." Alternatively, from the range of predicates that common sense attaches to "men," we select only those predicates suggested by "birds." My understanding of "birds," involving as it does the idea of flight, suggests to me an idea of spiritual aspiration that is conventionally predicable of "men," and I then assume that this predicate is the one for which "birds" has been substituted. Once I have fixed upon this point of its conventional history, "men" in turn suggests other properties conventionally predicable of "birds"—perhaps that they sometimes soar beyond eye's reach. Thus I reconstruct, as an object of belief made available through a reasoned or common sense guesswork, the grounds of the substitution that gave rise to the simile.

As the trope leads back to a determinate awareness of the conventional histories of the likened terms, it also leads forward, as does Whitman's unconventional combination of conventional elements, to a vision of something new. After I have chosen from the available alternatives a particular property of the tenor (or a number of its properties), the vehicle ceases to be suggestive (though its suggestiveness may be revived at any time). To me, and in this case, the vehicle "birds" designates the spiritual aspirations that it once only suggested. Properties conventionally belonging to "men" accordingly supplement the conventional definition of "birds."[10] This event of mutual redefinition reconciles what the trope, considered as a *representation,* posits as its own past and present. Because the vehicle re-presents the properties of the tenor, the tenor belongs to a past re-presented and the vehicle to a present that re-presents. The representation that links past and present belongs to an emerging modernity.

The difference that generates the argument is thus a similarity-in-difference, the broadest or most fundamental kind of relation capable of being affirmed. Difference implies relation; non-relation is indifference. Since to say that two things differ is to say that they are not the same, the relation between them must be such that there might be some possibility of confusing them. I will say that the moon is different from a mandrake only if they might be thought to be the same. If they were not similar, or thought to be similar, the question of their sameness or difference could not arise. As similarity implies difference, difference implies similarity. A text begins in an "understanding-as."

By understanding Emerson's truth and Wordsworth's each as the other, Whitman commits himself to both. He argues just these two sides of the question because the representation demands that he do justice to only the past and present that it postulates. He thus commits himself to a particular historical sequence. As it distinguishes between a past represented and a present representing, Whitman's trope projects a future born of their mutual redefinition. His representation of the Wordsworthian past in the Emersonian present commits him to a modernity of fixed dimensions.

Familiar experience, conventional common sense, restricts the poet's freedom to affirm the new. In the formation of simile, the availability of an unconventional substitute breaks the bond between a subject and its conventional predicate. The subject becomes the simile's tenor as it captures the substitute, which becomes the vehicle, in the displaceable energies freed by the breaking of the conventional bond. But the energies displaced onto the vehicle "properly" belong elsewhere. The gravity of the familiar draws them back to the conventional predicates for which the vehicle has substituted. The vehicle is suggestive precisely to the extent that the voice of common sense insists on being heard. Freeplay exhausts itself in doing justice to familiar experience. The representation liberates energies from the constraints of orthodoxy while preserving its accomplishment.

A representation of the past in the present is thus the text's constitutive moment, the first cause of the new. Because it liberates the energies and tensions that animate Whitman's world, the trope that joins Wordsworthian and Emersonian discourses awakens Whitman both to his own rhetoric and to the new community it envisions. Any "Whitman" prior to his own rhetoric, a creative spirit or imagination that might be viewed as the maker of the poem, coincides with one or another of the conventional experiences that the poem puts in question. An ego or maker or imagination is in question, in other words, only to the extent that it has been constituted by conventional discourses that are supported by the communal labor—a labor that will be variously defined by the bond in question—of binding a subject to a predicate. Because this labor defines the members of the community as subjects of a certain kind, the availability of an unconventional substitute for the subject's conventional predicates frees the labor consumed in the task of conventional self-definition to a task of redefinition and change. The possibility of "understanding-as," in short, awakens the conventional "I" to new life, and the representation, pulling the subject toward the conventional and unconventional simultaneously, constitutes the imagination's will to reconcile the opposition in a new whole.

Whitman's question is a large one—"What is the truth of things?" Acting as the spokesman of the first, and attributing the second to his alienated soul and reader, he has to do justice to both the Wordsworthian experience and the Emersonian experience because his answer can only be that the truth comprehends both. That the halves of his and his community's experience are substantially one he does not recognize fully until Section 5, when the Emersonian soul, belonging to the living present of his audience, recollects and revives the Wordsworthian past. He sees and asserts the larger truth, which has been eclipsed by the temporality of experience, that the past and present and all their properties make up the predicates of "Life."

This truth figures as the thesis of Whitman's argument. The rhetorical project of the rest of the poem is to defend this truth, and we may suppose that the poet achieves the traditional rhetorical aims by observing the traditional rhetorical means. However we conceive them, they are necessarily enclosed, constituted, and made available by the metaphoricity that grounds his argument and asks the question that he seeks to answer. In particular, the "agreement" that marks the end of persuasion is a resource of simile. Subject and object, author and audience, past and present, each understands itself *as* the other and so comes to recognize itself in the other. Because a vehicle's conventional definition is supplemented by what it suggests about the tenor, the two terms mutually redefine one another and thus resolve their differences. The author agrees with the audience, and the audience, if it understands what the author has said, and if it acknowledges that he has done justice to both sides of the question, agrees with the author. The freedom that a poem makes available to its readers may be a threat to their experience, but by doing justice to its alienated halves, the poem preserves it transfigured in an emerging modernity.

IV. Representation and Interpretation

The metaphoricity in which the text begins, and which challenges the author to argue both sides of the question, challenges the interpreter to understand both sides of the question. Metaphoricity embraces the text on two registers. As it posits a difference in the sphere of truth, it also posits a difference in the sphere of meaning. "Song of Myself," for example, posits a difference in the meaning that Emerson and Wordsworth give to the words "life" or "experience." The difference puts meaning in question. Of virtually any word in "Song of Myself," two different accounts, Emersonian and Wordsworthian, can be given. This kind of metaphoricity—metaphoricity in the sphere of meaning—accounts for and justifies the interpreter's inescapable hypothesis that the text's meanings are questionable and indeterminate. The text is opaque because it understands one order of meaning as or in terms of another order of meaning. The text does not insist on just one meaning; it both dissembles and suggests a whole range of meanings.

To settle the question of meaning, the interpreter enters into the text's representation of meaning as meaning. The text speaks suggestively, and the interpreter responds to its suggestions. The vehicle of the representation, speaking within the interpreter's familiar experience, asks him to recall a past that it suggests. Because the tenor of a simile may at any time function as a vehicle—if A is like B, B is like A—this recovered past reciprocally suggests something about the present. These suggestions put in question his initial understanding of the present. The interpreter's corrected or revised or expanded understanding of the present may then suggest a new range of properties that put in question his initial understanding of the past.

The text's suggestiveness thus gives the interpreter access to his own experience, to what he already understands. As it gives access to familiar meanings, the text's suggestiveness exercises a selective surveillance that singles out meanings that are adequate to the clarification of the text. The criterion of adequacy is twofold: a meaning must be suggested by the text, and what is suggested must agree with common sense. The meanings that the interpreter attaches to the text must belong, according to the judgment of common sense, to the familiar experiences, past and present, that the suggestive play of representation makes available to reflection. A suggestion is valid, in other words, if it does not, in the judgment of common sense, contradict other suggestions.

The judgments of common sense make interpretation inseparable from criticism. If the interpreter happens to be the author of the text, these judgments give him the opportunity to revise his interpretation of the arguments that his own argument puts in question. Any revision in the sphere of meaning will of course require him to rework his argument. If he is not the author, the interpreter can justify criticism of the text on the grounds that its author has misinterpreted the arguments that he, as author, questions. The critic then judges that the meanings attached by the author to familiar experience, and thus to the modernity to which the author's representation is committed, cannot stand the test of common sense.

An interpreter of Whitman, for example, might object that Whitman's interpretations of the conventional experiences that he attributes to his community do not agree with his community's interpretations. The criticism, I emphasize, applies not to the author's argument, but to his interpretation of the two sides of the question that he argues (though a criticism of the argument may follow). In his exploration of the question of truth, the author recovers, reconstructs, or "does justice to" two arguments, two rhetorical commitments, which he has already interpreted. By contrast, the interpreter's exploration of the question of meaning recovers and reconstructs a conventional interpretation of the two sides of the question. Because the interpreter's exploration unfailingly presents to reflection alternative interpretations of the two sides, it puts in question the author's interpretation of them. Since an argument can appear to reflection only "inside" an understanding of its two sides, the interpreter's criticism—a criticism specifically of the author's interpretation of the two sides—also applies to what the interpreter will take to be the author's interpretation of his own text.

V. The Destiny of the Text

An author must insist that he understands his own argument. Lest he undercut both his own ground and the future that it foresees, the author cannot question his interpretation of the arguments that he questions. An argument accordingly represses the possibility of questioning its own self-understanding. No argument can free itself from this dogmatism. The author denies, at least provisionally and until he becomes once again his own interpreter, that meaning is questionable. His text thus tacitly affirms that it grounds itself in certainty and self-evidence. To say that the understanding that grounds the argument is unquestionable is to say that the author understands his argument unquestionably and truly. By declaring that it appears fully in the light of its own self-evidence, the text repudiates its opacity and its status as a representation waiting to be clarified. The text claims to be a locus of meaning.

It is if we grant this claim that we follow Brooks and Miller in collapsing the difference between texts and interpretations. The difference reappears, however, in the conclusions that can be drawn from the hypothesis of the equivalence of texts and interpretations. Brooks, for example, tacitly defines a text as an interpretation. If interpretations achieve meaning, the author, considered as an interpreter, achieves meaning, and the reader or critic, whose role has been usurped by the author, can only hope to appropriate the understanding that the author has already achieved. By contrast, Miller tacitly defines an interpretation as a text. Neither authors nor readers can ever really understand because, whenever they interpret, they author another text whose meanings must be interpreted in yet another text, which likewise remains to be understood. In the one account, a text is the locus of achieved meaning; in the other, a text is the locus of failed meaning.

The act of interpretation, however, always amounts to a practical denial of the text's claim to meaning. One does not interpret that which is already clear. The interpreter enters into the text's representation of meaning as meaning to determine what it suggests. And if a text's meanings, apart from interpretation, are therefore indeterminate, interpretation does not change them. Something indeterminate cannot be changed. By entering into the questioning of meaning repressed by the author, the interpreter makes the text fulfill the destiny anticipated by the metaphoricity of its origins. Interpretation produces a transparent text. The text appears to reflection in the familiar experience made available to us by its suggestiveness, and as the text appears it changes, or its rhetoric seeks to change, our experience of truth. As our experience brings the argument to reflection, the argument, in partnership with our experience, bequeaths not only a past and a present that we are asked to view as our own, but also a modernity that we are yet to live.

I emphasize that a text hopes to reconcile a conflict in *communal* experience. Whitman's community is divided, at least as he understands it, because it urges contradictory claims that constitute the indubitable "truths" of the community's experience. To clarify these truths, and to make the modernity that emerges from them available to reflection, the interpreter must appeal to his own experience: we understand the new in terms of what we already understand. Thus I appealed to my understanding of Emerson and Wordsworth. But the two criteria that an interpretation must meet—that it be suggested by the text and that it agree with common sense—leave room for the widest spectrum of different and equally valid interpretations. A Marxist critic might characterize Whitman's argument differently. Had he met these criteria, however, his interpretation would tend to make available to reflection, though in different terms, the same two sides of the question and the same answer. Meeting these criteria is not easy. The metaphoricity of the text asks the interpreter to question the presuppositions that he brings to it. These presuppositions are determined by experiences that have already been made available to reflection. They constitute his "common sense." If the text, as it appears to reflection, disconfirms the interpreter's "common sense," he usually abandons the text, not his own common sense.

What links all interpreters, regardless of their presuppositions, is a shared, or potentially communicable, historical experience that can be recognized, and which to that extent remains the same, in the different languages that make it available to reflection. The sum of this experience, as it appears to reflection in the sum of the languages of criticism, comprehends the whole of common sense. Beginning with his allotted portion, the interpreter reconstructs the text's historical ground by listening to its suggestions. By judging according to common sense, he acts in behalf of the community. Hence the final arbiter of the validity of an interpretation is the community, the reservoir of common sense. Ideally, an interpretation should be judged against all possible interpretations of the same text. In practice, we judge it against the available interpretations. Hence, not only is a wide spectrum of competing interpretations inevitable; it is essential to the community's task of self-understanding. A pluralistic community, unsubdued by dogma, has the best chance of knowing what to believe about itself.

Communal assent to an interpretation makes a text's modernity available to communal reflection. The whole process of raising and settling a question of truth then becomes an actual communal resource available to actual communal experience. The question may belong to our past: the moment of change, whatever its place in history, makes itself available to actual experience only through interpretation. But change takes place only if we agree to change. As we reflect upon the text, we ask whether it speaks for us. Is its question our own? Does it, as it observes the two sides of the question, observe a difference within our own experience? In short, does it make possible an authentic transformation of our own experience? We assent to change and arrive at the experience of the new if we decide that the text argues its question of truth in our behalf and argues it fairly. We assent to a change located in our past—to Whitman's vision of Democracy, for example—if we decide that the text argues fairly a question of truth in behalf of the community it addresses. We assent if the text does justice to a difference between moments of our collective past. We then arrive at the experience of a living and changing past different from our own present.

NOTES

[1] *Rhetoric*, 1355a. The passage in question runs as follows: "We must be able to employ persuasion, just as strict reasoning can be employed, on opposite sides of a question, not in order that we may in practice employ it in both ways (for we must not make people believe what is wrong), but in order that we may see clearly what the facts are, and that, if another man argues unfairly, we on our part may be able to confute him."

[2] *The Well Wrought Urn* (New York: Reynal & Hitchcock, 1947), pp. 186–87. Further references to this volume are indicated in the text by page number.

[3] This "decentering" is the primary concern of Jacques Derrida's "White Mythology," *New Literary History*, 6 (1974), 5–74. For a more focussed account of "difference" see his essay "Différance" in *Speech and Phenomenon*, trans. David P. Allison (Evanston: Northwestern University Press, 1973), and Lacan's "The Agency of the Letter in the Unconscious" in *Ecrits*, trans. Alan Sheridan (New York: Norton, 1977).

[4] "The Critic as Host," in *Deconstruction and Criticism* (New York: Seabury, 1975), pp. 247–48.

[5] *Leaves of Grass*, ed. Harold W. Blodgett and Sculley Bradley (New York: Norton, 1968), p. 28. Further references to "Song of Myself" are from this edition and are indicated in the text by line number.

[6] *The Poetical Works of William Wordsworth*, ed. E. de Selincourt (Oxford: Clarendon Press, 1940–1949), IV, 279.

7 Ibid., II, 279–80.

8 *The Complete Works of Ralph Waldo Emerson*, The Centenary Edition, 12 vols. (Boston: Houghton Mifflin, 1903–1904), I, 64. Further references to Emerson's writings are from this edition and are indicated in the text by volume and page number.

9 *The Philosophy of Rhetoric* (London: Oxford University Press, 1936), pp. 95–112. I use the term "simile" where Richards uses the term "metaphor" to distinguish the trope in question from another trope, more properly termed "metaphor," that effectively identifies two things by giving the name of the one to the other.

10 The mutual redefinition of a simile's terms gives rise to what is known technically as a "transfer." For a discussion of "transfer," see William Empson, *The Structure of Complex Words* (London: Chatto & Windus, 1951), pp. 334–36.

RALPH WALDO EMERSON

Letter to Walt Whitman
(1855)

Letter from Ralph Waldo Emerson to Whitman, 21 July 1855. Transcribed from facsimile copy in *Walt Whitman: A Selection of the Manuscripts, Books and Association Items.* Gathered by Charles E. Feinberg. Catalogue of an Exhibition Held at The Detroit Public Library, Detroit, Michigan, 1955. The Introduction to this Catalogue by David C. Mearns, Chief of the Manuscripts Division of the Library of Congress, notes that 'This has been called "probably now the most famous letter in American literary history."'

Concord 21 July
Massts 1855

Dear Sir,
    I am not blind to the worth of the wonderful gift of *Leaves of Grass*. I find it the most extraordinary piece of wit & wisdom that America has yet contributed. I am very happy in reading it, as great power makes us happy. It meets the demand I am always making of what seemed the sterile and stingy Nature, as if too much handiwork or too much lymph in the temperament were making our western wits fat & mean. I give you joy of your free & brave thoughts. I have great joy in it. I find incomparable things said incomparably well, as they must be. I find the courage of treatment, which so delights us, & which large perception only can inspire. I greet you at the beginning of a great career, which yet must have had a long foreground somewhere for such a start. I rubbed my eyes a little to see if this sunbeam were no illusion; but the solid sense of the book is a sober certainty. It has the best merits, namely, of fortifying & encouraging.

I did not know until I, last night, saw the book advertised in a newspaper, that I could trust the name as real & available for a post-office. I wish to see my benefactor, & have felt much like striking my tasks, & visiting New York to pay you my respects.

R. W. Emerson.

Mr. Walter Whitman.

RUFUS W. GRISWOLD

Unsigned Review
(1855)

An unconsidered letter of introduction has oftentimes procured the admittance of a scurvy fellow into good society, and our apology for permitting any allusion to the above volume in our columns is, that it has been unworthily recommended by a gentleman of wide repute, and might, on that account, obtain access to respectable people, unless its real character were exposed.

Mr. Ralph Waldo Emerson either recognizes and accepts these 'leaves,' as the gratifying result of his own peculiar doctrines, or else he has hastily indorsed them, after a partial and superficial reading. If it is of any importance he may extricate himself from the dilemma. We, however, believe that this book does express the bolder results of a certain transcendental kind of thinking, which some may have styled philosophy.

As to the volume itself, we have only to remark, that it strongly fortifies the doctrines of the Metempsychosists, for it is impossible to imagine how any man's fancy could have conceived such a mass of stupid filth, unless he were possessed of the soul of a sentimental donkey that had died of disappointed love. This *poet* (?) without wit, but with a certain vagrant wildness, just serves to show the energy which natural imbecility is occasionally capable of under strong excitement.

There are too many persons, who imagine they demonstrate their superiority to their fellows, by disregarding all the politenesses and decencies of life, and, therefore, justify themselves in indulging the vilest imaginings and shamefullest license. But Nature, abhorring the abuse of the capacities she has given to man, retaliates upon him, by rendering extravagant indulgence in any direction followed by an insatiable, ever-consuming, and never to be appeased passion.

Thus, to these pitiful beings, virtue and honor are but names. Bloated with self-conceit, they strut abroad unabashed in the daylight, and expose to the world the festering sores that overlay them, like a garment. Unless we admit this exhibition to be beautiful, we are at once set down for non-progressive conservatives, destitute of the 'inner light,' the far-seeingness which, of course, characterizes those gifted individuals. Now, any one who has noticed the tendency of thought in these later years, must be aware that a quantity of this kind of nonsense is being constantly displayed. The immodesty of presumption exhibited by those *seers;* their arrogant pretentiousness; the complacent smile with which they listen to the echo of their own braying, should be, and we believe is, enough to disgust the great majority of sensible folks; but, unfortunately, there is a class that, mistaking sound for sense, attach some importance to all this rant and cant. These candid, these ingenuous, these honest 'progressionists'; these human diamonds without flaws; these men that have *come*—detest furiously all shams; 'to the pure, all things are pure'; they are pure, and, consequently, must thrust their reeking presence under every man's nose.

They seem to think that man has no instinctive delicacy; is not imbued with a conservative and preservative modesty, that acts as a restraint upon the violence of passions, which for a wise purpose, have been made so strong. No! these fellows have no secrets, no disguises; no, indeed! But they do have, conceal it by whatever language they choose, a degrading, beastly sensuality, that is fast rotting the healthy core of all the social virtues.

There was a time when licentiousness laughed at reproval; now it writes essays and delivers lectures. Once it shunned the light; now it courts attention, writes books showing how grand and pure it is, and prophesies from its lecherous lips its own ultimate triumph.

Shall we argue with such men? Shall we admit them into our houses, that they may leave a foul odor, contaminating the pure, healthful air? Or shall they be placed in the same category with the comparatively innocent slave of poverty, ignorance, and passion that skulks along in the shadows of byways; even in her deep degradation possessing some sparks of the Divine light, the germ of good that reveals itself by a sense of shame?

Thus, then, we leave this gathering of muck to the laws which, certainly, if they fulfil their intent, must have power to suppress such obscenity. As it is entirely destitute of wit, there is no probability that any would, after this exposure, read it in the hope of finding that; and we trust no one will require further evidence—for, indeed, we do not believe there is a newspaper so vile that would print confirmatory extracts.

In our allusion to this book, we have found it impossible to convey any, even the most faint idea of its style and contents, and of our disgust and detestation of them, without employing language that cannot be pleasing to ears polite; but it does seem that some one should, under circumstances like these, undertake a most disagreeable, yet stern duty. The records of crime show that many monsters have gone on in impunity, because the exposure of their vileness was attended with too great indelicacy. *Peccatum illud horribile, inter Christianos non nominandum.*[1]

NOTE

[1] "That horrible sin not to be mentioned among Christians."

D. R. JARVIS

Whitman and Speech-Based Prosody
(1981)

Whitman's "free verse," wrote William Carlos Williams in his "Essay on *Leaves of Grass,*"

> constituted a direct challenge to all living poets to show cause why they should not do likewise. It is a challenge that still holds good. . . . From the beginning Whitman realized that the matter was largely technical.[1]

Whitman's importance as an innovator in versification has been directly and indirectly acknowledged by the subsequent generation of American poets which called for the development of a speech-based prosody, including such diverse figures as Charles Olson and Allen Ginsberg. Charles Olson in his "Projective Verse," a statement on poetics to which Robert Creeley, Robert Duncan and Denise Levertov have all at some time given their assent and allegiance, declared that the ear and the units of ordinary speech should provide the rhythm of future verse and that modern devices such as the typewriter had again made this possible:

> For the ear, which once had the burden of memory to quicken it (rime & regular cadence were its aids and have merely lived on in print after the oral necessities were ended) can now again . . . be the threshold of projective verse.[2]

The argument is identical to Whitman's in an early note where he says that prescribed forms like rhyme and metre are outmoded mnemonic devices left over from the "days before the printing press."[3] Allen Ginsberg in "Notes for *Howl* and Other Poems," records that around 1955 he began to experiment with Whitman's long line. "I realised," he continued, that Whitman's form had rarely been further explored (improved on even) in the U.S. . . . . No attempt's been made to use it in the light of early XX Century organization of new speech-rhythm prosody.[4]

In view of acknowledgements such as these it is surprising that little attention, beyond the recognition of his use of biblical parallelism, has been given to Whitman's poetry as the outcome of his own theory of a speech-based prosody. Critics have only vaguely appreciated how the phonic elements of Whitman's style, iterated syntactic structures, the organization of stresses, and "rhyme," are combined in speech-based yet rhythmical units. The critics have ranged from the view, on the one hand, that Whitman's poetry is mere prose dressed-up, to the view, on the other hand, that it is really metrical.[5] Both extremes neglect Whitman's own technical theory and his call for a "speaking" style. The former contrasts with his unequivocal statement in "Ventures, on an Old Theme" that true poetry is "necessarily always rhythmic," the latter with his equally unequivocal statement that "arbitrary and rhyming metre" had nothing to do with his kind of rhythm.[6]

Here, then, a twofold problem needs to be confronted. Not only is it necessary to seriously consider whether Whitman's rhythms correspond with the ideal he outlines in theory, but also to consider the purely descriptive and linguistic problem. To establish whether Whitman's prosody achieved his aims it is first necessary to define the basic constitutive units of his rhythms and how they are organised.

Many commentators have pointed to Whitman's use of (syntactic) parallelism as the outstanding feature of his style, and some, notably Gay Wilson Allen, have declared it to be the basic constitutive device of his poetry.[7] Whitman's use of parallelism is responsible, says Allen, for the overwhelming predominance of end-stopped lines in the mature Whitman. "The line," says Allen, "is the unit."[8] E. C. Ross also found that "the line" was the unit in Whitman, and argued that this feature distanced his poetry both from prose and from ordinary metrical poetry. "Whitman's verse," wrote Ross, "is further removed from prose than is traditional verse itself, for the reason that the traditional verse is, like prose, composed in sentences, whereas Whitman's verse is composed in lines."[9] Allen makes a similar observation when he traces the development of Whitman's mature syntactic style from early imitations of biblical prose:

> Of the olden time, when it came to pass
> That the beautiful god, Jesus, should finish his work on earth
> Then went Judas, and sold the divine youth,
> And took pay for his body.[10]

Here Whitman seems to be experimenting with clausal and phrasal units rather than using sentences. This is suggested by his punctuation which separates "Of the olden time" from "when it came to pass" and "Then went Judas" from "and sold the divine youth" for no other apparent reason than to emphasise the phrasal cadences. As Allen notes, it is the run-on line ("it came to pass/That . . .") which distinguishes this passage from the mature Whitman.

However, in "Biblical Analogies for Walt Whitman's Prosody," Allen also pointed to some departures on Whitman's part from the biblical model. He observes that in the mature Whitman the parallelism has a "phonic" component.[11] He also noted "one other dissimilarity between the biblical parallelism and Whitman's. As a rule it is easier to break Whitman's long lines into shorter parallelisms.[12] Unfortunately, Mr. Allen did not explore the consequences of these observations. For, as will be seen, both phonic indicators and the "shorter parallelisms" make it impossible to accept the view that "the line" is the unit in Whitman.[13]

While E. C. Ross recognised the differences between Whitman's poetic syntax and that of normal prose, Mr. Allen's tendency, especially in the influential *Walt Whitman Handbook,* is to diminish them. In Whitman's notebooks for the 1850s there are several prose pieces which were later reworked in "Song of Myself." These provide a unique opportunity for comparing the prose and poetry in this regard:

S. 1   I want that tenor, large and fresh as the creation, the parting of whose mouth shall lift over my head the sluices of all the delight yet discovered for our race.

S. 2   I want the soprano that lithely overleaps the stars, and convulses me like the love-grips of her in whose arms I lay last night.[14]

In the 1855 edition of *Leaves of Grass* these two sentences were pared down to:

A tenor large and fresh as the creation fills me,
The orbic flex of his mouth is pouring and filling me full. [p. 1]
I hear the trained soprano . . . she convulses me like the climax of my
    love-grip. [p. 2]

The differences here are not only the result of the removal in p. 1 and p. 2 of some of the detail present in the prose versions, but also of differences in the kind of syntactic structures. S. 1 and S. 2 feature hypotaxis. They consist of main and subordinate structures which are linked by explicit linguistic connectors. P. 1 and p. 2, on the other hand, feature parataxis. They feature simple, independent clausal units placed alongside one another without explicit connectors.

These differences between the syntactic style of Whitman's prose and poetry are typical, and help to create a greater rhythmicality, but Mr. Allen seems to ignore them. The reason for this lies in Mr. Allen's interpretive procedure in the *Handbook*. He sees Whitman's style as an index to the author's mind. He must diminish differences between the prose and the poetry because of his view that Whitman's form "arises" from his "psychological impulses."[15] It would, of course, be inconsistent for Mr. Allen to argue that such impulses were reflected in the poetry and not the prose, or vice versa. This procedure is an example, in the best of Whitman critics, of the tendency not to give Whitman credit for his own form. It is also true, however, that Whitman himself invited such criticism because, despite his many prose pieces and notes dealing overtly with technical matters, such as "Ventures, on an Old Theme," he frequently disclaimed such concerns in more public statements.

Now Mr. Allen and Mr. Ross both noted the typicality of end-stopped lines in Whitman. But a cursory glance at Whitman's poetry shows that such junctures are by no means confined to the ends of lines, as Allen, Ross and many others seem to assume. As in the above examples, two or three may occur within a single line. That is, a line in Whitman may consist of two or three shorter parallelisms. In the following lines, for example, the equivalence and parallelism surely operate not between lines but between shorter units:

> I loafe and invite my soul,
> I lean and loafe at my ease . . . , observing a spear of summer grass.

> Over the growing sugar . . . over the cotton plant . . . over the rice in its low
>   moist field;
> Over the sharp-peaked farmhouse with its scalloped scum and slender shoots
>   from the gutters;
> Over the western persimmon . . . over the longleaved corn and the delicate
>   blueflowered flax.

Whitman's 1855 punctuation much more clearly preserves these divisions, and thus it is reproduced here. These lines consist, like the previous examples, of simple phrasal or clausal units placed side by side in parataxis. In the first example especially, there are two lines but, clearly, three rhythmical units.

Syntactic parallelism furnishes Whitman with the constitutive unit of his rhythm. In order to justify this claim it is necessary only to consider the second aspect of Whitman's parallelism that Allen noted as a departure from the biblical model, that is, the organisation of "phonic" elements. Consider again,

```
x  /   x  x /  x  /
I loafe and invite my soul
x /   x  /   x x  /
I lean and loafe at my ease
x /  x x  /  x  /  x  /
observing a spear of summer grass
```

The distance between stresses, that is, the number of syllables between stresses is only approximately regulated, limited to one or two syllables. It may be noted, preliminarily, that this variability is in accord with Whitman in "Ventures" where he says that the metrical convention of strict feet, "the measurement-rules of iambic, spondee, dactyl, &c.," furnish a medium only "for interior writers and themes." [16]

Since Whitman declares that "metre" has no relevance to his rhythm it is useful, in further examining phonic elements, to apply some other method of analysis. David Abercrombie, in "A Phonetician's View of Verse Structure," outlines such a method which is simple and readily applicable to Whitman. [17] Mr. Abercrombie defines three formal devices which he calls "end-markers" and which, he maintains, can be used to define the rhythmical units of most English verse, regardless of whether it is strictly metrical. The first is rhyme or some other sound scheme; the second is a "silent final stress"; the third is a final monosyllabic measure used seldom or not at all elsewhere in the unit. These devices may occur, Mr. Abercrombie explains, individually or in combination.

In the same lines there is a repetition of sounds which, although not conventional rhyme, is, like rhyme, closely related to the rhythmic structure and involves the last stressed syllable of a unit.

I *loa*fe and invite my *soul*
I *lea*n and loafe at my *ea*se

In each case the repetition involves the first and last stressed syllables of two successive units and may be regarded as an end-marker. This pattern, which may be designated A B A, is a common one in Whitman:

The mach*i*nist rolls up his sl*ee*ves
the pol*i*ceman travels his b*ea*t
the gatekeeper m*a*rks who p*a*ss

The last of these three units (which make up a single line in Section 15 of "Song of Myself") presents a variation, A B B. This pattern is also found elsewhere in Section 15:

> The malformed limbs are *t*ied to the ana*t*omist's *t*able
> What is removed dro*p*s horribly in a *p*ail
> The quadroon girl is *s*old at the *s*tand

Although in this last example the first unit clearly has more stresses than the subsequent ones the A B B pattern occurs in syntactically parallel parts of the unit, that is, the verb and final noun. This serves to reinforce the equivalence despite variation.

A similar variation occurs in the following units from Section 33:

> Where the *ch*eese-*c*loth hangs in the *k*it*ch*en   (A B A)
> and *a*ndirons stra*d*dle the hearth-sl*a*b   (A A A)
> and cobwebs *f*all in *f*es*t*oons from the ra*ft*ers   (A B B B)

The last unit has one more stress than the first two but preserves the pattern in which the final stressed syllable involves a repetition.

These patterns, of course, are only rhythmically significant insofar as they correspond with other indicators. They do correspond with the syntactic parallelism and, as will now be seen, with the organisation of stresses. Returning to the first example, one can readily observe the use of the second end-marking device, a silent final stress. Each of the units has four stresses (/ denotes the beginning of a measure and is placed immediately before a stressed syllable; ∧ denotes a silent stress);

> I /loafe and in /vite my soul / ∧
> I / lean and /loafe at my /ease / ∧
> Ob /serving a /spear of /summer /grass.

The silent stress, of course, is felt as a pause between each unit when reading the lines aloud. This can be simply demonstrated by tapping one's fingers in time with the stresses. One's fingers want to tap, it is soon found, at the point marked by a silent stress. In the last unit this pause is filled in with the syllable *grass*, thus bringing the short stanza to an end.

In each of these units the use of the third type of end-marker, a final monosyllabic measure, can be clearly seen. This requires no further comment. Instead, consider some further examples and the subtle variations Whitman typically uses with these devices.

The pause with its silent stress may, as in the above example, share a measure with the anacrusis of the subsequent unit, that is, with the initial unstressed syllable of the next unit. This can be more clearly observed when they are written as follows:

I /loafe and in /vite my soul / ∧ I / /lean and /loafe at my /ease
/ ∧ ob/ /serving a /spear of /summer /grass.

The pause may also occupy a measure of itself:

I /hear bra/vuras of /birds / ∧ / / bustle of /growing /wheat
/ ∧ / / gossip of /flames / ∧ / / clack of sticks cooking my meals.

Notice how, in typical fashion, Whitman varies his rhythm in these units. The first two are the characteristic four measure units. The third has only three. The fourth fills in the final stress with *meals*, being the end of a short stanza. Monosyllabics end each unit.

Sometimes Whitman varies his rhythm with a shorter pause which can be thought of as containing a silent unstressed syllable:

The /blab of the /pave (✕) / /tires of /carts (✕) / /sluff of
/bootsoles (✕) / /talk of the /promenaders

These, of course, are two measure units. More characteristic of Whitman is to introduce extra stresses. This can be seen in

The malformed limbs are tied to the anatomist's table
What is removed drops horribly in a pail
The quadroon girl is sold at the stand
the drunkard nods by the barroom stove

A number of qualifiers expand these lines from the basic four-measure pattern: "malformed" and "anatomist's" in the first unit; "horribly" in the second; "quadroon" in the third; and "barroom" in the fourth. Because most of these items do not receive *major* stresses while the common elements of the repeated syntactic pattern do (subject noun, verb, final noun), the rhythmical impression is maintained. This is a good example of how syntactic parallelism plays a part in the regulation of phonic materials, that is, of major stresses.[18] The units which follow, moreover, return to the basic four stress pattern:

The ma/chinist /rolls up his /sleeves / ∧
the po/liceman /travels his /beat / ∧
the /gatekeeper /marks who /pass / ∧

Another typical variation can be seen in Whitman's use of compounds which are often substituted for the terminal monosyllabic. Many of these can be found in Section 33 of "Song of Myself ":

     A   B   A
Where the life-car is drawn on the slipnoose
     A   B   A
Where the hay-rick stands in the barnyard
     A
and the drystalks are scattered
     A [?]
and the brood cow waits in the hovel

Here again, Whitman uses, in the main, the four-measure unit. The A B A pattern recurs with compound nouns whose conspicuous stress pattern provides an interesting repetition of sounds. It is interesting that there is a strong desire when reading the lines to pronounce "brood cow" as a compound, that is, as bróod còw and not brôodców (adjective + noun). This seems to testify to the part these items are playing in the rhythmic structure.

Enough material has now been gathered to justify some conclusions about how Whitman's versification meets the requirements he outlined in theory. Whitman's theory of poetry, taken as a whole, is a theory of the function of the poem in a democratic society. He is fundamentally concerned with the poem's social and moral utility to the nation. Similarly, the characteristic and chief requirement Whitman made of the poem's rhythms was that they should be "necessary" as opposed to "arbitrary." Whitman's attitude in "Ventures, on an Old Theme" is simply an elaboration of his attitude in the early note where he talks about metre and rhyme as mnemonic devices belonging to the days before the printing press. His view is, as Charles Olson was later to put it, that metre and rhyme no longer have the justification of "oral necessity." For Whitman, art for art's sake, ornament for ornament's sake, are aesthetic heresies.

It was argued above that the analysis of phonic materials would bear out the claim that the short syntactic units or, as Gay Wilson Allen termed them, "shorter parallelisms," provide the basic rhythmic unit in Whitman. The analysis of end-markers clearly shows that this is the case, that units of rhythm defined on phonological grounds coincide with these syntactic units. It is important to remember that this means that the typographical line is not a reliable guide to rhythmic structure in Whitman. Whitman's punctuation (commas and, in the 1855–1860 editions, dashes or four spaced periods) is more reliable but can be misleading. Consider the opening of "Song of Myself":

> I /celebrate my/self (and /sing my/self)
> And what /I as/sume (✕) /you shall as/sume
> For /every /atom be/longing to /me
> / ∧ as /good be/longs to /you.

In these lines Whitman uses a four-measure unit with a short pause between each unit, that is, not a pause containing a whole silent stress. The exception, of course, is the last line—analysed above as two units. The pronounced caesura after "me" clearly demands a longer pause and indicates, in accordance with end-marking criteria, that this is the end of a rhythmic unit. This segmentation of the line parallels the syntactic juncture marked by (✕) in the previous line. The shorter pause (✕) separates the line at a parallel grammatical point (but not at a parallel rhythmical point). The monosyllabics *me* and *you* also support the division of the line into two rhythmic units.

Consider, as a final example, the following lines which occur in "Song of Myself" not long after the above example:

> I will /go to the /bank by the /wood / ∧ and be/ /come undis/guised
> and /naked / ∧ I am/ / mad for /it to be in /contact /with me.

Despite the typography and the lack of punctuational indication the phonological units of verse are clearly defined as:

> I will /go to the /bank by the /wood / ∧
> and be/come undis/guised and /naked / ∧
> I am /mad for /it to be in /contact /with me.

Such an analysis shows the typical four-measure unit (although the last line is admittedly a questionable reading); it coincides with the syntactic junctures of *clause/clause/clause;* and it coincides also with the monosyllabic indicator of *wood* in the first line.

Many of Whitman's longer lines, apparently irregularities, can be segmented in this way to show the rhythmic units. Invariably, these units are "end-stopped," that is, they coincide with a syntactic juncture marked phonologically by a pause. Many of Whitman's long lines, however, cannot be thus divided. Whitman does not always maintain numerical equivalences. The point is that a rhythmical impression persists despite variations.

The coincidence of syntactic and rhythmic units in Whitman points to how his rhythm is necessary and not arbitrary. This is hinted at by Roman

Jakobson in his "Linguistics and Poetics" although no Whitman critic seems to have taken it up. Mr. Jakobson observed that

> it would be an unfortunate mistake to deny the constitutive value of intonation in English meters. Not even speaking about its fundamental role in the meters of such a master of English free verse as Whitman, it is impossible to ignore the metrical significance of pausal intonation . . . in a poem like "The Rape of the Lock" with its intentional avoidance of enjambements.[19]

In the first part of this statement Mr. Jakobson points to the regulative effects of syntax on intonation. In verse like Whitman's which employs such syntactic parallelism this regularity is even more marked. As was suggested earlier, this is a phonic or echoic aspect of syntactic parallelism, and it undoubtedly contributes to rhythmic equivalences even when strict numbers are not maintained.

The second part of the statement suggests how Whitman's rhythm is "necessary" and speech-based. The avoidance of enjambments or run-on lines is, of course, a salient feature of Whitman's verse. Now in poetry where there is much enjambment the metric units tend to become obscured, as, for example, in the later blank verse of Shakespeare. When the metric units become obscured the "prose" or ordinary speech intonation takes over the sentence. This gives rise to debate as to whether the poetry should be read so as to emphasise the metre (with a slight pause at the line-end) or read "normally" as in prose. This is a problem for the Shakespearean actor. This prose intonation factor is also alluded to by Benjamin Hrushovski when he says that one of the major tools of rhythmic expression is "the characteristic emphasis of each word and a bringing of local elements . . . into relative, temporary independence and isolation from the long linear flow of the sentence."[20]

This suggests the "arbitrary" nature of metric units in combination with long sentences. The numerical basis of the metric unit has no essential relation with the normal prose intonation and, in metrical verse, is often in conflict with it. (Of course, the skilful metrical poet can put this conflict to fruitful and expressive use. The intention here is not to deprecate conventional metre by the use of Whitman's term "arbitrary.") Such conflicts, however, do not arise in Whitman. His poetry is not composed in long sentences; he has no run-on lines. In Whitman the rhythmic unit is always coincident with syntactic and, therefore, with intonational factors. His poetry may be spoken "normally" without obscuring the rhythm. In this sense Whitman's rhythm is speech-based; it is a "necessary" and not an "arbitrary" feature of his verse. Whitman, indeed, says as much in "Ventures" when, after rejecting "arbitrary" and "chiming" versification, he declares that poetry should soar "to the freer, vast, diviner heaven of prose."[21] And, of course, he had begun by announcing that "the time has arrived to essentially break down the barriers of form between prose and poetry."[22]

The pertinence of Whitman's speech-based prosody lies in the testimony with which this article was begun. Whitman's prosody, his commitment to "free verse" and the poetic use of common speech, has been much more fruitful and influential among subsequent American poets than his "philosophy" or views on "democracy." Once an understanding of Whitman's prosody has allowed us to take his theory seriously, the way is open for the recognitioin of Whitman as something more than only a "spiritual" father, as Pound put it,[23] of the modern American "free verse" and speech-rhythm experimentalists. He can be seen as the first to isolate the technical and theoretical issues and the first to provide a practical demonstration.

To illustrate the former, by way of conclusion, it is only necessary, as Allen Ginsberg suggests, to look at "early XX Century" verse experiment. The "free verse" controversy engendered by Imagism throws up the same issues that Whitman identified in "Ventures." The Imagists provide a point of continuity between Whitman and the twentieth century and, in Amy Lowell, the first of those incongruous disclaimers of Whitman which have been partly responsible for the prevalent neglect of his prosodic theory and practice.[24]

A diminishing of the "barriers of form" (in Whitman's phrase) between prose and poetry is a central issue raised both by Whitman (in "Ventures") and by the later "free verse" movement. Their common desire to use the language and rhythms of ordinary speech and to rid poetry of stock diction and ornament (a fairly new term at the time much vaunted by the Imagists was "cliché") led Whitman and the Imagists to an awareness of the rhythms available in the "vast, diviner heavens of prose." To objections that theirs was not poetry but prose the Imagists replied "So be it!" thereby indicating that, like Whitman, they saw the distinction as an arbitrary "barrier." Amy Lowell dealt with such objections in a reply to Livingston Lowes's article, "An Unacknowledged Imagist," in *The Nation*, 26 March 1916. In the article Lowes had taken some excerpts from George Meredith's prose and arranged it into lines to make some excellent imagistic poems. He followed this exercise by printing some of Lowell's poetry as prose and concluded, "Which is which?"

Amy Lowell answered in a *New York Times* interview that

there is no difference. Typography is not relevant to the discussion. Whether a thing is written as prose or as verse is immaterial. But if we would see the advantage which Meredith's imagination enjoyed in the freer form of expression we need only compare these lyrical passages [the ones made into imagistic poems by Lowes] with his own metrical poetry.²⁵

Although Lowell was to deny Whitman's influence specifically on free verse (she accepted it in other areas) the parallel with Whitman here is obvious. Whitman's poetry could also be arranged typographically to highlight the rhythmical units but this would also be an arbitrary exercise. Clearly, Whitman and Amy Lowell felt that other advantages were to be gained by printing the poetry otherwise, and were aware that this would not affect a speech-based or "prose" rhythm.

NOTES

¹ William Carlos Williams, "Essay on *Leaves of Grass*," in *Walt Whitman: A Collection of Critical Essays*, edited by Roy Harvey Pearce (Englewood Cliffs, N.J.: Prentice-Hall, 1962), p. 146.

² Charles Olson, "Projective Verse," reprinted in *The New American Poetry*, edited by Donald M. Allen (New York: Grove Press, 1960), p. 394.

³ *The Complete Writings of Walt Whitman*, edited by Richard Maurice Bucke, Thomas B. Harned and Horace L. Traubel (Boston: Small, Maynard, n.d.), "Notes on the Meaning and Intention of *Leaves of Grass*," 9:36.

⁴ Allen Ginsberg, "Notes for *Howl* and Other Poems," in *The New American Poetry*, edited by Donald M. Allen (New York: Grove Press, 1960), p. 416.

⁵ Harvey Gross, in his *Sound and Form in Modern Poetry* (Ann Arbor: University of Michigan Press, 1968), p. 83, emphasizes the prosaic aspects of Whitman's poetry, rhetorical figures, biblical phraseology and incantatory syntax, "Whitman's prosody," he writes, "shows no development from traditional syllable-stress metric." Sculley Bradley, in "The Fundamental Metrical Principle in Whitman's Poetry," *American Literature*, 10 (1938–1939), 437, writes that "We can at once discard many of the theories . . . that [Whitman] wrote 'prose-poetry.'" Professor Bradley then goes on to argue that Whitman's accentual metre can be traced to Old English verse types.

⁶ *Prose Works 1892: Collect and Other Prose*, edited by Floyd Stovall (New York: New York University Press, 1964), "Notes Left Over," 2:519.

⁷ Gay Wilson Allen, "Biblical Analogies for Walt Whitman's Prosody," *Revue Anglo-Americaine*, 10 (August 1933), 490–507, and *American Prosody* (1935; rpt. New York: Octagon Books, 1966), pp. 217–243.

⁸ Gay Wilson Allen, "Biblical Analogies," p. 491; and *American Prosody*, p. 221.

⁹ E. C. Ross, "Whitman's Verse," *Modern Language Notes*, 45 (June 1930), 363.

¹⁰ Gay Wilson Allen, *Walt Whitman Handbook* (New York: Hendricks House, 1962), pp. 393–394.

¹¹ Gay Wilson Allen, "Biblical Analogies," p. 492.

¹² *Ibid.,* p. 494.

¹³ Mr. Allen's assertion that the line is the rhythmical unit is largely based on the highly problematical notion of "thought-rhythm" (*American Prosody,* p. 221), a not dissimilar idea to Basil de Selincourt in "The Form," *A Century of Whitman Criticism,* edited by Edwin Haviland Miller (Bloomington: Indiana University Press, 1969), p. 139. While it is possible that each line in Whitman is a unit of thought, if such a unit could ever be defined, the units of *rhythm* must be defined on some more precise grounds.

¹⁴ *The Uncollected Poetry and Prose of Walt Whitman,* edited by Emory Holloway (1921, rpt. New York: Peter Smith, 1932), 2:53.

¹⁵ Gay Wilson Allen, *Handbook,* p. 399.

¹⁶ *Prose Works 1892,* "Notes Left Over," 2:519.

¹⁷ David Abercrombie, "A Phonetician's View of Verse Structure," in *Studies in Phonetics and Linguistics* (London: Oxford University Press, 1965), p. 20f.

¹⁸ See David Crystal, *Prosodic Systems and Intonation in English* (Cambridge: At the University Press, 1969), an exhaustive account of intonational factors in English (for example, levels of stress) and their relation to syntax and meaning. The term "prosodic," as used by Crystal, does not refer to versification (as "prosody" does in this article) but to systems of intonational factors generally. It follows from Crystal's discussion of syntax and intonation that a repetition of a given syntactic structure, as in parallelism, must involve repetitions, in the phonological realm, of intonational factors. The relevant factor for the purposes of versification is the parallel positioning of major stress.

¹⁹ Roman Jakobson, "Linguistics and Poetics: Concluding Statement," in *Style in Language,* edited by Thomas A. Sebeok (New York: John Wiley, 1960), p. 365.

²⁰ Benjamin Hrushovski, "On Free Rhythms in Modern Poetry," *Style in Language,* p. 189.

²¹ *Prose Works 1892,* "Notes Left Over," 2:520.

²² *Ibid.,* p. 519.

²³ Ezra Pound, "Walt Whitman," in *Walt Whitman: A Collection of Critical Essays,* p. 9.

²⁴ Amy Lowell makes a general acknowledgement of Whitman as a poetic precursor in "Walt Whitman and the New Poetry," *Yale Review,* 16 (1927), 502–519. With regard to "free verse" specifically, however, she denies that the new poetry owes any of its form to Whitman. As has been noted by Glenn Hughes in *Imagism and the Imagists: A Study in Modern Poetry* (New York: Humanities Press, 1960), p. 128, Amy Lowell had also curiously denied the influence of Whitman on John Gould Fletcher, a self-confessed and "ardent Whitmanite," in her *Tendencies in Modern American Poetry* (Boston: Houghton Mifflin, 1921), p. 296. The most notable subsequent disclaimer of Whitman was made, of course, by T. S. Eliot in his introduction to Ezra Pound's Faber *Selected Poems* (1928): "[I]t is indeed obvious—that Pound owes nothing to Whitman. This is an elementary observation." Two recent studies which subject Eliot's disclaimer to considerable critical scrutiny are S. Musgrove's *T. S. Eliot and Walt Whitman* (Wellington: University of New Zealand Press, 1952) and Ronald Hayman's *Arguing With Walt Whitman: An Essay on his Influence on 20th Century American Verse* (London: Covent Garden Press, 1971). Amy Lowell's remarks, in 1921 and

1927, take precedence. It is possible that both her and Eliot's remarks have their origin in the controversy between Fletcher and Eliot in *The New Statesman* in 1917. Eliot (3 March 1917) had said that good free verse secured charm by "the constant suggestion and skilful evasion of iambic pentameter." Fletcher replied (24 March 1917) by calling up Blake and the "rough hexameters of Whitman."

25 *New York Times*, 26 March 1916.

DANA PHILLIPS

Nineteenth-Century Racial Thought and Whitman's "Democratic Ethnology of the Future"
(1994)

If he knew that an Eskimo sat in a kyak, immediately there was Walt being little and yellow and greasy, sitting in a kyak.

—D. H. LAWRENCE, "WHITMAN,"

STUDIES IN CLASSIC AMERICAN LITERATURE

Many readers of Walt Whitman's poetry would agree with the statement that "the poet sings of an America where people of all colors come together, mixing indiscriminately in a great democracy yet respecting each other's rich cultural heritage and diversity."[1]

This judgment of Whitman's racial politics may be taken as representative of the consensus of Whitman scholars. But what nowadays might be called Whitman's "multiculturalism" (the all-inclusive embrace of the world's folk that has seemed to many to be an essentially Whitmanian gesture) is revealed upon closer, more skeptical inspection to be something else entirely. I argue in this essay that Whitman's racial politics are more complicated, more conflicted, and considerably less admirable than his reputation for a broad and easy tolerance of others suggests. I try to show how Whitman's apparent "multiculturalism" actually functions as a means of specifying, despite all the evidence to the contrary, the singular culture of the United States and the common racial identity of its citizens.

Putting Whitman in a context of biological and racial thought as delineated by Michel Foucault and other historians, I argue that the poet wants to articulate the essential sameness-in-difference of America and

Americans, to record and celebrate the ways in which America is bound in political union and Americans are compounded as one people—and as one race. I am also taking issue, then, with Werner Sollors's identification of the "process of ethnic dissociation," in which, he says, literature "plays a central part." [2] The process of dissociation, according to Sollors, is essential to the formation of the modern idea of the nation. But while "the nation" is certainly one of its key terms, Whitman's poetry depends on an opposite strategy of ethnic and racial *association* in its definition of that term. This association, or synthesis, of Americans is then imagined by the poet to be America's unique contribution to the history of nation-states. With this conceptual framework in mind, "listen," if you will, to section three of the poem "Salut au Monde!":

What do you hear Walt Whitman?

I hear the workman singing and the farmer's wife singing,
I hear in the distance the sounds of children and of animals early in the day,
I hear emulous shouts of Australians pursuing the wild horse,
I hear the Spanish dance with castanets in the chestnut shade, to the rebeck
    and guitar,
I hear continual echoes from the Thames,
I hear fierce French liberty songs,
I hear of the Italian boat-sculler the musical recitative of old poems,
I hear the locusts in Syria as they strike the grain and grass with the showers
    of their terrible clouds,
I hear the Coptic refrain toward sundown, pensively falling on the breast of
    the black venerable vast mother the Nile,
I hear the chirp of the Mexican muleteer, and the bells of the mule,
I hear the Arab muezzin calling from the top of the mosque,
I hear the Christian priests at the altars of their churches, I hear the
    responsive base and soprano,
I hear the cry of the Cossack, and the sailor's voice putting to sea at Okotsk,
I hear the wheeze of the slave-coffle as the slaves march on, as the husky
    gangs pass on by twos and threes, fasten'd together with wrist-chains and
    ankle-chains,
I hear the Hebrew reading his records and psalms,
I hear the rhythmic myths of the Greeks, and the strong legends of the
    Romans,
I hear the tale of the divine life and bloody death of the beautiful God the
    Christ,

> I hear the Hindoo teaching his favorite pupil the loves, wars, adages,
> transmitted safely to this day from poets who wrote three thousand
> years ago.[3]

The question arises: what do *you* hear? Ostensibly, a dialogue—but it is a dialogue of a peculiarly Whitmanian sort, one in which the author takes all the roles. Such one-sided "dialogue" is common in Whitman's poetry: he often directs questions to himself or to the reader, questions to which he then proceeds to give the sort of fulsome answer recorded in section three of "Salut." This is a canny and, for all its expansiveness, economical piece of stage management: despite its many *dramatis personae,* "Salut" is a one-man show. Actually, this is suggested by the poem's very first line—"O take my hand Walt Whitman!" (p. 287). Given the odd visual image it evokes, the line underscores the circularity of the poet's address.

It is important to note the office this formal device performs: his "dialogue" with himself enacts Whitman's social function as the mediator of culture, the declared role of the bard in his 1855 preface. As a medium for and of culture, Whitman is in section three of "Salut" not a seer, as he is elsewhere in the poem, but a *hear-er* (a choice in keeping with his fondness for music and other forms of vocalism), and what he hears are the sounds of different cultures from all around the world—the voices of the folks. Yet Whitman makes few efforts to reproduce these sounds or voices for his reader. Consequently, the passage has a somewhat abstract quality. Readers must take these folk sounds at Whitman's word, and many of his words— "emulous shouts," "continual echoes"—convey very little concrete, empirical information. That is, they do not *sound like* anything. This lapse in the poem's contact with materiality may be intentional: the catalog is not intended to be a mimesis. But more important than their relative degree of onomatopoeia, or actual physical likeness to the sounds they ostensibly represent, is the logic of these representations. We listen to, or more likely we read (silently, to ourselves), the report of a man who claims, even as he speaks (or rather, writes), to be hearing things—things that except in a few instances ("chirp" and "wheeze") he does not bother to reproduce for us. Instead he merely *refers* to them.

So we cannot hear what Whitman hears; we can only read what he wrote. As readers we have to take his words for granted. The reader's subordinate role in the hierarchy of representation is a basic fact of Whitman's poetics, one he tries to obviate by adopting a sort of hail-fellow-well-met manner toward the poem's "you," whom he represents as his interlocutor. Dialogue is Whitman's way of avoiding some of the negative implications of the authority entailed by authorship. His poetry is filled with passages resembling section three of "Salut," and they not only raise complicated questions about Whitman's authorial relationship to his reader—questions of form—but equally vexing questions about content. One must not only ask why "Salut" takes the shape of a poem and not something else—a geography textbook, for example. One must also ask why Whitman wants to tell us about these so-called "savage types."

I would like to begin answering both of these questions by examining more closely the content of Whitman's report in "Salut." The poem's imagery is intended to convey the typical character of the exotic folks—exotic, at least, to an American—whom Whitman portrays.[4] The "sounds" Whitman cites in section three establish the essential difference of each of the nationalities and ethnicities he catalogs from all the others. For example, "the chirp of the Mexican muleteer" is meant to be the characteristic vocal expression of *all* Mexican muleteers. The representative principle operating here is much the same as in a birdwatcher's field guide: just as geese cry "yahonk" (as Whitman tells us in "Song of Myself"), so too do Mexican muleteers "chirp"; Australians utter "emulous shouts" (at least when pursuing horses); and slaves wear "coffles" that "wheeze." The same principle is at work in section ten of "Salut," where Orientals swarm; Ashantee, Dahomans, and Krumans sit in huts; and Turks smoke opium (p. 293). In short, concepts of natural history are employed in "Salut" as the instruments of a rather crude kind of "anthropology."[5] The sounds and the sights Whitman references are intended to type the nationalities and ethnicities he documents—that is, to stereotype them: to identify their "species" and fix them in place, so that they might then be deployed as the relatively stable terms of an implicit comparison.

This comparison becomes explicit in section twelve of "Salut" when the speaker, as a representative of a more advanced "type," addresses the assembly of others he has cataloged: "I do not prefer others so very much before you either, / I do not say one word against you, away back there where you stand, / (You will come forward in due time to my side.)" (p. 296). Whitman treats his images of The Other—the "Austral negro, naked, red, sooty, with protrusive lip, groveling, seeking your food!" and the "haggard, uncouth, untutor'd Bedowee!" (p. 296), for example—as basic "specimens," to use one of the poet's favorite words. They are like the contents of a storage cabinet in a museum of natural history that the magisterial savant can arrange and rearrange according to his understanding of the place of each being in the evolutionary scale.

But otherwise the rhetoric of catalogs like this one suggests that Whitman has little real desire to understand The Other in a disinterested, "scientific" fashion. The characters recorded in "Salut" are not allowed to be heard (or seen) by anyone other than their ostensible auditor (and surveyor), Wait Whitman, who reports on their sounds—not at all the same thing as their *words*—in a monologue that masquerades as a dialogue, as something more sociable, more polyvocal, and more "democratic" than it really is. The poet's privileged knowledge of these mute foreign characters extends to every aspect of their existence: only the poet explores at first hand the full range of the world's sensorium, and only he can make sense of it. The poetic sensibility—the poet's identity—is the unifying element of the poem's argument. Thus it is as both representative *principle* and *principal* that Whitman offers the salutation that closes the poem: "Toward you all, in America's name, / I raise high the perpendicular hand, I make the signal, / To remain after me in sight forever, / For all the haunts and homes of men" (p. 297).

Whitman's catalogs of race seem even more significant—and less the pure products of his eccentric overestimate of the importance of poetry and the "prophetic" powers of poets—when viewed from the perspective Foucault adumbrates in *The Order of Things*. There Foucault describes a change that he says is definitive of modernity: by the early nineteenth century, rigidly fixed schemes for viewing the world—for example, that of "the book that one opens, that one pores over and reads in order to know nature"— had been swept away by the idea of the living organism, which is born, develops, and dies, only for its experience to be reiterated by another life form that inaugurates another cycle of flux.[6] The modern discovery of what Foucault calls "life" or more broadly "the murmur of the ontological continuum" (*Order*, p. 207) proved, however, to be both enabling and disabling— the former because it gave knowledge an impetus toward a more direct encounter with the natural world (of a sort that many of Whitman's catalogs reflect); and the latter because language seemed, for the first time, to go skittering across the surface of that world even as it undeniably was penetrating its depths in new and productive ways (an inability to achieve closure that is also characteristic of Whitman's catalogs). According to Foucault this dilemma arose when the essential role that perception plays in all knowledge was foregrounded: no longer was knowledge a relatively simple matter of citing the interpretation that nature seemed to wear so plainly on its face. In order to know, one now had to discover the secret linkages and hidden exchanges of energy across an apparently infinite continuum. But the facticity of this continuum was placed in doubt by a new sense of nature as the endless unfolding of becoming rather than as the fixed arrangement of stable identities that it formerly had seemed. Awareness of the potential infinity of the field of knowledge leads, according to Foucault, to a peculiarly modern sense of alienation, a feeling that man's epistemological continuity with the world has somehow been ruptured: "What modern thought is to throw fundamentally into question is the relation of meaning with the form of truth and the form of being: in the firmament of our reflection there reigns a discourse—a perhaps inaccessible discourse—which would at the same time be an ontology and a semantics" (*Order,* p. 208).

This doubling of the discourses of modernity—their ambition on the one hand "as analytics of finitude" (*Order,* p. 317) to make an exhaustive description of the world and their assertion on the other hand that any given comprehension of totality would be merely putative, would be nothing but "a veil of illusion" (*Order,* p. 317) and would be (culpably) metaphysical—is a recurrent source of anxiety in Whitman's poetry. He attempts, especially in catalogs like the one from "Salut au Monde!" that I began this essay by quoting, a grand survey of life's mutability of the sort that Foucault identifies as one of the new techniques of knowledge. But at the same time, Whitman also attempts to unify the field of his survey of "life" by discovering (or at the very least asserting) that one or another cherished term—body, soul, America—stands for the most important aspect of that field: that it is, in fact, its essence. Thus Whitman, who identified with figures from the Age of Reason (like Thomas Paine) as well as with figures from the new age of science (like the phrenological Fowlers), combined the precritical belief in a human essence with a fascination for what Foucault calls "the analytic of everything." We discover this combination encoded everywhere in Whitman's poetry: for example, in a line like "The loose drift of character, the inkling through random types, the solidification" from "Song of the Broad Axe" (p. 332). Recognizing the importance of this combination can give us the means of unlocking Whitman's catalogs of race. The prospect of a "solidification" of "random types" is one of the central themes of Whitman's poetry, entailed by his claim in "Song of Myself" to "contain multitudes" (p. 87). "Salut au Monde!" gives us an "inkling" of who those multitudes are.

By Whitman's day racial theorizing—the new science of ethnology, the study of the unfolding of the becoming of man—had been encouraged not only by the shift in epistemological outlook described by Foucault but by advances in scientific understanding (of heredity, for example) as well. Such theorizing was also encouraged by several popular forms of scientific *mis*understanding (such as phrenology and craniometry, both of which under the new conditions of knowledge proved to be relatively short-lived). To try to define the races in terms of their inherent differences (or relative degrees of superiority and inferiority) had come to seem a crucial, as well as a *natural,* undertaking.[7] By the 1850s race had become in the minds of many

Europeans and Americans *the* distinctively anthropic quality. It was certainly the central term of anthropological study. "Race" was for Whitman and his contemporaries a means of accounting for the greater or lesser possession of those qualities that were said to be "racy"—in the case of (white male) Americans such qualities as vigor, manliness, a predisposition to make war and conquer new territories, and even business acumen were all comprehended by this term.

Other literary examples of the era's obsession with racial definition are not far to seek. Consider Emerson's *English Traits,* which was published in August 1856, approximately one year after the first edition of the *Leaves.* In it Emerson expresses the racial theories of Anglo-Saxonism in a remarkably undiluted fashion; ironically, however, the book is despite its title an essay on the problem of American racial and cultural identity. Also worth remarking is the degree to which *English Traits* is devoid of Emerson's usual self-erasing, riddling assertions. Its author was aware of the book's forthright character; he writes that in the lectures he gave while visiting England, "I hesitated to read and threw out for its impertinence many a disparaging phrase, which I had been accustomed to spin, about poor, thin, unable mortals;—so much had the fine physique and the personal vigor of this robust race worked on my imagination."[8] This reworking of Emerson's imagination is evident on almost every page of his book: he was renewed by his British experience in something other than the Transcendentalist way. Accordingly, in *English Traits* he ponders the issue of race in what is for him an unusually forthright manner:

> It is race, is it not? that puts the hundred millions of India under the dominion of a remote island in the north of Europe. Race avails much, if that be true, which is alleged, that all Celts are Catholics, and all Saxons are Protestants; that Celts love unity of power, and Saxons the representative principle. Race is a controlling influence in the Jew, who, for two millenniums, under every climate, has preserved the same character and employments. Race in the negro is of appalling importance. The French in Canada, cut off from all intercourse with the parent people, have held their national traits. I chanced to read Tacitus "on the Manners of the Germans," not long since, in Missouri, and the heart of Illinois, and I found abundant points of resemblance between the Germans of the Hercynian forest, and our *Hoosiers, Suckers,* and *Badgers* of the American woods. (p. 792)

As the last sentence of this passage hints, Emerson's true subject is America and the racially determined American character. In the mid nineteenth century Americans understood themselves to be Anglo-Saxons with the bark still on; they, more than the English, were the true heirs of primordial (i.e., Germanic) Anglo-Saxon will and ability. Moreover, the American had insured the realization of his potential for superiority by following a more "natural" path of development than his English relative, emigrating to the New World and eliminating the tradition of unnatural, top-heavy aristocratic privilege. Emerson, like Whitman, thought that Americans would develop their racial identity far better than their old-world relatives had. Americans would become more and more characteristic and soon supplant their forebears as world leaders; or, as Emerson puts the case in *English Traits:* "The Russian in his snows is aiming to be English. The Turk and Chinese also are making awkward efforts to be English. The practical common-sense of modern society, the utilitarian direction which labor, laws, opinion, religion take, is the natural genius of the British mind. . . . The American is only the continuation of the English genius into new conditions, more or less propitious" (p. 785).

Emerson concludes, after a long conversation on the subject of America with one "C." (Carlyle), that despite its present crudity and the merely embryonic state of its culture America is destined to surpass Britain someday: "England, an old and exhausted island, must one day be contented, like other parents, to be strong only in her children" (p. 916). But it is the ambiguity of Emerson's meditations on racial character and history that I wish to emphasize: on the one hand he marvels at the vigor and common sense of the English, which he adduces as evidence of the superiority of the Anglo-Saxon race; on the other hand he offers a shrewd Yankee's appreciation of Britain's economic and military prowess. The question that arises, and that at some points in his text Emerson struggles to answer, is whether it is what the English *do* that counts or is it who they *are?* In the *Leaves,* and elsewhere, Whitman struggles with similar questions in relation to Americans.

This struggle underscores the paradox central to the nineteenth century's conception of race: everything seemed to be racial, or "racy"; but (especially in polyglot America) no one thing by itself seemed to be "race." The question that arose, then, was whether "race" should be considered as a (biological) factor inherent in human history or as merely a supple and fairly comprehensive category of interpretation. Was race *real*, or was it only a heuristic, rhetorical means of making sense of the political and economic dominance of any given people? These questions were of great concern to Whitman, who as something of a scientific dilettante was aware of the work being done by ethnologists and of the new evolutionary theories that Darwin would be the first to synthesize successfully in his epoch-making 1859 book (three years after the initial publication of "Salut au Monde!").

Whitman struggled, then, to come to terms with both the newly historical nature of human existence and with the questions of racial identity it raised. The epistemic shift from an older to a newer and more scientific form of knowledge described by Foucault may be echoed in the last three lines of the passage from section twelve of "Salut" that I quoted above: "I do not prefer others so very much before you either, / I do not say one word against you, away back there where you stand, / (You will come forward in due time to my side.)" (p. 296). Earlier in the poem Whitman offers a taxonomy of humankind, one in which each of the beings cataloged seems to exist contemporaneously with the speaker. In these three lines this classificatory scheme is historicized. A vision of The Other is projected into the past (or "away back there"), and what appear to be crude racial stereotypes now become examples of the poet's evolutionary optimism. The Austral negro, the Berber, the Patagonian, the Feejeeman, and many others suddenly appear to occupy different rungs (different from the speaker's, at any rate) on the evolutionary ladder—which means, of course, both that they are (for the time being) his inferiors but also that they will not always be so. The speaker's confidence in racial progress, however, is inversely proportional to the abject barbarity of the "haggard, uncouth, untutor'd" peoples he addresses and dependent on its continuation until the "due time" for their advance "Forward" to his "side" has arrived. It is possible for him to meet the Caffre and the "plague-swarms in Madras, Nankin, Kaubul, Cairo" (p. 296) on such friendly terms only because he greets them from a distance (they are "away back there"). They do not threaten him. And although his parenthetical invitation to "come forward in due time to my side" suggests that the speaker is rather kindly, if not fondly, disposed toward the particular others he addresses, the use to which proto-evolutionary theory is put here does suggest that he is taking a suspect form of comfort from it if his admiration for these others is based on a conviction that they are conforming to the model that *he* provides.

The speaker in "Salut au Monde!"—the one who answers the question "what do you hear?"—is identified as "Wait Whitman"; he is intended to be not just a representative of Euro-American civilization but more particularly a representation of "the poet" as well and thus a specimen of a more "poetic" kind of being. This stereotype brings into focus all the other stereotypes cataloged in the poem. It gives them the freedom of *its* speech. In short, the images of racial others in "Salut" work contrarily, against their own interests, to suggest the summary, synthesizing identity of the speaker, figured as the poet himself. The poem is about the search for a new model of humanity, one that will flourish under new and different conditions of historical and cultural development. Whitman always identifies this new model of humanity as an American model: in his hymn to Manifest Destiny, "Song of the Redwood-Tree" (1874), Whitman calls the American "*the new culminating man*" (p. 352). And in "By Blue Ontario's Shore" (1856) he identifies this new man with the figure of the poet, who is "typical, before all" (p. 479). The latter phrase is an apt gloss on the poet's role in "Salut."

Whitman's cataloging of "the precedent dim ages" (the phrase occurs in "A Broadway Pageant" [p. 387]) could be described as empiricist. But his attempt to identify a single containing form—a "culminating man," often implied to be himself—in order to give meaning to the information he gathers in his catalogs is idealist. Thus Whitman thinks in a way that according to Foucault demonstrates the ideological continuity of apparently opposed forms of knowledge: "The anthropological configuration of modern philosophy consists in doubling over dogmatism, in dividing it into two different levels each lending support to and limiting the other: the precritical analysis of what man is in his essence becomes the analytic of everything that can, in general, be presented to man's experience" (*Order*, p. 341). The eighteenth century's belief in Man persists despite the nineteenth century's discovery of men—this is one of the many constitutive contradictions that Foucault discovers at the heart of the modern *episteme*. It is also a constitutive contradiction at the heart of *Leaves of Grass*. There is, however, a price to be paid for this philosophical confusion. As Foucault puts it, "we find philosophy falling asleep once more in the hollow of this Fold; this time not the sleep of Dogmatism, but that of Anthropology" (*Order*, p. 341). In Whitman's case, philosophy's anthropological slumber becomes most troubling when he abandons the "analysis of actual experience"—especially of immediate bodily life—with which much of his *Leaves* is concerned and then attempts to found, in *Democratic Vistas*, a discourse that he calls "the democratic ethnology of the future."

Unfortunately, Whitman cannot point to any obvious, undebatable examples of The American—not in the same way he can point to clear examples of The Other, like the Austral Negro or the Feejeeman. Those others share certain cultural habits and, most importantly, distinctive racial features (skin color and physiognomy). Americans were a heterogenous-looking lot, and it became of special concern to Whitman how Americans should look if they all could look the same. As a result, much of his work is marked by a concern for the physical appearance—the physiognomy and physiology—of Americans. This is not surprising, since "the body" was a central term of Whitman's imagination.[9]

In the Whitmanian concept of the body, the body serves as the epistemological clearinghouse for managing one's relations with the social and natural worlds. In the nineteenth century, as Foucault has shown, the body became the nexus where biological, linguistic, and economic issues had their origins. The body was also the site where those who sought to resolve the crisis of epistemological rupture, of the gap between ontology and semantics, set busily to work. And insofar as attempts to close this gap became embroiled in issues of public policy, the body is also where what Foucault in his later work comes to call "power" is focused.[10] The concept of the body politic seems inevitably to raise the issue of the body's racial status. The term Whitman uses to describe his intellectual exploration of the American body politic in its racial aspect is "ethnology";[11] he sets himself early in his career the task of identifying the essentially American body, of discovering what he will eventually call "the democratic ethnology of the future."

But this discovery proved a difficult one to make. Not even that American icon Abraham Lincoln is an unambiguous specimen of the American body. Whitman identifies Lincoln—whose physiognomy and physiology he admired—as a Southerner; and this is something of a paradox, whether or not it is literally true that Lincoln was born in the South and of Southern parents. In his lecture on "The Death of Abraham Lincoln" Whitman praises the Great Emancipator's Southern roots. Lincoln's death, he says,

> belongs to these States in their entirety—not the North only, but the South—perhaps belongs most tenderly and devoutly to the South, of all; for there, really, this man's birthstock. There and thence his antecedent stamp. Why should I not say that thence his manliest traits—his universality—his canny, easy ways and words upon the surface—his inflexible determination and courage at heart? Have you never realized it, my friends, that Lincoln, though grafted on the West, is essentially, in personnel and character, a Southern contribution? (p. 1037)

How warmly Whitman's Northern audiences may have welcomed this particular line of reasoning is a good question.[12] But certainly the form his reasoning takes would have been familiar to them: it rehashes the sentimental Civil War motif of "brother against brother" in terms of the mixed (but not divided) character of one man. More importantly, Whitman's argument for Lincoln's fitness as a symbol of America is couched in terms of the notion of "birthstock," a familiar one in the nineteenth century. He identifies

Lincoln's Southern "birthstock" as the source of what seem to be characteristically American traits: "canny, easy ways and words upon the surface," "inflexible determination and courage at heart." "Birthstock" translates here into "manifest destiny": as a man born on the frontier who had helped to develop the region west of the Alleghenies (always a mythical topography for Whitman), Lincoln was in Whitman's eyes the born leader of the nation during the Civil War and not merely its elected president. He was—as many critics have noted—precisely the sort of charismatic, unifying figure Whitman had called for in his poetry. But this hermeneutic—using the personality traits of an exceptional man like Lincoln as a key to American cultural identity—does not do everything Whitman needs done. Lincoln may have had what we might call Southern traits, and those traits might have contributed to the composite identity of The American. But did Lincoln look like a Southerner? And how does a Southerner look?

The answer to these questions makes it clear that the assumptions about race that inform Whitman's effort to outline "the democratic ethnology of the future" recognize differences that to us no longer seem racial. For example, in a fragment collected in *Specimen Days* Whitman praises a group of men from the American South whom he saw one day in a Washington street. Of this Union regiment made up of Tennessee volunteers he writes: "They were all of pleasant physiognomy; no refinement, nor blanch'd with intellect, but as my eye pick'd them, moving along, rank by rank, there did not seem to be a single repulsive, brutal or markedly stupid face among them" (p. 754). The humanity of Southerners comes as something of a surprise to Whitman, as if he had *expected* them to be "repulsive, brutal" and "markedly stupid." As he describes them, Southerners figure as the anthropological equivalents of the "dim-descended, black, divine-soul'd African, large, fine-headed, nobly-form'd, superbly destin'd, on equal terms with me!" whom Whitman apostrophizes in "Salut au Monde!" (p. 294); or, much more immediately and closer to home, of the African-American First United States Colored Troops he writes about in "Paying the 1st U.S.C.T.," a scrap of his Civil War reminiscences included in *November Boughs* (1888). There Whitman records his thoughts after witnessing payday among a unit of colored troops: "we cannot find fault with the appearance of this crowd—negroes though they be. They are manly enough, bright enough, look as if they had the soldier-stuff in them, look hardy, patient, many of them real handsome young fellows . . . there are some thoroughly African physiognomies, very black in color, large, protruding lips, low forehead, etc. But I have to say that I do not see one utterly revolting face" (pp. 1182–83).

This depiction of black men may seem to jar with the sympathetic depictions of Africans and African Americans (the distinction is an important one) in some passages of Whitman's poetry—such as the line from "Salut" I have just cited above. But for Whitman, and for his contemporaries, the transformation of blacks from slaves to freedmen did not negate the fundamental inferiority of American and other blacks as a race. Because science had justified belief in the inferiority of blacks, there was in the 1850s and 1860s widespread consensus on the subject.[13] This consensus obtained even among those we would like to think of as having known better: as Stephen Jay Gould notes, "all American culture heroes embraced racial attitudes that would embarrass public school mythmakers"[14] and Whitman is no exception.

Because racial thinking had been legitimated by contemporary science, Whitman judges both the "divine-soul'd African" and the Colored Troops according to a physiological and physiognomic standard—that is, he judges them according to an image of what he regards as their specific biology. This image is, as he says, "thoroughly African" but not yet "heroic"—however "superbly destin'd" it may be. The white men from Tennessee are judged by a similar standard, one that also involves an image of a lowest common human denominator. In describing the Tennesseans, Whitman uses criteria and adjectives much like those he applies to the Colored Troops (some of the Colored Troops have "protruding lips" and a "low forehead"; the Southerners' faces are, unexpectedly, neither too refined, "nor blanch'd with intellect," nor "repulsive, brutal or markedly stupid"). This implicit equation, at some level, of the Colored Troops and the Tennessee volunteers suggests that Whitman expected the latter to be not just different from Northerners, and thus from himself, but nearly as different as were the Colored Troops— that is, he expected Southerners to be physically and even racially different (and thus inferior). He could expect Southerners to be racially different because he assumed that racial and national or cultural identity were the same things—and Southerners had recently declared themselves a separate nation, after all. Thus Lincoln is an interesting case, because he was indisputably a great American with the kind of noble physiognomy that Whitman admired while at the same time he was of mixed birth—a "Southern American," if you will.

As Whitman's observations of these men demonstrate, the possibilities for racial difference seemed much greater in the nineteenth century than they do today. This kind of difference was one presumably always apparent to the eye, and in notes Whitman made during a trip to Canada and included in *Specimen Days* he marveled at the quality of Canadian brood stock and at the fact—to him, astonishing—that Canadians looked just like Americans: young Canadians were "forming a hardy, democratic, intelligent, radically sound, and just as American, good-natured and *individualistic* race, as the average range of best specimens among us. . . . I find smiles and courtesy everywhere—physiognomies in general curiously like those in the United States—(I was astonished to find the same resemblance all through the province of Quebec.)" (pp. 880–83). Whitman did not think, as one would expect him to have thought, of Canadians as fellow "Caucasians": "Caucasian" was not an ultimate category of race for Whitman.[15] But "Canadian" was: Canadians—much more clearly than Southerners—were to be counted among The Other not just as foreigners but as members of another race. This entailed a difference that should show itself in their very bodies, a difference that was fundamentally biological.

Thus the question that Whitman inevitably faced as a result of his understanding of race as a matter of both national and biological identity, or consanguinity, is this: what race is an American? America seemed—to Whitman and others—somewhat undefined nationally. He knew that the American population was multiracial in its origins (and it had, in the 1840s, experienced the first wave of large-scale "foreign" immigration, complicating its racial and ethnic profiles), and his inability to reason around this obstacle to American racial identity caused him to stumble in his celebration of the American future. According to nineteenth-century assumptions about culture, without a racial identity all its own America could never become a nation in any meaningful sense of the term: Kwame Anthony Appiah has explained the appearance of Martin Farquhar Tupper's poem "The Anglo-Saxon Race" in 1850 by arguing that "by Tupper's day a distinctively modern understanding of what it was to be a people—an understanding in terms of our modern notion of race—was beginning to be forged: that notion had at its heart a new scientific conception of biological heredity. . . . But it was, also . . . interwoven with a new understanding of a people as a nation and of the role of culture—and, crucially for our purposes, of literature—in the life of nations."[16] Whitman shared this understanding and sought far and wide—at home and abroad—for a model of the racy individuality he thought the country and his poetry needed. Since the country was, relatively speaking, still a new one, it really had not had time to evolve an identity through some process of natural selection of favorable racial traits. Thus in his poetry Whitman was forced to take self-identical figures like the "Chinaman and Chinawoman of China" and the "Tartar of Tartary" from "Salut" (p. 295) and the well-bearded, brawny roughs of "Song of Myself" and—to borrow a phrase from Foucault—"fold one over the other as though they were equivalents" (*Order,* p. 9) so that the one could serve as an analogy for the other, if not as its ground.

A problem arises, however, when Whitman's figures seem like mere names, when they seem to have too little meaning (this is an inherent limitation of the catalog as a literary form). A passage near the beginning of "Song of Myself" may demonstrate Whitman's awareness of this problem: there a child asks "What is the grass?" (p. 31). The poet then offers a variety of possible meanings for the "symbol" of the grass. It is, he writes, "the flag of my disposition, out of hopeful green stuff woven"; or "the handkerchief of the Lord"; or "itself a child . . . the produced babe of the vegetation" (p. 31). But significantly for the present discussion, the grass—in addition to being any number of other things—is said to be "a uniform hieroglyphic, / And it means, Sprouting alike in broad zones and narrow zones, / Growing among black folks as among white, / Kanuck, Tuckahoe, Congressman, Cuff, I give them the same, I receive them the same." Arguably, then, the grass is not a "symbol" so much as it is a *figure of similitude:* one might almost say it is a figure of a symbol, given that the root meaning of the word from which "symbol" derives is "to throw together" or "compare" different things—to create a "sign-ball." Whitman "throws together" a bunch of different meanings—and different people: "Kanuck, Tuckahoe, Congressman, Cuff"—in the figure of the grass; but he also suggests that they are interchangeable, that ultimately they all mean and are the *same* thing.

In "Salut au Monde!" this "symbolism" extends even to those peoples Whitman cannot name: "All you continentals of Asia, Africa, Europe, Australia, indifferent of place! / All you on the numberless islands of the archipelagoes of the sea! / And you of centuries hence when you listen to me! / And you each and everywhere whom I specify not, but include just the same!" (p. 295). This way of apprehending similitude—specifying not, including "just the same"—is the habit of thought central to Whitman's conception of racial identity. As a "uniform hieroglyphic" the grass exemplifies the ideal form of writing, which is nondiscursive or symbolic—that is, associative and synthetic. The grass manages to communicate its meanings without involving itself in the frustrations of difference: "it means . . . the same," and wherever it sprouts it sprouts "alike." It provides a sort of common ground for "black folks" as well as "white." The "Congressman" and "Cuff" may not be of the same race (as we have seen, Whitman preserves the distinction between black and white) but both are equally "racial"—which, given Whitman's anthropological assumptions, means that both are equally human (if not equal *as* humans: one is a congressman, after all, and the other is probably a slave). For Whitman, then, the issue is ultimately not racial difference but racial sameness.

Despite Whitman's intentions, what actually emerges in the *Leaves* is not one "type of the modern," not one type or "eidólon" of The American, but any number of American types. This proliferation of American images and identities causes a problem with which Whitman struggles throughout his career: in order to explain how America is different from other countries and Americans are different from other people, he must first be able to identify—as I have suggested—the ways in which they are the same. Since Americans share neither common blood nor common folkways, this is not easy to do. And a variety of American types is tantamount to none at all: each proves to be, upon closer scrutiny, isolated from the others by—for example—regional, political, sexual, and/or other differences. A western hunter or a trapper may have nothing in common with, say, a physician or a priest, but all four figures occur in one of the catalogs in "Song of Myself"—a catalog that represents one of Whitman's earliest attempts to define American types. It is similar to the American cultural sampler that he will later use in his survey of world peoples in "Salut"; and in the catalog in "Song of Myself" the poet claims that he is "One of the great nation, the nation of many nations—the smallest the same and the largest the same" (p. 42). And then he names the specific identities that are fused in his person:

> A Yankee bound my own way . . . ready for trade . . . my joints the limberest
>   joints on earth and the sternest joints on earth,
> A Kentuckian walking the vale of the Elkhorn in my deerskin leggings,
> A boatman over the lakes or bays or along coasts . . . a Hoosier, a Badger,
>   a Buckeye,
> A Louisianian or Georgian, a poke-easy from sandhills and pines.
>   (p. 42)

By asserting that for him all of these apparently different persons, personalities, and cultural or racial identities are interchangeable—"the smallest the same and the largest the same," one identity "soon as" another—Whitman tries to avoid some of the darker implications of American history (regional rivalry over slavery, to pick an obvious example). Here he uses nicknames like "Hoosier" and "Badger" or "Buckeye" and "poke-easy" (two of these are also cited by Emerson as naming representative Americans) rather than more proper names. Such names might mark the social distinctions that these particular nicknames conveniently elide. An epithet like "poke-easy from sandhills and pines" equates English or Scotch-Irish "poor whites" of Georgia and the two Carolinas with their Hoosier, Badger, and Buckeye fellow Americans to the northwest. These nicknames create a vernacular democratic space.

But the creation of a vernacular democratic space has a deeper ideological motivation, one that may be at work even in what would seem to be the most politically innocent of Whitman's works, "I Hear America Singing" (1860). This poem may insist that each of the persons it names sings a "varied carol" or "what belongs to him or her and to none else" (p. 174), but it nevertheless gives the dominant impression of a grand democratic chorus ringing with one voice throughout the land. The question it raises, in short, is whether it is the difference of all these democratic personalities that is being memorialized or their sameness: is what is represented in the poem "just folks" or the more portentous phenomenon of The Folk? The answer is that Whitman wants to have it both ways, but he will settle for the latter. In the poem a single entity performs for a single auditor: the poem's title, after all, is *"I* hear *America* singing" (emphasis added). "I Hear America Singing" employs much the same strategy as "Salut," but in this case we "hear" a chorus not of The Other but of The Same. In both poems, however, the catalog functions as a means of eliding differences: it operates on the principles of assimilation and homogenization. But the catalog works at the level of appearance only: it is a means of making the many *seem* like one.

Whitman's desire for genuinely American persons is complicated, however, not only by the diversity of the nation's immigrant citizenry but also by the presence of indigenous peoples. They would seem, after all, to have some claim to being the only authentic, the only native, Americans. Whitman recognized this claim: he had encountered representatives of the western tribes during his tenure as a clerk in the Indian Bureau in the 1860s. In a short piece entitled "An Indian Bureau Reminiscence" (published in *November Boughs*) Whitman wrote that he thought the western tribesmen were "the most wonderful proofs of what Nature can produce, (the survival of the fittest, no doubt—all the frailer samples dropt, sorted out by death) . . . the full exploitation and fruitage of a human identity, not from the culmination-points of 'culture' and artificial civilization, but tallying our race, as it were, with giant, vital, gnarl'd, enduring trees" (pp. 1170–71). By the end of this passage Whitman's analogy has converted the initially human chiefs into veritable wooden Indians: they "tally" humanity with "giant, vital, gnarl'd, enduring trees." And by so characterizing the chiefs he also apotheosizes them as models of "racy" individuality: he sees the chiefs not as proofs of the strength of another culture but as "wonderful proofs of what Nature can produce." Whitman attributes superlative qualities to these men, but the terms of his praise set the stage for their potential dismissal as *no more than* "natural."

In his poetry Whitman finesses his way around the obstacle of a truly native American identity—one in which he and the overwhelming majority of his peers cannot share—by announcing that, just as the era's conventional wisdom about the "vanishing redman" had it, the aboriginals soon will conveniently fade away. In "Starting From Paumanok" (1860) Whitman rather neatly reads "the red aborigines" out of existence. Like a natural historian, he lists their names as if they were the calls and cries—the "natural breaths"—of so many soon-to-be-extinct birds and mammals:

> The red aborigines,
> Leaving natural breaths, sounds of rain and winds, calls as of birds and
>   animals in the woods, syllabled to us for names,
> Okonee, Koosa, Ottawa, Monongahela, Sauk, Natchez, Chattahoochee,
>   Kaqueta, Oronoco,
> Wabash, Miami, Saginaw, Chippewa, Oshkosh, Walla-Walla,
> Leaving such to the States they melt, they depart, charging the water and
>   the land with names.

> (p. 186)

Acknowledging the "charging" of "the water and the land with names" while dismissing the bearers of those names is an ironic gesture, though perhaps unconsciously so. But a similarly evasive tactic serves Whitman equally well when his desire for real American paragons is frustrated by the debased existence of many western settlers, whom he had long idealized as the country's great hope but who could not measure up to the standard set by "those great aboriginal specimens."

"The women of the prairie cities"—Kansas City and Denver—proved a particular disappointment to him. In 1879, during his trip out West, Whitman was sorry to learn that these women were as thin, pale, and conventional as their counterparts in the East, and he recorded their shortcomings in a journal passage on "The Women of the West" reproduced in *Specimen Days*: "they do *not* have, either in physique or the mentality appropriate to them, any high native originality of spirit or body, (as the men certainly have, appropriate to them.) They are 'intellectual' and fashionable, but dyspeptic-looking and generally doll-like; their ambition evidently is to copy their eastern sisters. Something far different and in advance must appear, to tally and complete the superb masculinity of the West, and maintain and continue it" (p. 868). Whitman's desire to invigorate women is related to his desire to have them inseminated: especially in the great American West, women were to be the means for breeding the well-muscled Americans (that is, the "superb" males) of the future. And so, for the sake of the nation, the women there ought to be encouraged to appear in public as something other than "dyspeptic-looking and generally doll-like."

Democratic Vistas addresses faults like the dyspepsia of the women of Kansas City and Denver as well as the ailments and other shortcomings of the body politic more generally—"the people's crudeness, vice, caprices" (p. 930). Whitman thought these faults might be addressed and redressed by a "divine literatus" (p. 932) or, failing that, by a group of "mighty poets, artists, teachers, fit for us, national expressers, comprehending and effusing for the men and women of the States, what is universal, native, common to all, inland and seaboard, northern and southern" (p. 935). He advocates a cultural revolution that would complete the political revolution of the previous century: "Our fundamental want to-day in the United States . . . is of a class, and the clear idea of a class, of native authors, literatures, far different, far higher in grade than any yet known, sacerdotal, modern, fit to cope with our occasions, lands, permeating the whole mass of American mentality, taste, belief, breathing into it a new breath of life" (p. 932). Whitman did not believe (in the late 1860s) that anyone had managed yet to breathe "a new breath of life" into an authentic American culture. American democracy lacked "the new blood, new frame" it needed—"the lack of a common skeleton, knitting all close," Whitman writes, "continually haunts me" (p. 935). D. H. Lawrence, writing sixty years later, tended to agree with Whitman: the rebirth of American literature was more hopeful than real. Lawrence thought it "no good *asserting*" that such a rebirth had occurred, and he demanded, "Where is this new bird called the true American? Show us the homunculus of the new era. Go on, show us him. Because all that is visible to the naked European eye, in America, is a sort of recreant European. We want to see this missing link of the next era."[17]

Lawrence's evocation of "this missing link of the next era" is a canny, intuitive choice of the perfect emblem for nineteenth-century America's obsession with race, racial others, and its own racial character. Whitman has to settle in *Democratic Vistas* for a (merely) prophetic announcement of the future identity of America and Americans as one country and one people: "To-day, ahead, though dimly yet, we see, in vistas, a copious, sane, gigantic offspring" (p. 929). Whitman looks to the future because the specifics of actual democracy—for example, the sharp practices associated with presidential elections—tend to disgust him. This disgust also has as one of its main causes his revulsion for the raddled and unhealthy bodies, as he saw them, of American citizens—he claims to be examining the country "like a physician diagnosing some deep disease" (p. 937). At times this is more than just one of the essay's controlling metaphors, as the following passage demonstrates:

> Confess that everywhere, in shop, street, church, theatre, barroom, official
> chair, are pervading flippancy and vulgarity, low cunning, infidelity—every-
> where the youth puny, impudent, foppish, prematurely ripe—everywhere
> an abnormal libidinousness, unhealthy forms, male, female, painted, padded,
> dyed, chignon'd, muddy complexions, bad blood, the capacity for good
> motherhood deceasing or deceas'd, shallow notions of beauty, with a range
> of manners, or rather lack of manners, (considering the advantages enjoy'd,)
> probably the meanest to be seen in the world.
>   (p. 939)

Whitman's "average" man and woman prove too true to type, or no better than average—the mean is too mean, "the meanest to be seen in the world." This failure of the democratic experiment to produce a new, healthier, and better-looking body politic—a term he understands as referring to a biological as well as a civil entity—is something Whitman cannot accept.

Because he was frustrated in his attempt to win the hearts and minds and reform the bodies of his contemporaries, Whitman claimed in *Democratic Vistas* that he was projecting "the democratic ethnology of the future" (p. 963). Accordingly, in this essay Whitman expends more of his energy in sketching hortatory democratic "vistas" than in making the sort of closely observed case studies of actual democratic life that he had come by then to find so depressing. In the course of the essay he shifts from offering a diagnosis of America's ills to offering a prognosis of its chances for good racial health (and the good cultural health that would entail). In his embrace of an "ethnology of the future"—of what amounts to a national eugenic policy—Whitman sought what in its immediate historical context must have seemed a utopian rationalization of the failure of democracy to sooner fulfill its great human potential. But in retrospect his "democratic ethnology of the future" seems less than benign: it seems to call for a prescriptive form of physical anthropology (i.e., eugenics). Like many another nineteenth-century reformer, Whitman urges his fellow citizens to meddle with not just the lives of individual human beings but with the genetics of entire human populations.[18]

At the root of his coming to favor a concept of culture as grounded in the national body (individual and collective) over a concept of culture as arising on higher and less material grounds is Whitman's lifelong worry over the distortions he thought inherent in the latter notion. He feared, as he put it in "By Blue Ontario's Shore," "grace, elegance, civilization, delicatesse" and "the mellow sweet, the sucking of honey-juice" (p. 470) that was characteristic of the culture of polite society. "Culture" was something he associated with the artificiality and antidemocratic social hierarchy of Europe and, more particularly, of England. In *Democratic Vistas* he renews this criticism of "culture": "This word Culture, or what it has come to represent, involves, by contrast, our whole theme, and has been, indeed, the spur, urging us to engagement. Certain questions arise. As now taught, accepted and carried out, are not the processes of culture rapidly creating a class of supercilious infidels, who believe in nothing?" (p. 962). Whitman urges his fellow Americans to come to a more implicit, more basic, and more organic understanding of cultural life: "I should demand a programme of culture, drawn out, not for a single class alone, or for the parlors or lecture-rooms, but with an eye to practical life, the west, the working-men, the facts of farms and jack-planes and engineers, and of the broad range of the women also of the middle and working strata, and with reference to the perfect equality of women, and of a grand and powerful motherhood" (p. 962). But Whitman was—as we have seen—doubtful of the grandeur and power of "motherhood" as it was then incarnate in America: American women were gripped by "incredible holds and webs of silliness, millinery, and every kind of dyspeptic depletion" (p. 940). He had to admit that his was a "programme" not currently practicable: democratic ethnology is intended to produce what Lawrence identifies as the "missing link" of American identity, but only in the future. More immediately, Whitman may have recognized how his appeal to "practical life" and to the elemental forces of nature might suggest more direct forms of cultural activism: the violent weeding out, for example, of those decadent "supercilious infidels, who believe in nothing." That is, it might produce the more toxic variety of nationalism with which we are familiar.[19]

Thus when Whitman cries, in one of the most oratorical passages in his essay, "I demand races of orbic bards, with unconditional uncompromising sway. Come forth, sweet democratic despots of the west!" (p. 974), we cannot—because of the dire cultural and political conflicts that inform his plea—blandly assure ourselves that his utterance is as merely rhetorical as we would like to think. It is informed by assumptions about race (and gender) quite different from our own. Whitman's invocation of "democratic despots"—"sweet" though they may be—implies a certain impatience with actual democratic processes and a preference for more immediate and potentially oppressive means of achieving consensus. But *Democratic Vistas* is not essentially different from Whitman's earlier work, only more explicit in its prescriptive tendencies. This seems clear enough when one reads Whitman's newspaper editorials written for the *Brooklyn Daily Times* during the years when he was also putting together the early editions of *Leaves of Grass*. These editorials often take up matters of public health, which they treat as matters of great importance for the body politic. In one editorial Whitman calls for the physical development of the nation's male youth: "Here, in this young, vigorous country we want no spoonies and milksops—better have a little too much of the animal physique, with its accompanying propensities, than be narrow in the chest, shaky in the legs and pusillanimous in self-defence and self-assertion!" One does not normally associate this sort of machismo with the Good Gray Poet, but it is quite in keeping with the nationalist fervor of the younger Whitman, who was also capable at this time of editorializing against the public blight of so-called "Ugly Women"—Ugly Women being yet another threat to eugenically conceived national security.[20] Of course, Whitman was not alone among American writers in his awareness of mid-century discourses of women's health. Consider the following speech about the "nervous," delicate young women of New England made by Professor Westervelt in *The Blithedale Romance* (1852): "Some philosophers choose to glorify this habit of body by terming it spiritual; but, in my opinion, it is rather the effect of unwholesome food, bad air, lack of out-door exercise, and neglect of bathing, on the part of these damsels and their female progenitors; all resulting in a kind of hereditary dyspepsia. Zenobia, even with her uncomfortable surplus of vitality, is far the better model of womanhood."[21] It is important to realize, however, that Hawthorne is satirizing the kind of reformer's discourse that Whitman took quite seriously.

Democratic Vistas thus represents more than a temporary lapse of political judgment and expresses more than the feeling of conservative reaction that swept over Whitman after the war. Its political impatience and its concern with race and the racial body cannot be dismissed as quaint relics of the perfervid enthusiasm of the radically chauvinist Democrat of the 1840s. Nor can they be said to be the mere unconscious by-products of a disease-stricken old man's crabbed meditations on subjects about which he really knew very little. Figures created in the early years of the poet's career—figures like the athletic Western heroes of "Song of Myself"—are neither politically innocent nor politically insignificant. They, too, represent

Whitman's deep yearning for American racial vitality, perennially the subject of his work. What emerges from *Democratic Vistas*, then, and in less obvious ways from the *Leaves* as well, is Whitman's desire "to formulate beyond this present vagueness—to help line and put before us the species, or a specimen of the species, of the democratic ethnology of the future" (p. 963). This is a project for which Whitman thought his poetry had performed at least some of the initial ground breaking in its celebration of figures like the racy types we encounter in "Salut" or the fallen president of "O Captain! My Captain!" and "When Lilacs Last in the Dooryard Bloom'd." Identifying "a specimen of the species" meant discovering the sort of paradigmatic being of whom he had always dreamed. But it meant no more than that: until some program of the sort he outlined was actually realized in America, Whitman thought that "our triumphant modern civilizee, with his all-schooling and his wondrous appliances, will still show himself but an amputation" (p. 964). But as Whitman only too well knew, the average American "civilizee" did not think of his body as disabled, nor of his cultural life as unnatural, and was much more interested in developing "his wondrous appliances" than he was in becoming a reader of that would-be improving text, *Leaves of Grass*.

NOTES

[1] Ronald T. Takaki, *Iron Cages: Race and Culture in Nineteenth-Century America* (New York: Alfred A. Knopf, 1979), p. 281. There have been remarkably few attempts on the part of Americanists to call into question Whitman's use of images of "America" as a paradise of race relations and of the "American" as a person who somehow cancels out the history of racial conflict in his very being. Critics have been aware of the importance of evolutionary theory to the poet's thinking but tend to treat Whitman's use of that theory as a question of general intellectual influence or as evidence of his conceptual sophistication; examples of this tendency can be found in David Charles Leonard, "Lamarckian Evolution in Whitman's 'Song of Myself,'" *Walt Whitman Review*, 24 (1978), 21–28; and Hertha D. Wong, "'This Old Theory Broch'd Anew': Darwinism and Whitman's Poetic Program," *Walt Whitman Quarterly Review*, 5, no. 4 (1988), 27–39. A remarkable instance of someone citing Whitman in an argument that openly relies on dated racial stereotypes (e.g., Negroes are natural athletes, Native Americans are technologically retarded) can be found in Perry Miller, "The Shaping of the American Character," *The New England Quarterly*, 28 (1955), 435–54. Miller echoes Whitman in more than one respect: like the poet, he is also forced to conclude that Americans do not really have an identifiable character and that this apparent lack is actually their special virtue.

[2] "Ethnicity," in *Critical Terms for Literary Study*, ed. Frank Lentricchia and Thomas McLaughlin (Chicago: Univ. of Chicago Press, 1990), p. 290.

3 "Salut au Monde!" in *Complete Poetry and Collected Prose,* ed. Justin Kaplan (New York: Library of America, 1982), pp. 288–89. Further references to Whitman's poetry and prose, unless otherwise noted, are from this edition and are cited parenthetically in the text.

4 Of course, the poem is also interested in the geology, place names, flora and fauna, history, and daily life of the exotic locales it catalogs; its "salute," then, is addressed not only to the world's folk but to the entire material existence of what is for Whitman an American imperium, the Earth itself. He is everywhere welcomed on his grand progress around the globe as if he were some visiting White Father come to view the assembled natives: "What do you see Walt Whitman? / Who are they you salute, and that one after another salute you?" (p. 289).

5 That Whitman's ethnological poetry should remind one of the work of natural historians is not surprising: an overlap between ethnology and natural history was common, as the two disciplines bore a strong family resemblance. Lewis Henry Morgan, a founding father of American anthropology, worked at both an ethnologist and a natural historian. His *League of the Iroquois,* published in 1851, was followed in 1868 by *The American Beaver and His Works.* One might also cite, in this connection, gifted amateurs like George Bird Grinnell, who was both an authority on the Northern Plains Tribes (he accompanied Custer on his 1874 Black Hills Expedition) and the editor of a popular fishing and hunting magazine.

6 *The Order of Things: An Archaeology of the Human Sciences* (New York: Vintage Books, 1970), p. 35.

7 One might consult, in this connection, Thomas F. Gossett's *Race: The History of an Idea in America* (Dallas: Southern Methodist Univ. Press, 1963). For a detailed account of a racialist discourse that enjoyed great vogue in the United States, see Reginald Horsman's *Race and Manifest Destiny: The Origins of American Racial Anglo-Saxonism* (Cambridge, Mass.: Harvard Univ. Press, 1981).

8 *English Traits,* in *Essays and Lectures,* ed. Joel Porte (New York: Library of America, 1983), p. 824.

9 For discussion of Whitman and the body, one might consult M. Jimmie Killingsworth, *Whitman's Poetry of the Body: Sexuality, Politics, and the Text* (Chapel Hill: Univ. of North Carolina Press, 1989). Most discussions of Whitman's "poetry of the body" are celebratory and limit their conception of the body to the sexual body without considering too carefully, or at all, the body's other qualities—its racial characteristics, for example.

10 Knowledge of the body—of its needs as a natural organism, of its pleasures as the instrument of sexual desire, and of its utility as a means both of sexual reproduction and of productive labor—becomes in the nineteenth century the essential tool for preserving the power of the state. This change coincides with the epistemic shift I have been detailing: the disinvestments of power in the body of the king and its reinvestment in the body politic— the body/bodies of the nation-state and its people/citizens—are the political cognates of the rearrangement of knowledge in the disciplines of biology, linguistics, and economics. Foucault describes the reimagination of the body politic in the opening chapters of *Discipline and Punish: The Birth of the Prison,* trans. Alan Sheridan (New York: Vintage Books, 1979).

11 This is in accord with contemporary usage. "Ethnology" did not originally mean the study of the cultural practices of primitive peoples, the sense in which we ordinarily use

this word today (when, in any case, the word "ethnography" is preferred). Instead, "ethnology" meant the study of the physiology and physiognomy of other peoples (not just "primitives") in hopes of defining their biologically inherent racial character. Only gradually did the term "ethnology" come to mean the sort of culturally oriented study we are more familiar with today, but the validity of "ethnology" as a biological science was being seriously questioned not long after Whitman wrote *Democratic Vistas:* "Dr. John Wesley Powell, Director of the Bureau of Ethnology of the Smithsonian Institution in the 1880s, flatly declared that 'there is no science of ethnology,' by which he meant the determination of race differences" (Gossett, *Race,* p. 83).

   12   The speech was given on several occasions from 1879 to 1881 and was published in the *Collect* that follows *Specimen Days* in 1882. It was last delivered publicly in 1890 in Philadelphia.

   13   "By the early 1850s the inherent inequality of races was simply accepted as a scientific fact in America, and most of the discussion now concerned either the religious problem of accepting polygenesis as an explanation of racial differences or the problem of exactly defining the different races" (Horsman, *Race and Manifest Destiny,* p. 134).

   14   *The Mismeasure of Man* (New York: W. W. Norton, 1981), p. 32.

   15   This racial division was only elucidated in the latter half of the nineteenth century, based largely on the not-very-reliable research of the craniometers. A good account of their work can be found in Gould's *The Mismeasure of Man.*

   16   "Race," in *Critical Terms for Literary Study,* p. 276. Appiah traces the pairing of race and literature as the ostensible creators of national identity back to Johann Gottfried Herder (whom Whitman mentions once or twice but probably never read). It is interesting to note on the other hand that Tupper's poetry is sometimes cited as possibly having had an influence on *Leaves of Grass.* See, for example, David S. Reynolds, *Beneath the American Renaissance: The Subversive Imagination in the Age of Emerson and Melville* (New York: Alfred A. Knopf, 1988), p. 313.

   17   Foreword to *Studies in Classic American Literature* (New York: Viking Press, 1961), p. vii.

   18   The disgusted tone of many passages in *Democratic Vistas* is echoed—and becomes much more virulent and openly antidemocratic—in the twentieth century in the work of sociobiologists like the crusty Earnest Albert Hooton, who was Professor of Anthropology at Harvard as well as Curator of Somatology at Harvard's Peabody Museum. In *Apes, Men, and Morons* (New York: G. P. Putnam's Sons, 1937) Hooton admits that precise racial definition is impossible and dismisses the idea of racial superiority—"every man is his own Nordic" (p. 231). But he argues that within racial (and/or national) groups an effort should be made to improve the breeding stock lest society be overburdened with "those tainted with hereditary disease" and "those who are insane, feeble-minded, and antisocial" (p. 236). Hooton believed that this issue was of particular concern in a democracy (prone as democratic nations are to pusillanimous humanitarianism): "We must either do some biological housecleaning or delude ourselves with the futile hope that a government of the unfit, for the unfit, and by the unfit will not perish from the earth" (p. 294). It should be noted that Hooton decried the growing disciplinary split between cultural and physical anthropology (he saw cultural

anthropology as a spurious science anyway, concerned only with epiphenomena rather than biological fact).

[19] Whitman's nationalism can be glossed by the following words from Foucault's *The History of Sexuality*, which describe the genealogy of the racial thinking that eventually erupted in the late nineteenth and early twentieth centuries in overtly malevolent forms: "The bourgeoisie's 'blood' was its sex. And this is more than a play on words; many of the themes characteristic of the caste manners of the nobility reappeared in the nineteenth-century bourgeoisie, but in the guise of biological, medical, or eugenic precepts. . . . But there was more to this concern with the sexual body than the bourgeois transposition of themes of the nobility for the purpose of self-affirmation. A different project was also involved: that of the indefinite extension of strength, vigor, health, and life" (*The History of Sexuality, Volume I: An Introduction,* trans. Robert Hurley [New York: Vintage Books, 1980], pp. 124–25). This obsession with the management of the body correlates with what Foucault calls "a type of 'racism'"—and he adds that "it was a dynamic racism, a racism of expansion, even if it was still in a budding state, awaiting the second half of the nineteenth century to bear the fruits that we have tasted" (p. 125). Of course, there are important differences between Whitman's and other, later forms of nationalism. I am not trying here to suggest that the poet was a Fascist—he would have been horrified by their violence and anti-Semitism. His racial thinking, as I have argued, is more concerned with the forging of racial semblances than it is with the eradication of differences. Thus Whitman, in the poem "Race of Veterans" (1865–66), can appeal to something much like the "blood and soil" concept later championed by the German fascists *without* necessarily embracing related concepts of, say, genocide: "Race of veterans—race of victors! / Race of the soil, ready for conflict—race of the conquering march! / (No more credulity's race, abiding-temper'd race,) / Race henceforth owning no law but the law of itself, / Race of passion and the storm" (p. 452). But that he does not construe this rhetoric as it will later be construed does not mean that it is not a dangerous way to talk. Whitman is parroting the discourse of Anglo-Saxonism, which historians do recognize as a precursor of National Socialist racial philosophies. On the importance of "blood and soil" to the Nazis, see Herbert Marcuse's essay on National Socialist discourse, "The Struggle Against Liberalism in the Totalitarian View of the State," in his *Negations: Essays in Critical Theory,* trans. Jeremy J. Shapiro (Boston: Beacon Press, 1968), pp. 3–42.

[20] The first quote is from Whitman's editorial "Pugilism and Pugilists," 23 August 1858; the second is from "Can All Marry?" dated 22 June 1859. Both are quoted from *I Sit and Look Out: Editorials from the "Brooklyn Daily Times,"* ed. Emory Holloway and Vernolian Schwarz (New York: Columbia Univ. Press, 1932), pp. 106, 121. It is during this period that Whitman's association with the phrenological Fowlers was strongest: the *Leaves* was sold in their bookshop, where one could also purchase Orson Fowler's tracts on female beauty and its significance for the future of the race. On Whitman's relationship with the Fowlers, see Harold Aspiz's *Walt Whitman and the Body Beautiful* (Urbana: Univ. of Illinois Press, 1980).

[21] Nathaniel Hawthorne, *The Blithedale Romance,* ed. William Charvat, et al., vol. 3 of *The Centenary Edition of the Works of Nathaniel Hawthorne* (Columbia: Ohio State Univ. Press, 1964), pp. 95–96.

CARMINE SARRACINO

Figures of Transcendence
in Whitman's Poetry
(1987)

Make no puns
funny remarks
Double entendres
"witty" remarks
ironies
Sarcasms
Only that which
is simply earnest
meant,—harmless
to any one's feelings
—unadorned
unvarnished
nothing to
excite a
laugh
silence
silence
silence
silence
laconic
taciturn.[1]

Perhaps one of the oddest features of "Song of Myself" is that this apparent formula for blandness, scribbled in a notebook, produced instead one of the most compelling and controversial poems in American literature. The poem does excite a laugh, and was not harmless to the feelings of such as Whittier, who threw his complimentary copy of *Leaves of Grass* into the fire. But as we look over Whitman's list we see that the poem succeeds not because Whitman abandoned or violated these tenets; it succeeds even though he remained remarkably true to them.

Whitman repeated four times the quality he wanted to communicate more than any other: silence. Here we find ourselves with no mere oddity, but with an apparent impossibility. Silence cannot be communicated by language, since to talk or to listen or to read is to destroy silence, to shift attention from the thing pointed at—silence—to the finger pointing—the poem. How could Whitman hope to resolve this paradox? How could silence sing? The more fundamental question is: Why would he draw up such a strange list of tenets anyway? Why should silence preoccupy a singer?

These questions go to the heart of the creative process Whitman experienced as a poet, and more, to the heart of the so-called mystical experience that recurred throughout his life, the great secret he repeatedly hinted about in his poetry, especially "Song of Myself." Although "ineffability" is the byword of mysticism, Whitman's mystical experiences need not be banished, as they largely have been, to critically inaccessible realms. To do so is a loss to Whitman readers and scholars. Yet most attempts at explication have resulted in the substitution of one set of ambiguous terms for another. Little is cleared up by defining "cosmic consciousness" as ". . . the consciousness of the self that is the cosmos, the one that is the all, the *atman,* the internal principle which is also the mighty universal *Brahman.*"[2]

If Whitman did experience higher states of consciousness, can we talk about it critically? For example, do these states have an analyzable structure? If so, does the structure of a higher state of consciousness in some describable way influence the structure of what is created from that level of consciousness, in Whitman's case, his poetry? The answers I will propose shed some light on the odd list of tenets Whitman drew up in his notebooks, and also suggest a solution to the impasse of his apparently contrary impulses for song and for silence.

This approach might seem naive, since I implicitly accept the possibility that Whitman was what he seemed, and that his "mystical experiences" were neither invented nor pretended, nor misunderstood bouts of epilepsy. In 1980s America, dominated as it is by a celebrity culture, by advertising "images," we regard Whitman as a *poseur,* or an artist who fabricated an image to match his poetic voice. Two recent biographies, Justin Kaplan's *Walt Whitman: A Life,* and Paul Zweig's *Walt Whitman, the Making of the Poet* take this approach. Thus what friends regarded as Whitman's Christlike self-sacrifice in the army hospital wards becomes sublimated homosexuality; his countenance of Buddhalike tranquility, a mask. Mrs. Gilchrist, R. M. Bucke, Horace Traubel, and others who revered Whitman we dismiss as "overheated minds," "true believers" who gullibly bought the whole show. Whitman was a bit of a phony, a troubled man, a careerist—in short, a lot like us.

Another motivation for this somewhat cynical portrayal of Whitman stems from our desire to rescue him from the curse of "the good gray poet."

Our belief in the redeeming value of evil was noted recently in a review of a biography of Strindberg:

> Since Delacroix's day, we have lived under the sign of one of his immediate successors, Arthur Rimbaud, who wrote that the poet, albeit a sage, was the great Sick Man, the great Criminal, the great Accursed. This conception, for a while startling, is by now a received idea. By the standards of the modern man on the street, a Dylan Thomas is obviously a poet while a William Carlos Williams is not. To justify his men or women, the biographer has to go back to the detail of their lives and discover the sinister, or at least the scandalous, element. Ruskin, who has seemed one's primmest uncle, is brought back—vindicated-—as a child molester.[3]

So, although Whitman repeatedly reminds himself in notebooks and journals to be plain and simple, to be non-literary, Zweig, for example, sees this intention as a kind of gimmick, like the novelist's pose of "telling the facts." Zweig concludes, with a distinctly contemporary paranoiac knowingness, that Whitman's bag of tricks is deep. Alternatively, I hope that an understanding of Whitman's experiences of expanded awareness will shed light on his desire for simplicity, and at the same time disclose the depth and profundity of these experiences.

A stock criticism of Whitman, his supposed lack of artistic polish, refinement of craft, and subtlety, stems directly from the mistreatment of the writing born of Whitman's expanded awareness. From Henry James on he has often disappointed the educated reader looking for the literary. In the list I have cited from his notebooks, he casts down most of the conventional techniques of modern literature, irony foremost among them. This does not, however, leave him without subtlety. Intuitively aware of the heuristic inadequacies of language on the level of meaning, Whitman shifted his attention to what his poem could reveal, not state outright. "Have you felt so proud," he asks with some forbidden sarcasm in section two of "Song of Myself," "to get at the meaning of poems?" What he promises in the next line is not meaning, but direct conveyance to "the origin of all poems," which for Whitman was the "mystical experience" of a fourth major state of consciousness, transcendental consciousness, a state of complete mental quietude, silence. We might recall another famous mystic, Gautama the Buddha, who when pressed to sermonize about his enlightenment remained silent and held up a flower. In an actual, nonsentimental sense, "Song of Myself" was the flower Whitman held up for those with eyes to see. In this way alone could he fulfill his promise in the "Preface" to the 1855 edition of *Leaves of Grass* to ". . . well nigh express the inexpressible."

Efforts to illuminate Whitman's mysticism have often failed because critics have taken classically hermeneutial approaches to this poet who insists that argument is futile and that only our presence itself convinces. In section twenty-five of "Song of Myself": "Writing and talk do not prove me, / I carry the plenum of proof and every thing else in my face, / With the *hush* of my lips I wholly confound the skeptic" (italics mine). For this reason Whitman went to extremes to make his presence visible in *Leaves of Grass,* to "show his face" not only by composing the poems, but then by incorporating those poems, that "soul" of his mind's creation, in a physical artifact, a body crafted with his hands. In an almost literal sense, Whitman tried to make his book a physiological extension of himself. He chose the paper and the typeface, set some of the type, printed and bound the pages, designed the unusual covers, and even included an engraving from a photograph of himself. Anyone can speculate about enlightenment. But the enlightened embody enlightenment. It is only necessary that they clearly show themselves, "hold themselves up" to the world, and with the hush of their lips convince or confound.

Whitman wanted his readers to respond to his book as they would respond to his actual presence. His book would contain the structure of his higher state of consciousness embodied in the structure of the poems themselves, in their "face," as it was in his own face. With Whitman, such encoding was not a deliberate technique but an inevitability, in much the way Frost describes how a poem comments on its creation by its very unfolding. "How can a poem have 'wildness' and at the same time a subject that should be fulfilled?" Frost asks. "It should be the pleasure of the poem itself to tell us how it can." This self-commenting quality of a poem he termed "the figure a poem makes."[4] John Burroughs, in his biography of Whitman, makes a similar point: "'Leaves of Grass' requires a large perspective; you must not get your face too near the book. . . . Looked at too closely, it often seems incoherent and meaningless; draw off a little and let the figure come out."[5]

It should be possible for us to see in the figures of poems in *Leaves* a kind of self-commentary on the structure of the higher state of consciousness that produced them, and that they embody. For the sake of clarity, I will first offer a model of consciousness based on those textbooks of higher states of consciousness, the *Vedas,* and then look at two main figures that emerge from "Song of Myself" and "A Song of the Rolling Earth" in light of this model—the circle and the broken line.[6]

Let me begin by explaining transcendental consciousness. Whitman repeatedly alludes to this state of silent inner-wakefulness (often termed *samadhi*"), calling it "the mere fact consciousness" or "interior consciousness," as in this excerpt from "Democratic Vistas":

> I should say, indeed, that only in the perfect uncontamination and solitariness of individuality may the spirituality of religion positively come forth at all. Only here, and on such terms, the meditation, the devout ecstasy, the soaring flight. Only here, communion with the mysteries, the eternal problems, whence? whither? Alone, and identity, and the mood—and the soul emerges, and all statements, churches, sermons, melt away like vapors. Alone, and silent thought and awe, and aspiration—and then the interior consciousness, like a hitherto unseen inscription, in magic ink, beams out its wondrous lines to the sense. Bibles may convey, and priests expound, but it is exclusively for the noiseless operation of one's isolated Self, to enter the pure ether of veneration, reach the divine levels, and commune with the unutterable.

The *Manduka Upanishad* recognizes the three usual states of consciousness (waking, sleeping, and dreaming) but adds to these a fourth state of union with the Absolute of Self. This additional state, which Whitman calls "interior consciousness," is termed "transcendental consciousness," or "pure consciousness."[7]

Usually when we are conscious, our consciousness has an object: we are conscious of some thing—a scene before our eyes, the sound of the wind, a thought, perhaps only a sensation. This consciousness is always limited, bounded by a finite object. For expedience, let us refer to this as the "conscious of x" model, where "x" is any object of consciousness. On the other hand, pure consciousness may be understood as consciousness *without* an object of consciousness: consciousness simply left alone by itself, undisturbed, silent. With no object to limit it, such consciousness is boundless, infinite.

But how can consciousness alone ever be known? Who, after all, would know it? The *Upanishads* themselves anticipate and frame just such questions: How can the eye see itself? How can the sword cut itself? By whom shall the knower be known?[8] The answer must lie in the notion of transcending, an answer Whitman expressed by means of a figure emblematic of transcendence: the circle. In transcendence, the linear "conscious of x" model of awareness simply does not apply. The usual "knower-knowing-known" distinctions dissolve. The *Upanishads* speak of meditation as a technique to turn the attention exclusively upon a mental object (a *mantra*) which is then systematically refined until it disappears altogether. At that point of transcendence, there would be awareness—one would not have blacked out—but awareness of what? If these conditions are allowed to be at least theoretically possible, then we have to say that the experiencer is experiencing himself—"the noiseless operation of one's isolated self"—as the object of experience. The knower is knowing himself in the act of knowing. The three distinctions—experiencer, experiencing, object of experience—merge into a transcendent unity which the *Upanishads* call pure consciousness.

The figure most clearly emblematic of the mechanics of transcendence is the circle. Awareness in this fourth state of consciousness, instead of moving outward in a linear direction to become lost in the object, loops back upon itself; it becomes aware of itself. This figure of the circle is repeated throughout "Song of Myself" and other poems as well. It is one of the two principal figures of transcendence in Whitman's poetry; the other is the broken line.

In the very first line "Song of Myself" projects an image of consciousness looping back on itself. "I" is the first word of this poem of the Self. "Celebrate" seems to draw consciousness outward in a linear way, but the final word bends the arc of consciousness back to its starting point: "myself." In this first line, then, we have the three components of ordinary waking-state awareness: experiencer (I), act of experiencing (celebrate) and object of experience (myself). The circle, however, fuses these separate components into a transcendent unity. If we read the line as Whitman revised it after 1855, allowing for the initial ellipsis we simply add another circle, ". . . and sing myself. . . ."

For many reasons, to call Whitman the poet of transcendent unity is no exaggeration. In the next line of the opening, for instance, he extends unity to the most immediate "other," the reader: "And what I assume you shall assume. . . ." The last word of the poem, in fact, is "you." By the time that last word occurs, however, the identity of the first word (I) and the last (you) should be established, unified within the transcendent Self. Thus the poem ends at its beginning point, describing a circle.

The fifth section of the poem deals most precisely with the actual experience of transcendence. The whole section is addressed to his "soul"—his essence, his consciousness—and he says: "I mind how once we lay such a transparent summer morning, / How you settled your head athwart my hips and gently turn'd over upon me. . . ." Again, we have an image of a turning back upon oneself, a circle, for his soul "turns over" upon him, turns inward in an experience of union tendered in sexual terms.[9]

Whitman's union, though, is of his self and his Self, the two selves, he tells us in a notebook entry, he had always been curiously aware of. The one self is factlike, limited, closed, comprised of specifics such as his six-foot height, his two-hundred-pound weight, his rosy complexion, his age and personal history. The other self, or Self as he often wrote it, could not be contained between his hat and bootsoles, but was a "kosmos," unbounded. He develops these two senses of selfhood very clearly in section four of "Song of Myself."

From the point of view of unboundedness, the bounded—any ordinary object of perception, including one's facticial self (to borrow a term from Sartre)—can appear "other." So section five begins: "I believe in you my soul, the other I am must not abase itself to you. . . ." In the experience that follows Whitman realizes experientially the identity of the bounded with the unbounded. The bounded, Whitman's physical nervous system, like a lover "contains" the unbounded, his consciousness: ". . . And parted the shirt from my bosom-bone, and plunged your tongue to my bare-stript heart, / And reach'd till you felt my beard, and reach'd till you held my feet."

The reality of blissful transcendent union of the bounded with the unbounded is Whitman's closing revelation in section five: "Swiftly arose and spread around me the peace and knowledge that pass all the argument of the earth. . . ." The images that follow hint of the identity of the infinite and the finite: ". . . the hand of God is the promise of my own, / . . . all the men ever born are also my brothers. . . ." And the adjective modifying the final catalog of concrete, obviously bound objects—". . . leaves stiff or drooping in the fields, / And brown ants . . . / And mossy scabs . . . heap'd stones. . . ."—is "limitless."

On the largest scale of its progressive unfolding also "Song of Myself" describes the figure of a circle, emblematic of the self-referential aspect of transcendence. We follow Whitman on a walk without destination, very much an Emersonian journey of the kind described in his essay "Circles" when he quotes Cromwell: "A man . . . never rises so high as when he knows not whither he is going." A loose definition of transcendence could be "self-forgetting," since the self is completely absorbed into the Self and is in a sense lost or abandoned. This may be part of Emerson's meaning when he says in the same essay, "The way of life is wonderful; it is by abandonment." When we "walk" this way, rather than feeling lost, we enjoy a sense of discovery. We find our Self everywhere. So Whitman, in a walk so free of self he deleted his name from the cover and title page of the first edition of *Leaves of Grass*, finds his Self everywhere ("every atom belonging to me as good belongs to you"). If he (and we) do not know where he is going, it is because really there is nowhere to go. The *Upanishads* say repeatedly "I am That" (unbounded pure consciousness), "Thou are That and all this is nothing but That." So Whitman closes his song, ". . . missing me one place, search another. . . ." The poem begins in the Self, returns repeatedly to the Self, and at the end comes around again to the Self, a circle of circles. The final line is a last hint—one of Whitman's favorite words—that his experience of unbounded Selfhood is not eccentric, but universal. We should be interested in his song, for it is our song too, even if we are not yet its singers. In the first section he told us that what he assumed, we too should assume. In the last section he promises that we too will one day discover the unbounded Self: "I stop somewhere waiting for you."[10]

Let us consider briefly a second figure of transcendence in Whitman's work, the infinite broken line. This figure emerges most clearly from Whitman's catalog technique and can be connected with the structure of the higher state of consciousness beyond transcendental consciousness: complete enlightenment, called in Vedic literature "all-time *samadhi*" or "*samadhi* without any seeds of ignorance" (*nirbija samadhi*). From R. M. Bucke onward, Whitman critics have favored the term "cosmic consciousness." In cosmic consciousness the silent, unbounded awareness of transcendental consciousness is never lost. In activity, it coexists with the bounded consciousness of specific thoughts, feelings, perceptions. *Manduka Upanishad* explains: "Like two birds of golden plumage, inseparable companions, the individual self and the immortal Self are perched on the branches of the self-same tree." The individual self is active; the unbounded self is silent. "The former tastes of the sweet and bitter fruits of the tree; the latter, tasting of neither, calmly observes."[11] Whitman wrote in his notebook, "I cannot understand the mystery: but I am always conscious of myself as two (as my soul and I)."[12] And throughout his poetry he uses the term "witness" to describe the curiously involved yet detached experience, "both in and out of the game" as he says in section four of "Song of Myself."

The catalog is an apt representation of the coexistence of pure consciousness along with thoughts, perceptions, and feelings, for it embodies the opposite and irreconcilable qualities of infinity and limitation. The catalog is composed of concrete objects, perceptions, and recollections; but the first item is simply the one Whitman has begun with, not a predictable or required starting point, and the last item does not exhaust the possibilities or reach a necessary conclusion. As Paul Zweig has observed, "A random list is, by definition, merely a sample of an unspoken list containing everything."[13] The catalog conveys the feeling of infinite extension preceding its beginning and following its ending. We might say that the catalog is finite in its elemental composition but infinite in its structure, and so combines without damage the irreconcilable opposites of Whitman's experience of cosmic consciousness: mortal body, and immortal soul; finite matter, and unbounded consciousness.

In another way, too, the catalog embodies the duality of the bounded versus the unbounded, or of the outer reality versus the inner. Not only does the catalog strike us as a segment lifted from an infinite sequence, but infinity is also interfused *among* elements. Because items in the catalog do not follow one another in any logical or even predictable sequence, the gaps between elements are not mere pauses, nor are they emptiness, but rather silences of all possibilities. Consider these excerpts from section fifteen of "Song of Myself":

> The pure contralto sings in the organ loft,
> The carpenter dresses his plank, the tongue of his foreplane whistles its wild
>   ascending lisp,
> The married and unmarried children ride home to their Thanksgiving dinner,
> The pilot seizes the king-pin, he heaves down with a strong arm,
> The mate stands braced in the whale-boat, lance and harpoon are ready . . .

And a bit later:

> The crew of the fish-smack pack repeated layers of halibut in the hold,
> The Missourian crosses the plains toting his wares and his cattle,
> As the fare-collector goes through the train he gives notice by the jingling
>   of loose change. . . .

We don't know what might emerge. Anything might. Each gap in a sense contains infinity, in immense richness of limitless possibility, while each item is concrete, specific, bounded. The unfolding of the catalog, then, expresses Whitman's total reality of coexistent boundaries along with unboundedness, a fifth state of consciousness which yokes (a word derived from the Sanskrit *yoga*) the ordinary waking state and the fourth state of transcendental consciousness. Just as Whitman is "both in and out of the game," so the catalog is both busy and, at the same time, silent.

Although "Song of Myself" is filled with insights and flashes of revelation, "Song of the Rolling Earth" ventures beyond hints and moves in the direction of explication. Whitman begins by announcing a language of nature, a language of perfection and silence: "Were you thinking that those were the words, those upright lines? Those curves, angles, dots? / No, those are not the words, the substantial words are in the ground and sea, / They are in the air, they are in you." Here we have the beginning of a philosophical rationale for why "our presence alone convinces." As he states a few lines later, "Human bodies are words. . . ." Our physical presence, then, is an undisguised statement. By extension, all forms of earth and sea are similarly full and true statements, so that the mere physical fact of "the rolling earth" becomes itself a complete song.

Whitman's ability to read this truest language, these hieroglyphs of the unmanifest manifesting, underlies his fascination with faces, each of which spoke to him of a complete personality or a personal history, as is most evident in his poem "Faces." Indeed, he often requested photographs from friends he could not otherwise see, as in a letter to Tennyson of 27 April 1872 when he repeats an earlier request for a photograph and ends with the admonition, "Don't forget the picture."[14] There is no evidence Whitman knew the famous story of the Buddha's silent sermon, but he says in the third verse of the first section of "Song of the Rolling Earth," "The masters know the earth's words and use them more than audible words."

As the title of the poem suggests, "Song of the Rolling Earth" also is built upon the figure of the circle, the round earth orbiting amid other spheres. The end of the first section elaborates the self-referential figure, placing circles within circles as Whitman had done in "Song of Myself." Amid "centripetal and centrifugal sisters" the "beautiful sister," earth, dances on. In the next verse, however, she is at rest, she "sits undisturbed," so that her motion, her dance, is relative only. Within herself she is quiet, holding in her hand "what has the character of a mirror," the moon. Again the figure here is self-referential, arching back upon itself as she sits "Holding a mirror day and night tirelessly before her own face." She is, we might say, both in and out of the dance.

The remaining lines of the first section present further cycles: the twenty-four hours of each day, the three hundred sixty-five days of each year. The final ten lines of this section bolster circularity auditorially. "Embracing," itself circular, is repeated three times in two lines. Internal rhyme ". . . the soul's realization and determination . . ." and the repeated "ing" sound of the present participle echo in the reader's ear. The simple present emerges, steady and silent amid a whirlwind, in the last line: "The divine ship sails the divine sea."

The second section begins to apply the metaphysical truths and the implied truths of section one to the individual: ". . . the song is to the singer, and comes back most to him, / The teaching is to the teacher, and comes back most to him, / The murder is to the murderer, and comes back most to him. . . ." Growth, development, the soul's journey, are circular, not only in the poetic sense of the soul's journey around the divine sea of the Self, but in an immediate ethical sense: our actions come back to us. We feed upon our own actions and are thereby nourished or poisoned: ". . . the gift is to the giver, and comes back most to him—it cannot fail. . . ." The final line opens out the implications of this view: "And no man understand any greatness or goodness but his own, or the indication of his own." Whitman will follow this thought to its furthest application in section three.

Whosoever is complete, to him or her "the earth shall surely be complete." Whose consciousness is linear, partial, bounded, for him or her the earth remains "jagged and broken." Through his experiences of transcendence Whitman connects this state of wholeness of awareness with silence, not an empty and dead silence but a lively and expanded silence of all possibilities. The sweetest love, then, is the wholeness of ". . . that which contains itself, which never invites and never refuses." And the poem concludes with praise of silence: "I swear I will never henceforth have to do with the faith that tells the best, / I will have to do only with that faith that leaves the best untold."

Whitman would labor to extend his presence to every aspect of his book itself and thereby transform it into a living natural object, an expression, as his body was an expression, of his boundless, silent soul. He tells us in "So Long!" "Camerado, this is no book, / Who touches this touches a man. . . ." As the form of his face inevitably expressed the wholeness of his being, he would trust that the figures, not the words of his poems, would similarly, in their own perfect and silent natural language, "express the inexpressible." If he could avoid the literary, could disdain the conventional, and simply extend himself into his creation, silence would speak, would sing. The song would be of himself.

NOTES

[1] Walt Whitman, *An 1855–56 Notebook Toward the Second Edition of "Leaves of Grass,"* ed. Harold W. Blodgett (Carbondale: University of Illinois Press, 1959), 7–8.

[2] Many of Whitman's contemporaries and friends attempted explication, especially Edward Carpenter and R. M. Bucke, both of whom were familiar with Vedic literature. William James dealt with Whitman's mysticism in *The Varieties of Religious Experience,* and in our own day there are several noteworthy studies: James E. Miller, "'Song of Myself' as Inverted Mystical Experience" in *A Critical Guide to Leaves of Grass* (Chicago: University of Chicago Press, 1957), 6–35; and more generally, Arthur Christy, *The Orient in American Transcendentalism* (New York: Columbia University Press, 1932). V. K. Chari, whose definition of "cosmic consciousness" I have quoted, has done the most thorough, systematic study in *Whitman in the Light of Vedantic Mysticism* (Lincoln: University of Nebraska Press, 1965). Chari's definition (p. 34) is inadequate, but his work remains an invaluable source.

[3] Eric Bentley, "Sweden's Nasty, Sexist, Racist Genius," *New York Times Book Review,* 1 September 1985.

⁴ Robert Frost, "The Figure a Poem Makes," in *Complete Poems of Robert Frost* (New York: Holt, Rinehart and Winston, 1949).

⁵ John Burroughs, *Whitman: A Study* (New York: William H. Wise and Co., 1924), 124.

⁶ The *Vedas* are immense and the *richas*, verses, sometimes impenetrably abstruse. *Rig Veda* alone contains more than ten thousand verses and is only one of four principal *Vedas*, to which we must add other lengthy works not technically part of the *Vedas*, but included in the broad category of "Vedic literature," such as the *Upanishads* and the *Bhagavad-Gita*. I must here acknowledge my indebtedness to Maharishi Mahesh Yogi for his formulation of "Vedic Science," a systematized and rationally comprehensible presentation of Vedic knowledge based upon the fourth major state of consciousness, transcendental consciousness. I should also point out that a great deal of empirical evidence exists for this fourth state of consciousness. Of the scores of published experiments, I might mention Wallace and Benson's "The Physiology of Meditation," *Scientific American*, 226 (1972) 84–90; also by Wallace et al., "A Wakeful Hypometabolic State," *American Journal of Physiology*, 221 (1971), 795–799.

⁷ "The life of man is divided between waking, dreaming, and dreamless sleep. But transcending these three states is superconscious vision—called the Fourth." The *Upanishads*, trans. by Swami Prabhavananda and Frederick Manchester (California: Mentor Classics, 1948), 49. All other references to the *Upanishads* are from this edition. The quotation from "Democratic Vistas" is in Floyd Stovall, ed., *Prose Works 1892* (New York: New York University Press, 1964), 2:398–399.

⁸ The *Brihadaranyaka Upanishad* says: "As long as there is duality, one sees the other, one hears the other, one smells the other, one speaks to the other; but when for the illumined soul the all is dissolved in the Self, who is there to be seen by whom, who is there to be smelt by whom, who is there to be spoken to by whom, who is there to be thought of by whom, who is there to be known by whom?" (*Upanishads*, 89).

⁹ The amorous image of section five was startling to many of Whitman's contemporaries and remains at least puzzling to modern readers. But the experience of the fourth state of consciousness, the *Upanishads* emphasize, is *ananda*, surpassing pleasure—bliss. What better concrete metaphor, then, for complete and blissful union than love play? There is, of course, in both Western and Eastern literature a long tradition of sexual religious poetry, especially in the work of Kabir, Mirabai, Rumi, St. John of the Cross, and John Donne, to name a few.

¹⁰ On this level of universal Self Whitman makes a similar appointment—to "meet" a prostitute, in "To a Common Prostitute," perhaps the most misread of his poems.

¹¹ *Upanishads*, 46–47.

¹² Walt Whitman, *The Uncollected Poetry and Prose of Walt Whitman*, ed. Emory Holloway (Garden City, New York: Doubleday, 1921), 66.

¹³ Paul Zweig, *Walt Whitman, The Making of the Poet* (New York: Basic Books, 1984), 248–249.

¹⁴ Walt Whitman, *The Correspondence*, ed. Edwin Haviland Miller (New York: New York University Press, 1964), 3:174–175.

Sample Student Research Paper

Sampson 1

LaTasha Priscilla Sampson

American Literature

Professor Léger

7 May, 2000

The Nature of the Poet:

Walt Whitman's 1855 Preface

and His Lifelong Poetic Practice

Like most poets who consider themselves innova-
tors, Walt Whitman formally describes his intentions for poetic practice at the start of his
career. In his introduction to the 1855 edition
of <u>Leaves of Grass</u>, Whitman outlines his ideas
about the character of the poet, the characteristics of a poem, and the processes of poetic creation. Whitman explicitly states that the poet is
a "seer" who conveys the wonder of all things and
who leads his people on "the path between reality
and their souls" (Preface 42). From Whitman's
work, a portrait of the artist emerges that is
consistent with his description of the artist in
his 1855 "manifesto." More importantly, Whitman
follows this artistic "script" throughout his
life and work. This essay will demonstrate that
Whitman himself follows the formula for poetic
practice that he outlines in his preface.

In the 1855 Preface, Whitman makes many claims
about himself, and in his poetry he insists upon

Thesis Statement:
Whitman outlines
his poetic formula
in the 1855
Preface and
adheres to
that formula in
his poetry.

Sampson 2

the same claims. He receives inspiration through
direct experience rather than as a result of
reading the works of previous thinkers. He celebrates natural beauty and commonplace human reality. He experiences the natural and the common
as supernatural and wondrous. He claims that
all natural phenomena are within him. His words
convey raw reality to others, so that they may
themselves "filter" it. And as one who contains
and transforms all reality, he becomes, despite
his repeated poetic protests to the contrary, a
supernatural being.

Whitman specifies, as many beginning poets
do, the philosophy that guides him. Although his
syntax and punctuation are as irregular in his
Preface as they are in his poetry itself, still
he clearly establishes his vision of the poet
in a few phrases within the otherwise rambling
discussion. The great poet, he writes, dismisses
nothing from his gaze: "The greatest poet hardly
knows pettiness or triviality. If he breathes
into any thing that was before thought small it
dilates with the grandeur of the life of the
universe" (Preface 42). The great (American) poet
receives "the essences of the real things and
past and present events" (Preface 40). Whitman
asserts this in the midst of a long catalogue
of just what those real things and events might
encompass. This catalogue in the Preface, and

What the poet
sees and who the
poet is, according
to Whitman

Sampson 3

others in the poetry itself, establish Whitman's
ability to focus his poetry on anything at all
and establish his supernatural capacity to contain all things. As clear as the divine size of
the poet, indicated by his capacity for containing worlds, is the divine creative capacity of
the poet, breathing grandeur into the commonplace
and knowing the "essences" of the phenomena which
enter him as though he were an all-knowing god.
For all of Whitman's protestations that the poet
is "one of the roughs" ("Song of Myself" 24) and
that "the others are as good as he, only he sees
it and they do not" (Preface 42), the poet in
Whitman's vision is a supernatural, divine being.

The poet is also a mediator, or interpreter
"of men and women and of all events and things"
(Preface 54). He is the sign post pointing the
way between the real and the soul of the reader
(Preface 42), who "exhibits the pinnacles . . .
and glows a moment on the extremest verge" and
at the same time "brings the spirit of any or all
events and passions and scenes and persons . . .
to bear on your individual character as you hear
or read" (Preface 44). He is transcendent, literally moving across levels of existence and experience. Like the Romantic poets, Whitman the poet
is fascinated by the transcendent state of death
(the word lisp'd by the ocean to the child at the
end of "Out of the Cradle Endlessly Rocking").
His insistence that the poet is a mediator, in

The poet's role
is a mediative,
redemptive, or
interpretive one.

Sampson 4

the 1855 Preface, makes Whitman's later focus
upon death ("Cradle" is first written in 1859) as
an important and transforming experience a natural focus. Also like the Romantic poets, Whitman
values the sensual and perceptual experience and
expression of the child or the common man, "that
indescribable freshness and unconsciousness about
an illiterate person that humbles and mocks the
power of the noblest expressive genius" (Preface
42). Later, Whitman praises as the "art of art,
the glory of expression and the sunshine of the
light of letters . . . simplicity," the poet who
is "the free channel of himself" (Preface 45).

Whitman's poetry fulfills all that his Preface
promises. He asserts his capacity to embrace all
of reality. He insists on the transcendent and
transformative value of each object upon which
his gaze rests. He constantly urges his readers
to appreciate the beauty of all that he shows
them. And he periodically assures the reader that
he is no more than a guide upon the common road
of human experience.

In Section 1 of "Song of Myself" Whitman
asserts "[m]y tongue, every atom of my blood
. . . [is] . . . form'd from this soil, this
air" (6), suggesting that his physical being is
indistinguishable from the essences of his natural surroundings. In fact, Whitman's speaker
asserts that he absorbs and contains Nature.
While he makes this self-identification with the

Whitman asserts
a transcendentalist
connection to
Nature.

Sampson 5

natural world, Whitman compares the atmospheres
of the drawing room and of a natural setting,
claiming that the first is an intoxicant and that
the second is harmless but necessary ("it is for
my mouth forever" [18]). This hint that he is potentially susceptible to the atmosphere of civilization insures his connection to the reader.
At the same time, Whitman reveals his preference
for the natural. He launches into a celebratory
description of himself in naked contact with Nature, his awareness focused upon his primal and
primary contact with it: breathing it, circulat-
ing it in his blood, encountering it with the
five senses: "[t]he sniff of green leaves . . . /
[t]he sound . . . of my voice . . . / . . . a few
embraces . . . / [t]he play of shine and shade
on the trees" (23-27).

In the brief poem "When I Heard the Learn'd
Astronomer," Whitman again contrasts the "civilized" to the natural experience of reality.
The speaker is overwhelmed by the symbols of
civilization—the auditorium filled with people
listening to a lecture delivered by an astronomer. The speaker insists on the comparison,
and on the relative negativity of the "civilization" experience versus the "natural" one. This
insistence is conveyed by sharp contrasts. The
catalogue of the astronomer's teaching aids,
the designation of the setting as a "lecture-
room," and the suggestion that in this room is

Whitman
contrasts the
civilized and
the natural.

Sampson 6

a <u>crowd</u> of attendees (a suggestion enforced by
the speaker's observation of "much applause")
are all pointedly contrasted to the relief with
which the speaker reports that he "ris[es] and
glid[es] out and wander[s] off" alone (8), to
"[l]ook in perfect silence at the stars" (10).
The implication is that aloneness and silence
represent a "perfect" state. In contrast, the
crowdedness and noise of the lecture and applause
are emphasized. The "silence" of the last line
also reinforces the speaker's preference for a
precivilized or natural encounter with reality
(versus a civilized encounter) because it depicts
an encounter with reality from which language
(the first indication of civilization) is absent.
This is ironic, since Whitman is a poet. On the
other hand, Whitman's seemingly unpoetic language
(a "speech-based" language as Jarvis calls it
[104]) may reflect his preference for natural,
precivilized experience.

In fact, Whitman's preference for common
language is stated directly in his poetry. In
"Had I the Choice," Whitman rejects the recog-
nizably "poetic" depiction of reality. Just as
the learned language of the astronomer has been
useless in conveying the reality of the stars,
language even in its most consciously poetic
form ("[m]eter or wit the best, or choice conceit to wield in perfect rhyme delight of singers" [5]) is incapable of describing the poet's

Whitman
rejects the
influence of
previous
poets.

Sampson 7

encounter with reality. Directly addressing
the sea, which so often symbolizes Nature for
Whitman, the speaker implies that the waves and
winds of the sea would produce poetry of higher
quality than that of the greatest bards.

> Whitman asserts that Poetry is derived directly from Nature.

Whitman is legendary for his love of common
reality, and for his celebration of the common
as the subject of poetry. Whitman's catalogues
are usually cited to demonstrate this tendency.
In the very brief and early "Cavalry Crossing
a Ford," Whitman demonstrates his capacity to
elevate the most common and uninteresting occurrences to artistic stature. In the poem, dated

> Whitman embraces common experience.

1865, Whitman simply records the mundane movement of a troop of cavalry. Amid all the drama
of the end of the Civil War, there is no drama,
no battle scene, no haste—nothing to suggest an
event out of the ordinary. There is no contest at
the crossing of the ford. Even the battle standard flutters, not bravely, but "gayly," <u>suggest-
ing</u> triumph or celebration, but not <u>insisting</u>
upon it. The casual wandering of the troop implies rather that the fluttering of the flag is
"gay" because of the velocity of the wind rather
than because of the spirit of the troop.

Whitman's "Song of Myself" again elevates the
mundane to the level of the poetic, both in its
emphases and in its language. Whitman's speaker
asserts that his poetry "celebrate[s] . . .
and sing[s]" himself, not as sharp-thinking and

Sampson 8

prophetic visionary, but as he is when at rest.
The opening lines of the poem depict the speaker
in a state as common and uninteresting as laziness, and as concrete as flesh: "I loafe and invite my soul, / . . . at my ease observing a
spear of summer grass," he rambles, and emphasizes his bodily existence as he does his relat-
edness with the dust. And he underscores that
relationship by asserting that the "atom[s] of
[his] blood [are] form'd from this soil" (4-6).
The refinements of civilized man are rejected by
the speaker here in favor of the grittiness of a
naked encounter with nature. The readers Whitman
addresses are no learned, polished connoisseurs
of poetry; Whitman assumes a common capacity to
interpret poetry and invites readers to "filter"
things for themselves (37).

   In "A Noiseless Patient Spider" Whitman compares the most ordinary of creatures performing
its most ordinary of operations, with the human
soul, which represents (arguably) the highest
of human capacities: the spiritual dimension of
human existence. The spider and its thread, of
which it weaves a web to capture and feed upon
other insects, is identified with the human soul
and its attempt to establish connection transcendentally. The comparison elevates the commonplace and renders common and universal the need
to establish relationship across all natural and
human divisions.

> The human soul
> is presented by
> Whitman in
> terms of the
> common *and*
> the extraordinary.

Sampson 9

Whitman's preference for the everyday is not
merely apparent in his choice of subject matter,
but in the choices that govern his style and
poetic forms. He dismisses the influence of the
"greatest bards" in favor of the almost banal
rhythm of ocean waves and the common breath of
sea air. And this rhythm and spirit organize
and punctuate the introductory lines of "Out
of the Cradle Endlessly Rocking," the poem in
which Whitman describes his transformation from
mere infantile human to poet, in the lonely midnight encounter with death on the shore of the
ocean.

> Simple rhythms as well as simple subject matter define the poetry of Whitman.

Whitman blends the objectivity of the reporter with the involvement of a mediator in
"Cavalry Crossing a Ford." Here Whitman acts as
the objective reporter of a commonplace, rather
uninteresting event, at the same time that he
dramatically occupies the central or threshold
position of the ford, a place of crossing "betwixt green islands" (1). From this position he
describes, again rather objectively, the scene
before him, leaving the reader to determine the
significance of the crossing itself. He also allows the reader to decipher the few details given
(such as the brownness of the faces, or the gay-
ness of the flag's fluttering).

> Whitman's function as poet is to occupy the central position between the reader and the subject matter of the poem.

In the selection from "Song of Myself," Whitman elaborately depicts the speaker's character

Sampson 10

as that of a common man. The poem emphasizes
the speaker's physical nature, his laziness,
his heredity, his attachment to the place "here"
by which he represents both "Paumanok" (Long
Island) and America. But at the same time, it is
this speaker who causes "Creeds and schools" to
be held in "abeyance," and who "harbor[s] [and]
permit[s]" Nature to speak "without check with
original energy" (10-13). This powerful being,
as well, goes on to contrast the perfumed houses
(that he will not let intoxicate him) with his
own naked sensual encounter with Nature. At the
end of the second section of "Song of Myself,"
Whitman returns to the place from which he can
mediate between reality and his reader, implying
a strict objectivity in placing all the facts
into his reader's hands:

> Stop this day and night with me and you
> shall possess the origin of all poems,
> You shall possess the good of the earth and
> sun, (there are millions of suns left,)
> You shall no longer take things at second
> or third hand, nor look through the eyes
> of the dead, nor feed on the spectres in
> books,
> You shall not look through my eyes either,
> nor take things from me,
> You shall listen to all sides and filter them
> for your self (33-37).

Yet Whitman asserts a certain authority for himself as poet.

Sampson 11

At the same time, as DeLancey asserts (83–84, 98), this objectivity still performs the feat of mediation, by bringing oppositions into the same space in the interest of community building, even as it elevates the reader herself into the position of interpretive authority.

Whitman's objectivity and authority as poet are sharply contrasted.

Whitman addresses his soul (a clear representation of the possibility of transcendence) directly in "A Noiseless Patient Spider" (1888). In this poem, the "soul" of the speaker is placed at the center of the universe ("[s]urrounded, detached, in measureless oceans of space" [7]). It occupies a central space in a fragmentary universe for which it feels the responsibility to find connection: "seeking the spheres to connect them" [8]). The comparison of the soul to the spider, who connects separated places with a web, further implies that the action of the soul is the central organizing action of the universe. The "web" Whitman weaves, with this comparison, between the reader and the speaker of the poem, is like a common spider web both connective and flimsy, as are Whitman's "figures of transcendence" (the ellipses, patterns of broken linearity, and circular rhetorical and image patterns, that Sarracino identifies [147 and elsewhere]). The poet/speaker, and his soul, clearly register the sense of poetic responsibility for mediating, transcendent action that Whitman has asserted

The soul of the poet is identified with the spider.

Sampson 12

earlier in his career, in the Preface to the 1855
edition.

Finally, in "Out of the Cradle Endlessly
Rocking" the poet steps into this mediating
space and becomes the means by which the possibility of transcendence is made available
to the common man. This happens to the speaker
(Whitman) when the child in the poem steps again
and again onto the beach, the threshold of sea
and land. The poem is pregnant, literally, with
images of transcendence. The endless rocking of
the cradle and the temporal setting of the poem
in the "ninth-month midnight," suggest procrea-
tion/generation (3). The second phrase suggests
sexual generation, or more simply, the sexual
itself, which as Aspiz argues is itself a perva-
sive figure of transcendence in Whitman's work
(Aspiz 58). The swollen moon (10), the heartbeat
of the speaker (12), the beach and the waves
(19), the contrast of "pains and joys . . . here
and hereafter" (20), and the foreshadowing and
retrospective ("leaping beyond . . . / . . .
reminiscence" [21-22]), all suggest a confusion
of time, a meeting of all times in a transcendent moment, as the poetic voice meets his current and past selves in the tears he sheds,
and so transcends memory and time to become something more than human: a poet. The transcendent
capacity of the poet is further emphasized by

The poet's
self-identity as
mediating figure
is created in
the encounter
between the
boy and death
in "Out of
the Cradle."

the mystic (6) and misty (11) setting he occupies
in this poem.

    Whitman's emphasis upon immediate and direct
experience of reality, and his desire to bring
the reader into such contact, is, in Whitman's
poetry, the fulfillment of the intention he asserts in the preface (Preface 43). In order to
assist readers in their contact with reality,
the poet must himself directly contact it. He
asserts his ability to touch reality directly
and to translate it for his readers without the
assistance or the wisdom of the philosophers,
poets who come before him, or the scientists of
his own day. Thus, he places his observer _in_ the
ford his cavalry is crossing. He must "barter"
"[m]eter or wit the best, or choice conceit
to wield in perfect rhyme delight of singers"
("Had I the Choice" 6, 5). He sets "[c]reeds and
schools in abeyance" ("Song of Myself" 1.10). He
leaves the "lecture-room" wherein he has become
"tired and sick" of "proofs . . . figures . . .
/ . . . charts and diagrams" ("When I Heard the
Learn'd Astronomer" 2-3). The poet must receive
directly from the encounter with Nature or Reality "the undulation of one wave, its trick"
and the "breath of [the sea] upon [his] verse,"
("Had I the Choice" 7-8). The poet, for Whitman,
must "undisguised and naked, / . . . be in contact" with nature ("Song of Myself" 19, 20); he
must "wander . . . off by [him]self,/ . . . [and]

Whitman fulfills his intentions as stated in the 1855 Preface, remaining faithful to those intentions throughout his career.

Sampson 14

[l]ook up in perfect silence at the stars" ("When I Heard the Learn'd Astronomer" 8, 10). Thus, Whitman's stated intention becomes a viable, present, and constructive force in his poetic expression, throughout his poetic life.

Works Cited

Aspiz, Harold. "Sexuality and the Language of
Transcendence." Léger 56.

DeLancey, Mark. "Texts, Interpretations, and
Whitman's 'Song of Myself.'" Léger 81.

Jarvis, D. R., "Whitman and Speech-Based Prosody." Léger 103.

Léger, J. Michael, ed. Walt Whitman: A Collection
of Poems. Harcourt Casebook Series in Literature. Fort Worth: Harcourt, 2000.

Sarracino, Carmine. "Figures of Transcendence in
Whitman's Poetry." Léger 142.

Whitman, Walt. "Preface to 1855 Edition Leaves of
Grass." Léger 38.

Bibliography

Biographical Sources

Allen, Gay Wilson. *The Solitary Singer: A Critical Biography.* New York: New York UP, 1967.

Babington, Douglass. "Whitman's Life and Art: The Precarious Boundary." *Canadian Review of American Studies* 17 (1986): 337–45.

Moder, Donna. "Gender Bipolarity and the Metaphorical Dimensions of Creativity in Walt Whitman's Poetry: A Psychobiographical Study." *Literature and Psychology* 34.1 (1988): 34–52.

Schmidgall, Gary. *Walt Whitman: A Gay Life.* New York: Dutton, 1997.

Mysticism, Spirituality, and Philosophy

Askin, Denise T. "Retrievements Out of the Night: Prophetic and Private Voices in Whitman's 'Drum Taps.'" *American Transcendentalist Quarterly* 51 (1981): 211–23.

Cederstrom, Lorelei. "A Jungian Approach to the Self in Major Whitman Poems." *Approaches to Teaching Whitman's Leaves of Grass.* Ed. Donald D. Kummings. New York: MLA, 1990. 81–89.

Corona, Mario. "'Whoever You Are Holding Me Now In Hand': A Book, A Body, and What Company To Keep." *Utopia in the Present Tense: Walt Whitman and the Language of the New World.* Ed. Marina Camboni. Rome: Calamo, 1994. 123–36.

French, R. W. "Whitman's Dream Vision: A Reading of 'The Sleepers.'" *Walt Whitman Quarterly Review* 8.1 (1990): 1–15.

Gilbert, Sandra M. "'Now in a Moment I Know What I Am For': Rituals of Initiation in Whitman and Dickinson." *Walt Whitman of Mickle Street.* Ed Geoffrey M. Sill. Knoxville: U of Tennessee P, 1994. 168–78.

Goodblatt, Chanita, and Joseph Glicksohn. "The Poetics of Meditation: Whitman's Meditative Catalogue." *Imagination, Cognition, and Personality* 9.1 (1989–1990): 75–86.

Hakutani, Yoshinobu. "Emerson, Whitman, and Zen Buddhism." *Midwest Quarterly* 31 (1990): 433–48.

Maslan, Mark. "Whitman and His Doubles: Division and Union in *Leaves of Grass* and Its Critics." *American Literary History* 6.1 (1994): 119–39.

Mulcaire, Terry. "Publishing Intimacy in *Leaves of Grass*." *ELH* 60 (1993): 471–501.

Schmidt, Bernard. "Whitman and American Personalistic Philosophy." *Walt Whitman Quarterly Review* 7.4 (1990): 180–90.

Schneidau, Herbert. "The Antinomian Strain: *The Bible* and American Poetry." The Bible *and American Arts and Letters*. Ed. Giles Gunn. Chico: Fortress, 1983. 11–32.

Stefanelli, Maria Anita. "'Chants' as 'Psalms for a New Bible.'" *Utopia in the Present Tense: Walt Whitman and the Language of the New World*. Ed. Marina Camboni. Rome: Calamo, 1994. 171–88.

Prosody, Form, and Influence Studies

Bidney, Martin. "Listening to Whitman: An Introduction to His Prosody." *Approaches to Teaching Whitman's* Leaves of Grass. Ed. Donald D. Kummings. New York: MLA, 1990. 90–8.

Christensen, Inger. "The Organic Theory of Art and Whitman's Poetry." *The Romantic Heritage: A Collection of Critical Essays*. Ed. Karsten Engelberg. Copenhagen: U of Copenhagen, 1983.

Forrey, Robert. "Whitman's 'Real Grammar': A Structuralist Approach." *Walt Whitman Review* 27.1 (1981): 14–24.

Hollis, C. Carroll. "Rhetoric, Elocution and Voice in *Leaves of Grass:* A Study in Affiliation." *Walt Whitman Review*. 2.2 (1984): 1–21.

———. "Whitman on 'Periphrastic' Literature." *Walt Whitman Quarterly Review* 7.3 (1990): 131–40.

Loving, Jerome. "Emerson, Whitman, and the Paradox of Self-Reliance." *Critical Essays on Walt Whitman*. Ed. James Woodress. Boston: Hall, 1983. 306–19.

Mainville, Stephen, and Ronald Schleifer. "Whitman's Printed Leaves: The Literal and the Metaphorical in *Leaves of Grass*." *Arizona Quarterly* 37.1 (1981): 17–30.

Nathanson, Tenney. "Whitman's Tropes of Light and Flood: Language and Representation in the Early Editions of *Leaves of Grass*." *ESQ* 31.2 (1985): 116–34.

Perry, Dennis. "Whitman's Influence on Stoker's *Dracula*." *Walt Whitman Review* 3.3 (1986): 29–35.

Pincus, Robert L. "A Mediated Vision, A Measured Voice: Culture and Criticism in Whitman's Prose." *Walt Whitman Review* 2.1 (1984): 22–31.

Schwiebert, John E. "Passage to More Than Imagism: Whitman's Imagistic Poems." *Walt Whitman Quarterly Review* 8.1 (1990): 16–28.

Thomas, M. Wynn. "Whitman's Achievements in the Personal Style in 'Calamus.'" *Walt Whitman Review* 1.3 (1983): 36–47.

Warren, James Perrin. "'Catching the Sign': Catalogue Rhetoric in 'The Sleepers.'" *Walt Whitman Review* 5.2 (1987): 16–34.

Weis, Monica R. "'Translating the Untranslatable': A Note on 'The Mystic Trumpeter.'" *Walt Whitman Review* 1.4 (1984): 27–31.

Political Interpretations
of Whitman and of His Work

Beach, Christopher. "'Now Lucifer Was Not Dead': Slavery, Intertextuality, and Subjectivity in *Leaves of Grass*." *Canadian Review of American Studies* 25.2 (1995): 27–48.

———. *The Politics of Distinction: Whitman and the Discourses of Nineteenth-Century America*. Athens: U of Georgia P, 1996.

Burrison, William. "Whitman's Drum Taps Revisited: The Good Gray, Tender Mother-Man and the Fierce, Red, Convulsive Rhythm of War." *Walt Whitman: Here and Now*. Ed. Joann P. Krieg. Westport, CT: Greenwood, 1985. 157–69.

Christophersen, Bill. "Singing the Body Eclectic: Walt Whitman's American 'Multitudes.'" *North Dakota Quarterly* 64.1 (1997): 51–8.

Erkkila, Betsy. *Whitman the Political Poet*. Oxford: Oxford UP, 1989.

Hoffman, Daniel. "'Hankering, Gross, Mystical, Nude': Whitman's 'Self' and the American Tradition." *Walt Whitman of Mickle Street*. Ed. Geoffrey M. Sill. Knoxville: U of Tennessee P, 1994. 1–17.

Hollis, C. Carroll. "'Tallying, Vocalizing All': Discourse Markers in *Leaves of Grass*." *Walt Whitman: The Centennial Essays*. Ed. Ed Folsom. Iowa City: U of Iowa P, 1994. 61–7.

Killingsworth, M. Jimmie. *Whitman's Poetry of the Body: Sexuality, Politics, and the Text*. Chapel Hill: U of North Carolina P, 1989.

Klammer, Martin. *Whitman, Slavery, and the Emergence of Leaves of Grass*. University Park: Pennsylvania State UP, 1995.

Loving, Jerome. "Whitman's Democratic Vista in the First *Leaves of Grass*." *Walt Whitman: Here and Now*. Ed. Joann P. Krieg. Westport, CT: Greenwood, 1985. 139–46.

Molesworth, Charles. "Whitman's Political Vision." *Raritan* 12.1 (1992): 98–112.

Newfield, Christopher. "Democracy and Male Homoeroticism." *The Yale Journal of Criticism* 6.2 (1993): 29–62.

Reynolds, David S. "Whitman the Radical Democrat." *The Mickle Street Review* 10 (1988): 39–48.

Scholnick, Robert J. "The American Context of Democratic Vistas." *Walt Whitman: Here and Now.* Ed. Joann P. Krieg. Westport, CT: Greenwood, 1985. 147–56.

———. "Toward a 'Wider Democratizing of Institutions': Whitman's Democratic Vistas." *American Transcendentalist Quarterly* 52 (1981): 286–302.

Schenkel, Elmar. "Walt Whitman and Fourth of July Rhetoric." *The Fourth of July: Political Oratory and Literary Reactions, 1776–1876.* Ed. Paul Goetsch. Tübingen: Narr, 1992. 205–17.

Thomas, M. Wynn. "Fratricide and Brotherly Love: Whitman and the Civil War." *The Cambridge Companion to Walt Whitman.* Ed. Ezra Greenspan. Cambridge: Cambridge UP, 1995. 27–44.

Trachtenberg, Alan. "Whitman's Visionary Politics." *Walt Whitman of Mickle Street.* Ed Geoffrey M. Sill. Knoxville: U of Tennessee P, 1994. 94–108.

Wiegman, Robyn. "Writing the Male Body: Naked Patriarchy and Whitmanian Democracy." *Literature and Psychology* 33.3–4 (1987): 16–26.

Gay Studies and Queer Theory Sources

Erkkila, Betsy. "Whitman and the Homosexual Republic." *Walt Whitman: The Centennial Essays.* Ed. Ed Folsom. Iowa City: U of Iowa P, 1994. 153–71.

Folsom, Ed. "Whitman Naked?" *Walt Whitman Quarterly Review* 11.4 (1994): 200–02.

Keller, Karl. "Walt Whitman Camping." *Camp Grounds: Style and Homosexuality.* Ed. David Bergman. Amherst: U of Massachusetts P, 1993. 113–20.

Martin, Robert K. "Whitman and the Politics of Identity." *Walt Whitman: The Centennial Essays.* Ed. Ed Folsom. Iowa City: U of Iowa P, 1994. 172–81.

Moon, Michael, and Eve Kosofsky Sedgwick. "Confusion of Tongues." *Breaking Bounds: Whitman and American Cultural Studies.* Ed. Betsy Erkkila and Jay Grossman. New York: Oxford UP, 1996. 23–9.

Moritz, William. "Seven Glimpses of Walt Whitman." *Gay Spirit: Myth and Meaning.* Ed. Mark Thompson. New York: St. Martin's, 1987. 131–52.

Olsen-Smith, Steven, and Hershel Parker. "'Live Oak, with Moss' and 'Calamus': Textual Inhibitions in Whitman Criticism." *Walt Whitman Quarterly Review* 14.4 (1997): 153–65.

Parker, Hershel. "The Real 'Live Oak, with Moss': Straight Talk about Whitman's Gay Manifesto." *Nineteenth-Century Literature* 51.2 (1996): 145–60.

Yingling, Tom. "Homosexuality and Utopian Discourse in American Literature." *Breaking Bounds: Whitman and American Cultural Studies.* Ed. Betsy Erkkila and Jay Grossman. New York: Oxford UP, 1996. 135–46.

Psychological and Psychoanalytic Readings of Whitman and His Work

Aarnes, William. "'Free Margins': Identity and Silence in Whitman's 'Specimen Days.'" *ESQ* 28 (1982): 243–60.

Askin, Denis T. "Whitman's Theory of Evil: A Clue to His Use of Paradox." *ESQ* 28 (1982): 121–32.

Bidney, Martin. "Structures of Perception in Blake and Whitman: Creative Contraries, Cosmic Body, Fourfold Vision." *ESQ* 28 (1982): 36–47.

Black, Stephen A. "Reading Whitman Psychoanalytically." *Walt Whitman: Here and Now.* Ed. Joann P. Krieg. Westport, CT: Greenwood, 1985. 43–8.

Haney, William S., II. "'Song of Myself': The Touch of Consciousness." *University of Mississippi Studies in English* 2 (1981): 64–70.

Moder, Donna. "Gender Bipolarity and the Metaphorical Dimensions of Creativity in Walt Whitman's Poetry: A Psychobiographical Study." *Literature and Psychology* 34.1 (1988): 34–52.

Pollack, Vivian R. "Death as Repression, Repression as Death: A Reading of Whitman's 'Calamus' Poems." *Walt Whitman of Mickle Street.* Ed. Geoffrey M. Sill. Knoxville: U of Tennessee P, 1994. 179–93.

Comparisons of Whitman with Other Poets, Contemporaneous and Later

Avi-Ram, Amitai. "Free Verse in Whitman and Ginsberg: The Body and the Simulacrum." *The Continuing Presence of Walt Whitman: The Life After the Life.* Ed. Robert K. Martin. Iowa City: U of Iowa P, 1992. 93–113.

Barrett, Faith. "Inclusion and Exclusion: Fictions of Self and Nation in Whitman and Dickinson." *The Emily Dickinson Journal* 5 (1996): 240–46.

Fontana, Ernest. "Whitman, Pater, and 'An English Poet.'" *Walt Whitman Quarterly Review* 14.1 (1996): 12–20.

Gilbert, Sandra M. "'Now in a Moment I Know What I Am For': Rituals of Initiation in Whitman and Dickinson." *Walt Whitman of Mickle Street.* Ed. Geoffrey M. Sill. Knoxville: U of Tennessee P, 1994. 168–78.

Meyers, Terry L. "Swinburne and Whitman: Further Evidence. *Walt Whitman Quarterly Review* 14.1 (1996): 1–11.

Shurr, William H. "The Salvation of America: Walt Whitman's Apocalypticism and Washington Irving's 'Columbus.'" *Walt Whitman of Mickle Street.* Ed. Geoffrey M. Sill. Knoxville: U of Tennessee P, 1994. 142–50.

Thurin, Erik Ingvar. *Whitman Between Expressionism and Impressionism: Language of the Body, Language of the Soul.* Lewisburg, PA: Bucknell UP, 1995.

Werlock, Abby. "Whitman, Wharton, and the Sexuality in Summer." *Speaking the Other Self: American Women Writers.* Ed. Jeanne Campbell Reesman. Athens: U of Georgia P, 1997. 246–62.

Feminist Criticism

Aspiz, Harold. "Walt Whitman, Feminist." *Walt Whitman: Here and Now.* Ed. Joann P. Krieg. Westport, CT: Greenwood, 1985. 79–88.

Killingsworth, M. J. "Walt Whitman's Prose and the Ethics of Sexual Liberation." *Walt Whitman: Here and Now.* Ed. Joann P. Krieg. Westport, CT: Greenwood, 1985. 69–78.

Loving, Jerome. "Whitman's Idea of Women." *Walt Whitman of Mickle Street.* Ed. Geoffrey M. Sill. Knoxville: U of Tennessee P, 1994. 151–67.

Mullins, Maire. "'Act-Poems of Eyes, Hands, Hips and Bosoms': Women's Sexuality in Walt Whitman's 'Children of Adam.'" *American Transcendental Quarterly* 6 (1992): 213–31.

Oakes, Karen. "'I Stop Somewhere Waiting For You': Whitman's Femininity and the Reader of *Leaves of Grass.*" *Out of Bounds: Male Writers and Gender(ed) Criticism.* Ed. Laura Claridge and Elizabeth Langland. Amherst: U of Massachusetts P, 1990. 169–75.

Reynolds, David S. "Whitman and Nineteenth-Century Views of Gender and Sexuality." *Walt Whitman of Mickle Street.* Ed. Geoffrey M. Sill. Knoxville: U of Tennessee P, 1994. 38–45.

Simons, John. "Edward Carpenter, Whitman and the Radical Aesthetic." *Gender Roles and Sexuality in Victorian Literature.* Ed. Christopher Parker. Hants: Scolar, 1995. 115–27.

Simpson, Louis. "Strategies of Sex in Whitman's Poetry." *Walt Whitman of Mickle Street.* Ed. Geoffrey M. Sill. Knoxville: U of Tennessee P, 1994. 28–37.

Warren, Joyce W. "Subversion versus Celebration: The Aborted Friendship of Fanny Fern and Walt Whitman." *Patrons and Protegées: Gender, Friendship, and Writing in Nineteenth-Century America.* Ed. Shirley Marchalonis. New Brunswick: Rutgers UP, 1994. 59–93.

World Wide Web Sites

Academy of American Poets. Online posting. 2 Aug. 1999. Worldnet. 5 Sept. 1999 <http://www.poets.org/poets/lit/POET/wwhitman.htm>.

Price, Kenneth M., and Ed Folsom. Public posting. 10 Aug. 1999. The Walt Whitman Hypertext Archive. Worldnet. 5 Sept. 1999 <http://jefferson.village.virginia.edu/whitman>.

Walt Whitman Home Page. Public posting 19 Oct. 1998. Worldnet. 5 Sept. 1999 <http://www.rs6.loc.gov/wwhome.html>.

Appendix: Documenting Sources

A Guide to MLA
Documentation Style

Documentation is the acknowledgment of information from an outside source that you use in a paper. In general, give credit to your sources whenever you quote, paraphrase, summarize, or in any other way incorporate borrowed information or ideas into your work. Not to do so—on purpose or by accident—is to commit **plagiarism,** to appropriate the intellectual property of others. By following accepted conventions of documentation, you not only help avoid plagiarism, but you show your readers that you write with care and precision. In addition, you enable them to distinguish your ideas from those of your sources and, if they wish, to locate and consult the sources you cite.

Not all ideas from your sources need to be documented. You can assume that certain information—facts from encyclopedias, textbooks, newspapers, magazines, and dictionaries, or even from television and radio—is common knowledge. Even if the information is new to you, it need not be documented as long as it is found in several reference sources and as long as you do not use the exact wording of your source. Information that is in dispute or that is the original contribution of a particular person, however, *must* be documented. You need not, for example, document the fact that Arthur Miller's *Death of a Salesman* was first performed in 1949 or that it won a Pulitzer Prize for drama. (You could find this information in any current encyclopedia.) You would, however, have to document a critic's interpretation of a performance or a scholar's analysis of an early draft of the play, even if you do not use your source's exact words.

Students of literature use the documentation style recommended by the Modern Language Association of America (MLA), a professional organization of more than twenty-five thousand teachers and students of English and other languages. This method of documentation, the one that you should use any time you write a literature paper, has three components: *parenthetical references in the text, a list of works cited,* and *explanatory notes.*

Parenthetical References
in the Text

MLA documentation uses references inserted in parentheses within the text that refer to an alphabetical list of works cited at the end of the paper. A typical **parenthetical reference** consists of the author's last name and a page number.

```
Gwendolyn Brooks uses the sonnet form to create
poems that have a wide social and aesthetic range
(Williams 972).
```

If you use more than one source by the same author, include a shortened title in the parenthetical reference. In the following entry, "Brooks's Way" is a shortened form of the complete title of the article "Gwendolyn Brooks's Way with the Sonnet."

```
Brooks not only knows Shakespeare, Spenser, and
Milton, but she also knows the full range of
African-American poetry (Williams, "Brooks's Way"
972).
```

If you mention the author's name or the title of the work in your paper, only a page reference is necessary.

```
According to Gladys Margaret Williams in "Gwendolyn
Brooks's Way with the Sonnet," Brooks combines a
sensitivity to poetic forms with a depth of emotion
appropriate for her subject matter (972-73).
```

Keep in mind that you use different punctuation for parenthetical references used with *paraphrases and summaries,* with *direct quotations run in with the text,* and with *quotations of more than four lines.*

Paraphrases and summaries

Place the parenthetical reference after the last word of the sentence and before the final punctuation:

```
In her works Brooks combines the pessimism of mod-
ernist poetry with the optimism of the Harlem Re-
naissance (Smith 978).
```

Direct quotations run in with the text

Place the parenthetical reference after the quotation marks and before the final punctuation:

> According to Gary Smith, Brooks's <u>A Street in Bronzeville</u> "conveys the primacy of suffering in the lives of poor Black women" (1980).

> According to Gary Smith, the poems in <u>A Street in Bronzeville</u>, "served notice that Brooks had learned her craft [. . .]" (978).

> Along with Thompson we must ask, "Why did it take so long for critics to acknowledge that Gwendolyn Brooks is an important voice in twentieth-century American poetry?" (123)

Quotations set off from the text

Omit the quotation marks and place the parenthetical reference one space after the final punctuation.

> For Gary Smith, the identity of Brooks's African-American women is inextricably linked with their sense of race and poverty:
>
>> For Brooks, unlike the Renaissance poets, the victimization of poor Black women becomes not simply a minor chord but a predominant theme of <u>A Street in Bronzeville</u>. Few, if any, of her female characters are able to free themselves from a web of poverty that threatens to strangle their lives. (980)

[Quotations of more than four lines are indented ten spaces (or one inch) from the margin and are not enclosed within quotation marks. The first line of a single paragraph of quoted material is not indented further. If you quote two or more paragraphs, indent the first line of each paragraph three additional spaces (one-quarter inch).]

SAMPLE REFERENCES

The following formats are used for parenthetical references to various kinds of sources used in papers about literature. (Keep in mind that the parenthetical reference contains just enough information to enable readers to find the source in the list of works cited at the end of the paper.)

An entire work

    August Wilson's play Fences treats many themes fre-
    quently expressed in modern drama.

[When citing an entire work, state the name of the author in your paper instead of in a parenthetical reference.]

A work by two or three authors

    Myths cut across boundaries and cultural spheres and
    reappear in strikingly similar forms from country to
    country (Feldman and Richardson 124).

    The effect of a work of literature depends on the
    audience's predispositions that derive from member-
    ship in various social groups (Hovland, Janis, and
    Kelley 87).

A work by more than three authors

    Hawthorne's short stories frequently use a combina-
    tion of allegorical and symbolic methods (Guerin
    et al. 91).

[The abbreviation *et al.* is Latin for "and others."]

A work in an anthology

    In his essay "Flat and Round Characters" E. M. For-
    ster distinguishes between one-dimensional charac-
    ters and those that are well developed (Stevick
    223-31).

[The parenthetical reference cites the anthology (edited by Stevick) that contains Forster's essay; full information about the anthology appears in the list of works cited.]

A work with volume and page numbers

> In 1961 one of Albee's plays, <u>The Zoo Story</u>, was
> finally performed in America (Eagleton 2:17).

An indirect source

> Wagner observed that myth and history stood before
> him "with opposing claims" (qtd. in Winkler 10).

[The abbreviation *qtd. in* (quoted in) indicates that the quoted material was not taken from the original source.]

A play or poem with numbered lines

> "Give thy thoughts no tongue," says Polonius,
> "Nor any unproportioned thought his act"
> (<u>Ham.</u> 1.3.59-60).

[The parentheses contain the act, scene, and line numbers, separated by periods. When included in parenthetical references, titles of the books of the Bible and well-known literary works are often abbreviated—*Gen.* for *Genesis* and *Ado* for *Much Ado about Nothing*, for example.]

> "I muse my life-long hate, and without flinch / I
> bear it nobly as I live my part," says Claude McKay
> in his bitterly ironic poem "The White City" (3-4).

[Notice that a slash (/) is used to separate lines of poetry run in with the text. The parenthetical reference cites the lines quoted.]

The List of Works Cited

Parenthetical references refer to a **list of works cited** that includes all the sources you refer to in your paper. (If your list includes all the works consulted, whether you cite them or not, use the title *Works Consulted.*) Begin the works cited list on a new page, continuing the page numbers of the paper. For example, if the text of the paper ends on page 6, the works cited section will begin on page 7.

Center the title *Works Cited* one inch from the top of the page. Arrange entries alphabetically, according to the last name of each author (or the first word of the title if the author is unknown). Articles—*a, an,* and *the*—at the beginning of a title are not considered first words. Thus *A Handbook of Critical Approaches to Literature* would be alphabetized under *H.* In order to conserve space, publishers' names are abbreviated—for example, *Harcourt* for Harcourt College Publishers. Double-space the entire works cited list between and within entries. Begin typing each entry at the left margin, and indent subsequent lines five spaces or one-half inch. The entry itself generally has three divisions—author, title, and publishing information—separated by periods.*

A book by a single author

Kingston, Maxine Hong. <u>The Woman Warrior: Memoirs of a Girlhood among Ghosts</u>. New York: Knopf, 1976.

A book by two or three authors

Feldman, Burton, and Robert D. Richardson. <u>The Rise of Modern Mythology</u>. Bloomington: Indiana UP, 1972.

[Notice that only the *first* author's name is in reverse order.]

A book by more than three authors

Guerin, Wilfred, et al., eds. <u>A Handbook of Critical Approaches to Literature</u>. 3rd ed. New York: Harper, 1992.

[Instead of using *et al.,* you may list all the authors' names in the order in which they appear on the title page.]

Two or more works by the same author

Novoa, Juan-Bruce. <u>Chicano Authors: Inquiry by Interview</u>, Austin: U of Texas P, 1980.

---

* The fifth edition of the *MLA Handbook for Writers of Research Papers* (1999) shows a single space after all end punctuation.

```
---. "Themes in Rudolfo Anaya's Work." Address
    given at New Mexico State University, Las
    Cruces. 11 Apr. 1987.
```

[List two or more works by the same author in alphabetical order by title. Include the author's full name in the first entry; use three unspaced hyphens followed by a period to take the place of the author's name in second and subsequent entries.]

An edited book

```
Oosthuizen, Ann, ed. Sometimes When It Rains:
    Writings by South African Women. New York:
    Pandora, 1987.
```

[Note that the abbreviation *ed.* stands for *editor.*]

A book with a volume number

```
Eagleton, T. Allston. A History of the New York
    Stage. Vol. 2. Englewood Cliffs: Prentice, 1987.
```

[All three volumes have the same title.]

```
Durant, Will, and Ariel Durant. The Age of Napoleon:
    A History of European Civilization from 1789 to
    1815. New York: Simon, 1975.
```

[Each volume has a different title, so you may cite an individual book without referring to the other volumes.]

A short story, poem, or play in a collection of the author's work

```
Gordimer, Nadine. "Once upon a Time." "Jump" and
    Other Stories. New York: Farrar, 1991. 23-30.
```

A short story in an anthology

```
Salinas, Marta. "The Scholarship Jacket." Nosotros:
    Latina Literature Today. Ed. Maria del Carmen
    Boza, Beverly Silva, and Carmen Valle. Bingham-
    ton: Bilingual, 1986. 68-70.
```

[The inclusive page numbers follow the year of publication. Note that here the abbreviation *Ed.* stands for *Edited by.*]

A poem in an anthology

> Simmerman, Jim. "Child's Grave, Hale County, Alabama." The Pushcart Prize, X: Best of the Small Presses. Ed. Bill Henderson. New York: Penguin, 1986. 198-99.

A play in an anthology

> Hughes, Langston. Mother and Child. Black Drama Anthology. Ed. Woodie King and Ron Miller. New York: NAL, 1986. 399-406.

An article in an anthology

> Forster, E. M. "Flat and Round Characters." The Theory of the Novel. Ed. Philip Stevick. New York: Free, 1980. 223-31.

More than one selection from the same anthology

If you are using more than one selection from an anthology, cite the anthology in one entry. In addition, list each individual selection separately, including the author and title of the selection, the anthology editor's last name, and the inclusive page numbers.

> Kirszner, Laurie G., and Stephen R. Mandell, eds. Literature: Reading, Reacting, Writing. 3rd ed. Fort Worth: Harcourt, 1997.

> Rich, Adrienne. "Diving into the Wreck." Kirszner and Mandell 874-76.

A translation

> Carpentier, Alejo. Reasons of State. Trans. Francis Partridge. New York: Norton, 1976.

An article in a journal with continuous pagination in each issue

Le Guin, Ursula K. "American Science Fiction and
    the Other." Science Fiction Studies 2 (1975):
    208-10.

An article with separate pagination in each issue

Grossman, Robert. "The Grotesque in Faulkner's
    'A Rose for Emily,'" Mosaic 20.3 (1987): 40-55.

[*20.3* signifies volume 20, issue 3.]

An article in a magazine

Milosz, Czeslaw. "A Lecture." New Yorker 22 June
    1992: 32.
"Solzhenitsyn: An Artist Becomes an Exile." Time
    25 Feb. 1974:34+.

[*34+* indicates that the article appears on pages that are not consecutive; in
this case the article begins on page 34 and then continues on page 37. An
article with no listed author is entered by title on the works cited list.]

An article in a daily newspaper

Oates, Joyce Carol. "When Characters from the Page
    Are Made Flesh on the Screen." New York Times
    23 Mar. 1986, late ed.: C1+.

[*C1+* indicates that the article begins on page 1 of Section C and continues
on a subsequent page.]

An article in a reference book

"Dance Theatre of Harlem." The New Encyclopaedia Bri-
    tannica: Micropaedia. 15th ed. 1987.

You do not need to include publication information for well-known reference books.

Grimstead, David. "Fuller, Margaret Sarah." Encyclo-
    pedia of American Biography. Ed. John A. Gar-
    raty. New York: Harper, 1974.

You must include publication information when citing reference books that are not well known.

A CD-ROM: Entry with a print version

> Zurbach, Kate. "The Linguistic Roots of Three Terms."
> <u>Linguistic Quarterly</u> 37 (1994): 12-47. <u>Infotrac:</u>
> <u>Magazine Index Plus</u>. CD-ROM. Information Access.
> Jan. 1996.

When you cite information with a print version from a CD-ROM, include the publication information, the underlined title of the database (*Infotrac: Magazine Index Plus*), the publication medium (CD-ROM), the name of the company that produced the CD-ROM (Information Access), and the electronic publication date.

A CD-ROM: Entry with no print version

> "Surrealism." <u>Encarta 1999</u>. CD-ROM. Redmond: Micro-
> soft, 1999.

If you are citing a part of a work, include the title in quotation marks.

> <u>A Music Lover's Multimedia Guide to Beethoven's 5th</u>.
> CD-ROM. Spring Valley: Interactive, 1993.

[If you are citing an entire work, include the underlined title.]

An online source: Entry with a print version

> Dekoven, Marianne. "Utopias Limited: Post-sixties
> and Postmodern American Fiction." <u>Modern Fiction</u>
> <u>Studies</u> 41.1 (spring 1995): 121-34. 17 Mar.
> 1996 <http://muse.jhu.edu/journals/MFS/v041/
> 41.1dekoven.html>.

When you cite information with a print version from an online source, include the publication information for the printed source, the number of pages or number of paragraphs (if available), and the date of access. Be sure to include the electronic address (URL) in angle brackets. Sometimes, you may use a commercial online service (America Online or LEXIS-NEXIS, for example) where you use a keyword, not an electronic address, to retrieve information. If you use a keyword to retrieve information, end your citation by typing *Keyword* followed by a colon and the word itself.

> "Gunpowder." <u>Compton's Encyclopedia Online</u>. Vers.
> 2.0. 1999. America Online. 28 Aug. 1999. Key-
> word: Compton's.

If, instead of a keyword, you use a series of topics to find your material, type *Path* followed by the topics (separated by semicolons) you used to locate your material.

> O'Hara, Sandra. "Reexamining the Canon." <u>Time</u> 12 May
> 1994:27. America Online. 22 Aug. 1994. Path:
> Education, Literature; <u>Time</u>.

An online source: Public posting

> Peters, Olaf. "Studying English through German."
> Online posting. 29 Feb. 1996. Foreign Language
> Forum, Multi Language Section. CompuServe.
> 15 Mar. 1996.
> Gilford, Mary. "Dog Heroes in Children's Literature."
> Online posting. 4 Oct. 1996. 23 Mar. 1996
> <News:alt.animals.dogs>. America Online.

WARNING: Using information from online forums and newsgroups is risky. Contributors are not necessarily experts, and frequently they are incorrect and misinformed. Unless you can be certain the information you are receiving from these sources is reliable, do not use it in your papers.

An online source: Electronic text

> Twain, Mark. <u>Adventures of Huckleberry Finn</u>. From
> <u>The Writing of Mark Twain</u>. Vol. 13. New York:
> Harper, 1970. <u>Wiretap.spies</u>. 13 Jan. 1996
> <http.//www.sci.Dixie.edu/DixieCollege/Ebooks/
> huckfin.html>.

This electronic text was originally published by Harper. The name of the repository for the electronic edition is Wiretap.spies (underlined).

An online source: E-mail

> Adkins, Camille. E-mail to the author. 8 June 1995.

An interview

>   Brooks, Gwendolyn. "Interviews." <u>Triquarterly</u> 60
>   (1984): 405-10.

A lecture or address

>   Novoa, Juan-Bruce. "Themes in Rudolfo Anaya's Work."
>   New Mexico State University, Las Cruces, 11 Apr.
>   1987.

A film or videocassette

>   "<u>A Worn Path</u>." By Eudora Welty. Dir. John Reid and
>   Claudia Velasco. Perf. Cora Lee Day and Conchita
>   Ferrell. Videocassette. Harcourt, 1994.

In addition to the title, the director, and the year, include other pertinent information such as the principal performers.

Explanatory Notes

Explanatory notes, indicated by a superscript (a raised number) in the text, may be used to cite several sources at once or to provide commentary or explanations that do not fit smoothly into your paper. The full text of these notes appears on the first numbered page following the last page of the paper. (If your paper has no explanatory notes, the works cited page follows the last page of the paper.) Like works cited entries, explanatory notes are double-spaced within and between entries. However, the first line of each explanatory note is indented five spaces (or one-half inch), with subsequent lines flush with the left-hand margin.

TO CITE SEVERAL SOURCES

In the paper

>   Surprising as it may seem, there have been many
>   attempts to define literature.[1]

In the note

>   [1]For an overview of critical opinion, see Arnold 72;
>   Eagleton 1-2; Howe 43-44; and Abrams 232-34.

TO PROVIDE EXPLANATIONS

In the paper

In recent years Gothic novels have achieved great popularity.[3]

In the note

[3]Gothic novels, works written in imitation of medieval romances, originally relied on supernatural occurrences. They flourished in the late eighteenth and early nineteenth centuries.

Credits

Harold Aspiz
"Sexuality and the Language of Transcendence" by Harold Aspiz from the *Walt Whitman Quarterly Review,* Vol. 5, No. 2, Fall 1987, pp. 1–7. Reprinted by permission of the *Walt Whitman Quarterly Review,* The University of Iowa, and the author.

William Birmingham
"Whitman's Song of the Possible American Self" by William Birmingham from *Cross Currents,* Vol. 43, No. 3, Fall 1993, pp. 341–357. Reprinted by permission.

Sculley Bradley, Ed.
"Preface to 1855 Edition 'Leaves of Grass'" from *Leaves of Grass and Selected Prose* by Walt Whitman. Preface copyright 1949 and renewed by Sculley Bradley, Ed. Reprinted by permission of Harcourt, Inc.

Mark DeLancey
"Texts, Interpretations, and Whitman's 'Song of Myself,'" American Literature, Vol. 61, No. 3, October 1989, pp. 360–381. Copyright 1989, Duke University Press. All rights reserved. Reprinted with permission.

Ralph Waldo Emerson
Emerson's Letter to Whitman, 1855 from *Walt Whitman: The Critical Heritage* edited by Milton Hindus. (International Thomson Publishing Services.)

Rufus W. Griswold
Rufus W. Grisold on Whitman, 1855, from *Walt Whitman: The Critical Heritage* edited by Milton Hindus. (International Thomson Publishing Services.)

D. R. Jarvis
Reprinted from "Whitman and Speech-Based Prosody" by D. R. Jarvis from *Walt Whitman Quarterly Review,* Vol. 27, No. 2 (1981) by permission of the Wayne State University Press.